Inside the
Writing Portfolio

Inside the Writing Portfolio

What We Need to Know to Assess Children's Writing

Carol Brennan Jenkins

HEINEMANN   Portsmouth, NH

HEINEMANN
361 Hanover Street
Portsmouth, NH 03801-3912
Offices and agents throughout the world

The author and publisher wish to thank those who have generously given permission to reprint borrowed material.

Excerpts from *The Diary of Thomas A. Edison* with Introduction by Kathleen L. McGuirk. Published by The Chatham Press, Inc. Copyright by Devin-Adair, Publishers, Inc., Old Greenwich, Connecticut, 06870. Reprinted by permission of Devin-Adair, Publishers, Inc. All rights reserved.

Writing Survey Form reprinted by permission of Nancie Atwell: *In the Middle: Writing, Reading, and Learning with Adolescents* (Boynton/Cook Publishers, A subsidiary of Reed Elsevier Inc., Portsmouth, NH, 1987).

CIP is on file with the Library of Congress
0-435-08893-9

Editor: Carolyn Coman
Production: Melissa L. Inglis
Cover Design: Jenny Jensen Greenleaf
Manufacturing: Elizabeth Valway
Interior photos by Michael Altfillisch

Printed in the United States of America on acid-free paper

Docutech RRD 2009

To Ted
the wind beneath my wings

To Tom
you continue to show me what it takes
to go the distance

Contents

Acknowledgments

As I try to find the words of gratitude for all those who have lived this book with me, I am reminded of Aristotle's teaching that "Without friends no one would choose to live, though he had all other goods. . . ." Writing this book has reaffirmed for me what a noble virtue true friendship is.

The best part of this adventure has been Shane Forsyth, whose insight and writing illuminates this text. Shane's unbridled enthusiasm for life, learning, and literacy carries this book. He embodies all that we know to be true about the intellectual and emotional powers of the young mind. To Shane's parents, Kathy and James Forsyth, I send my gratitude for raising a very special young man and for opening their home to me.

If it wasn't for Alice Earle, I wouldn't have met Shane. Alice invited me into her third-grade classroom many years ago and has continued to allow me to live and learn in her classroom. Alice is a wonderful teacher who believes that children bring a genuine love of learning to the classroom. She places a high premium on caring in her classroom—caring about each other, caring about the world around them. I remain indebted to Alice and thank her for her contribution to this book. I also thank her dad, Mr. Michael Altfillisch, for taking the photos of Alice's classroom for the chapter she contributed. I am grateful also to all of the other teachers who have shared their classrooms with me over the years. Of special note are Mary Leach at the Elihu Greenwood School; Angela Burgos, Mary Costello, Debbie Green, Lisa Lieberman, and Bill Murray at the Winship School; Becky Shepard at the Wildwood School; Lois Davenport, Gloria O'Brien, and the teachers at the T.C. Passios School; and Ginny Noiles and the teachers at the E.B. White and Willis Schools.

This book also is graced with the delightful writings of my friends and boat mates, Danielle, Vanessa, and Philip DeMeo. A special word of thanks to their parents, Pat and Lou DeMeo, who save every word that

Danielle, Vanessa, and Philip write, and who take great pleasure in watching their children grow as readers and writers. My gratitude also to James Cole, Jeffrey Desrosiers, Lauren Gray, Adam Schickedanz, Caitlyn Valanzola, and their parents for allowing me to include their writing samples in this book.

I am indebted to Avi, the award-winning children's author, for agreeing to share his literacy history and his early writing. His story stands as a painful reminder of the miseducation that occurs in some classrooms, and as a plea for teachers to accord children the highest levels of dignity and respect and to teach them well. Avi, I thank you for your passionate concern about children, your honesty, and your good will.

Judith Schickedanz, my mentor and friend, provided the intellectual sustenance and emotional support that I needed to bring this book to completion. Judy is a scholar of extraordinary intelligence. Her quick analytic powers and deep knowledge of the field of literacy guided my efforts. Her penetrating critique of the chapters in this book strengthened the manuscript immeasurably. Thanks to Judy, I am learning what it means to be a writer.

A debt of gratitude is extended to Edwin Delattre, Dean of the School of Education at Boston University. He has taken me under his wing in ways too numerous to count. He is one of those rare educators who emphasizes the intellectual life of an institution over administrative minutiae, who understands and appreciates the complexity of teaching, and who sets and expects the highest academic and ethical standards. I consider him one of my most important mentors for he is a man whose life is marked by intellectual fervor, probity, and professional excellence. Thanks, "Nag," for pushing me that extra mile.

Aristotle makes the case that friendship during times of misfortune is necessary, but that friendship during times of prosperity is noble. The sage counsel and warm friendship of Associate Deans Joan Dee and Boyd Dewey, of Thomas Culliton, and of Burleigh Shibles have seen me through the highs and lows of this writing venture, as well as many of life's other ventures. I am grateful also for the daily words of encouragement and vote of confidence of friends and colleagues at Boston University, in particular Roselmina Indrisano and Stephan Ellenwood. To Robert Kilburn, my gratitude for his computer wizardry and for his unending supply of good cheer—thanks, BF. To Judy Chambliss, many, many thanks for being your caring, compassionate self and for coaching me through my daily trials and tribulations. To Miriam Marecek, my gratitude for introducing me to Avi and for your kindness and support. To Diane Peterson, my former graduate assistant and now second grade teacher extraordinaire, many thanks for the computer searches, for hunting down resources, and so forth. Many thanks also to Janet Stankiewicz and Lisa Vidale who work tirelessly to keep (and to help me keep) my life under control. My gratitude also to Mel Howards whose passion about literacy enveloped me as an undergraduate and whose friendship has sustained me ever since.

A special thank you to Bobbi Fisher for sending me with manuscript in hand to Carolyn Coman, Acquisitions Editor, at Heinemann. Without Bobbi's spirit of generosity and words of encouragement, this book may not have found a home. When I think about Carolyn Coman, I count my blessings daily. I owe Carolyn an enormous debt of gratitude for believing in this book, and for her continual support, encouragement, and advice. Melissa Inglis, Production Editor, transformed this seemingly unwieldy manuscript into a readable text. I thank her for her magical touch and her gentle nature.

To my brother, Tom, I owe a special debt of gratitude for showing me how to stand tall in the face of life's challenges and for being there for me through thick and thin. Tom, you have more courage than anyone I know. I hope you know how much I admire you. I also want to thank my sisters, Patricia and Kate, for their support and for putting up with an absentee sister. To my nieces, Caitlyn and Kristin, and my nephew, Kyle, thanks for bringing such joy to our family. A special thank you is also sent to my in-laws, Flo and Joe, for their compassion and words of encouragement.

To my parents, Mary and Patrick Brennan, I send my deepest appreciation. My mother was pulled from school in Ireland in the third grade to work the farm and to take care of her younger siblings. My father was forced to leave school in the eighth grade to earn a wage for his family. I was not immersed in books as a young child. I did not see writing models around me. And yet I was given the greatest gift of all—parents who believed that I had the potential to make a difference in this world, who believed in the power of education, and who lived the ethic of hard work and of perseverance. Mom and Dad, all my love.

There are no words to thank Ted, my husband and my best friend. As I have told him on more than one occasion, if I were married to me, I would have divorced me a long time ago. He tolerates the endless hours I spend on the computer or at my desk with good humor. He drags me off for cherished walks on beaches when he thinks I am beginning to lose it. He listens hard, acknowledges my bouts of self-doubt, and offers words of encouragement. Ted, know always that you are my source of strength and sanity. I couldn't do this without you.

Portfolios and Learning to Write

Making the Case for the Collaborative Portfolio

A glance at the essay presented in Figure 1–1 takes many of us back to English class and the writing practices that prevailed until the 1970s. The teacher assigned a writing topic; we wrote our one-shot, get-it-right-the-first-time piece. The teacher applied the red pen to our draft, assuming sole responsibility for assessment. The teacher returned the piece, and we shrugged our shoulders in despair.

The essay in Figure 1–1 was written in grade 11 or 12 by Avi, the acclaimed author of award-winning books such as *The Barn*, *Nothing But The Truth*, and *The True Confessions of Charlotte Doyle*. At a conference in 1995, Avi spoke candidly and poignantly about his school history:

> . . . in 1951, I graduated from the 8th grade. At this time, I had not the slightest interest in writing. I was a voracious reader though. I was read to constantly as a kid and taken to the library every Friday. Books were enormously important. In 8th grade, though, I decided I wanted to be a scientist because I had won a science medal, and so I entered a major science high school in New York City. At the end of the first marking period, freshman year, I failed every class I had taken, and my parents yanked me out of that school. They enrolled me in a very small private school in Manhattan which had a great emphasis on reading and writing.
>
> At the end of the third year, my English teacher called my folks and told them that I was the worst student he had ever had. He said that unless I had tutoring or went to summer school, the school would not permit me to stay. Now I need to mention that I am dysgraphic. My parents knew it from a very early time in my schooling but chose not to tell me for reasons I truly don't know. Maybe it was the practice at that time. Maybe they were embarrassed. When I found out about the dysgraphia, my mother already had died. When I asked my father about it, he said that was my mother's decision not to tell me.
>
> It's important for you to understand that my parents had wanted to be writers. My aunt was a newspaper reporter. My grandmother was a playwright; my great grandparents were writers. I grew up in a family of writers, and now my parents were being told that I couldn't write. It

[handwritten annotations throughout]

M
_____
IRVING WORTIS

I am afraid that this is bloated, puffy with words that don't make any real sense —

ON ART

aesthetics mean more than self-expression. The word includes an ideal of beauty.

The aesthetic values of man *are* a problem, *a* question *no* that has been argued for many, *many* years. Each society, and each period of history has tended to find self expression in some kind of art form. Today, living in a world society, there is the unique situation in which all forms of art are being used for this expression. It is impossible therefore to judge decide what is the best, or the correct *no* form of art. Art, and the judgement of art, is a relationship that exists with each individual and is relative to that individual. There is no true art as sure as there is no dogmatic bad art. Art values can not be generalized. The aesthetic values of an art can not be argued, but, and it is an important but, art should be humanized. Not to say just *pictures* photographs, but there must be some contact and understanding between the art and the eye. I am not a person who feels a great deal of contact with what is called modern art, but occasionally I can enjoy such a painting. ~~In that case this case~~ I enjoy it because the color or pattern or (prehaps) style is nice. I can't say on the other hand that all realism appeals to me. It depends on my moods. I am fascinated by Dali's style but I can not take seriously what he has to say.

[handwritten margin notes: "You asked me yesterday if your writing was unclear — This is !"]
[handwritten: "clumsy sentence — Meaning unclear"]
[handwritten: "also confusing"]
[handwritten: "not a sentence"]
[handwritten: "Read Herbert Read on This subject. A book called Aesthetics"]

I do not believe that there is, or ever will be, a correct theory of art. Once in a while I like to paint or draw, prehaps mush around in some clay, mind you not well, but just because its fun to me. I can't (concieve) SP of art for art's sake. I have my own personal throry of art. It is totaly unscientific and I suppose *has* a touch of magic *belief* in it. That's what's nice about being young and *it* is my right. I like to think in these terms because it is a wonderful chalange and to me, very exciting.

I have a lump of clay in my hands. *an* It has no other form but prehaps odd-shaped ball. It has little or no eye appeal. Inside that clay is a

FIGURE 1–1   *Avi's high school essay*

was an insult to my culture and to my family. So my parents asked a friend of the family to tutor me that summer. She was a wonderful teacher who taught me more than the basics of writing. She did something that nobody had ever done before. She asked to see my writing. Now, just the thought of showing her my writing made me cringe. I couldn't bear the thought of showing my writing to anyone but I was given no choice. When I went to meet with her, she didn't talk about my terrible spelling or my bad grammar. To my amazement, all she did in that first session was talk about the ideas in the stories and plays I had written. And then she said the words that changed my life. She said, "You know, you're very interesting. If you wrote better, people would know that." All of a sudden, writing was not a thing in itself, but rather a system of communication. For a twelve-year-old-looking sixteen-year-old, the thought that people would think I was interesting because I wrote something was a revelation—it turned my life around.

When I tell this story to children, they really don't believe that I was a bad writer. So I bring along some of my high school papers to show them how much of a struggle writing was, and still is, for me. [See Figure 1–1.]

I then show the kids another longer piece that I wrote to get some extra credit, and I read my English teacher's comments:

> You are not a good enough student to take on this sort of work. From now on, write two page stories that are correctly spelled and punctuated, that show effective sentence construction and possess interesting word choice. A half page of good work is better than twenty pages of sloppiness.

There absolutely is nothing wrong with what my English teacher is saying but there is a good deal wrong with how he is saying it.

What is really interesting is that in my senior year I kept a diary, the only year I kept a diary. In March of 1955, I wrote, "I can't wait anymore. I'm going to be a writer." The diary has three interests: reading, writing, and girls. What I find fascinating is that there is almost no reference to this man, my English teacher. He is doing all this heavy criticism and I am paying no attention. It is so heavy that I've obliterated it. And I am totally consumed with reading and writing.

How, then, did I become a writer? That diary that I kept contains a list of books that I was reading—three or four books a week. I even put one of my own books—a short story—on the list. Next to this entry, I write, "That's nice to put down." I really believe I became a writer through my reading.

When I get to college, I spend all of my spare time writing. But I have been so traumatized by this English teacher that I take only one semester of English. I have a bachelor's degree and a couple of masters degrees but I've never taken another English class. And I never will. I just won't do it. I don't take writing classes either. But I am writing all the time while in college. I start off by writing plays. How clever of me to have done that because if I used bad grammar, I could say, "Well, that's how people talk." Writing plays represents one of the totally unconscious ways that I taught myself to write. When I was a junior in college at the University of Wisconsin, I submitted one of my plays to a playwriting contest. People judged the plays by writing anonymous comments. I didn't win the contest, of course, and one of the comments about my play was:

> This writer should be encouraged. Clearly, he is a foreign-born, non-English-speaking person, struggling to write in English and he should be encouraged.

However, the following year I did win that playwriting contest and that was my first taste of writing effectively.

It was not until I had kids of my own that I started to write for children. I wrote an animal story for my son, Shawn. The first book I published came out in 1970. It was a collection of very short stories for very short people—they were, in fact, stories that I have told to Shawn. Most of the copies sold are still in my basement—not too successful but I was enormously pleased. From that time on, I only wrote children's books. Since 1970, thirty-two books have been published, more than 100 editions, in this country and elsewhere, and I am very proud of them. It's wonderful to do something well, when you are told you can't do it at all.

On Becoming a Writer

Avi is not unlike many students who have endured the shackles of humiliation caused by stinging criticism. And yet, unlike so many others, Avi found within himself the strength to persevere. Avi attributes his staying power to stubbornness. There is no question that tenacity, girded by self-discipline, hard work, and a resilient spirit, propelled his writing efforts.

However, these virtues alone cannot account for Avi's compulsion to write. Indeed, his literacy history reveals that his passion for story was planted in his earliest years. Avi grew up in a family that valued literacy. He watched his parents read and write. He made weekly trips to the library. His parents constantly read to him. Soon, he became a voracious reader. A print-rich homelife laid the foundation for Avi's eventual success as a writer as it does for many young children. When young children are immersed in print, are surrounded by adults who engage in literate activity, and are responsive to children's inquiries and comments, they independently and joyfully pursue reading and writing endeavors (Bissex, 1980; Durkin, 1966; Schickedanz, 1990). Studies have shown that children who have been read to at home during their preschool years have larger vocabularies and experience a greater degree of success in learning to read than do children without a history of literacy experiences (Durkin, 1966; Snow, 1983).

But literacy development hinges not only on primary conditions such as immersion, emulation, and use (Cambourne, 1988; Holdaway, 1979) but also on the essential condition of demonstration. A demonstration is defined as an instructional encounter. For example, we learn to write in one of two ways—either through analysis of an author's text or through instruction (Smith, 1982). What Avi cites as the turning point in his life—the intervention of one teacher—speaks to the power of one kind of demonstration—instruction. Because one human being had the intuition to look beyond the surface level aspects of Avi's writing, to ferret out the substance of his thought, and to acknowledge his intellect, a writer was born. Because Avi's tutor showed him what he did well and what he needed to do to improve, he listened. She stands in stark contrast to Avi's English teacher. While she believed Avi could write, the English teacher believed that he couldn't. While she asked to see the writing Avi had done at home, the English teacher assumed Avi wrote only when directed to do so. While she allowed Avi to choose his topics, the English teacher assigned topics. While she conferred with Avi about his ideas, he swamped Avi with feedback at every level. While she taught Avi the basics of writing, he expected him to learn the conventions through the precision of a red pen. While she built Avi up, he tore Avi down.

Avi's English teacher was not an aberration. He did what many English teachers did in the 1950s. He cared about his subject area and wanted students to care. But he did not understand writing as the search for meaning. He did not instruct students in the art of topic choice, revision, and so forth. In essence, he prioritized product over process, mechanics over meaning. He taught whole class lessons but did not work with individual writers. Rather, he read each student's paper with great care and fixed everything in order to "teach" them. Avi's speculation is that even if this English teacher had the optimal situation of one-on-one tutoring, his approach to writing instruction would not have differed.

It took the wisdom of writers such as Peter Elbow and Donald Murray, during the late 1960s, to challenge these writing practices and to help English teachers reconceptualize the instruction of writing.

As positive as Avi's tutoring experience was, it was short-lived, and not repeated. Stung by the barrage of teachers' unrelenting criticism, Avi shunned all future formal writing instruction. Instead, he turned to the demonstrations of the writing masters themselves. As Avi notes, "I became a writer through my reading." It was through his study of the work by Dickens, Hemingway, and others that Avi learned the art of writing.

It was this fusion of factors—Avi's tenacity, a book-filled homelife, and the instruction of one teacher and of master writers—that enabled Avi to defy the odds, and eventually to earn critical acclaim:

> *The Fighting Ground*: Avi has written a taut, fastpaced novel that builds to a shattering climax. His protagonist's painful, inner struggle to understand the intense and conflicting emotions brought on by a war that spares no one is central to this finely crafted novel (Taxel, 1985, p. 23).

> *The Man who was Poe*: Avi recreates the gloom of 1840's Baltimore with a storyteller's ease, blending drama, history and mystery without a hint of pastiche or calculation (Sutton, 1989, p. 27).

> *The True Confessions of Charlotte Doyle*: "Not every thirteen-year-old girl is accused of murder, brought to trial, and found guilty." This direct opening line powerfully launches a novel of extraordinary achievement and resonance. . . . Expertly crafted and consistently involving, it is sure to excite, enthrall, and challenge readers (Mercier, 1991, pp. 56–57).

These reviews herald Avi's ability to craft memorable stories—stories with "spirited plots, believable characters, vivid atmosphere, accurate historical detail, and considerable irony and wit" (Senick & Gunton, 1991). But the appeal of Avi's work goes beyond his expert control of the literary elements. Readers are drawn to his stories because they penetrate the substance of our lives. They confront us with complex moral issues and force us to examine our own human frailties. It is these features that make Avi's books intellectually, emotionally, and morally compelling.

Critical acclaim has earned Avi two Newbery Honor books, two Children's Choice Awards (International Reading Association), a Scott O'Dell Award, a Horn Book–Boston Globe Award, and a host of other awards. For Avi, though, these awards represent not only a testimony to his talent and his dedication but also a triumph of personal fortitude and a vindication of a history of school failure.

One can only wonder how much richer the world of children's literature would be if young Avi had been allowed to write daily, to participate in minilessons on the craft and art of writing, to reread pieces in order to find topics of significance, to revise and edit pieces, to assess his progress as a writer, and to set challenging writing goals. Avi learned many of these critical writing dimensions on his own. Early on, for example, he made the decision to keep the artifacts that documented his evolution as a writer. While most of us would have taken a match to the red-stained pieces written in high school, Avi saved his. He also saved his diary. He saved the plays he wrote in college. He even saved a play he had written at home when he was nine or ten years old (Figure 1–2). He saved the first picture storybook he wrote for his son, Shawn. Thus, long before portfolios found their way into classrooms, Avi understood intuitively that in order to move forward as a writer, one must first look back.

Fortunately, today, because of educators such as Donald Graves and Lucy Calkins, children in many, many classrooms across the country are living the lives of writers. Central to the success of their writing endeavors is an assessment process that involves the creation of portfolios—collections of and reflections on their writings. These collections, housed in folders, binders, cereal boxes, or whatever, contain writing samples and other data which are analyzed to discover important insights about writers and about their writing progress. What data are collected and analyzed, when they are analyzed, and by whom they are analyzed varies from classroom to classroom. Because portfolio assessment is still in its infancy, answers to these questions and to the critical question of whether portfolios enhance children's learning are just beginning to be addressed by researchers (Valencia, Hiebert, & Afflerbach, 1994). Nevertheless, interest in this type of alternative assessment is strong and has resulted in emergence of three major models of portfolio assessment over the last ten years.

Models of Portfolio Assessment

We commit ourselves to portfolio assessment because we want children to learn to write well. We recognize that learning to write well requires the acquisition of certain habits of mind from the earliest years. Learning to write well requires daily effort, self-discipline, and resolve. It requires that children write in order to discover what they know and what they don't know. It requires the pursuit of embryonic ideas, unanswered questions, and unsettling notions. It requires reading extensively and intensively. It requires the engagement of intellectual powers in deliberate and reasoned ways. It requires that children distance themselves from their efforts in order to examine the clarity of their thoughts, the logic of their arguments, and the eloquence of their message. It requires learning from more knowledgeable others about the craft and art of writing. It also requires learning to take stock of themselves as writers—what they have written and why, what they need to write and why, the quality of their endeavors and so forth.

Efforts to help children become better writers have resulted in the development of three major portfolio models. Each model is based on a set of theoretical assumptions. Each has instructional implications. To

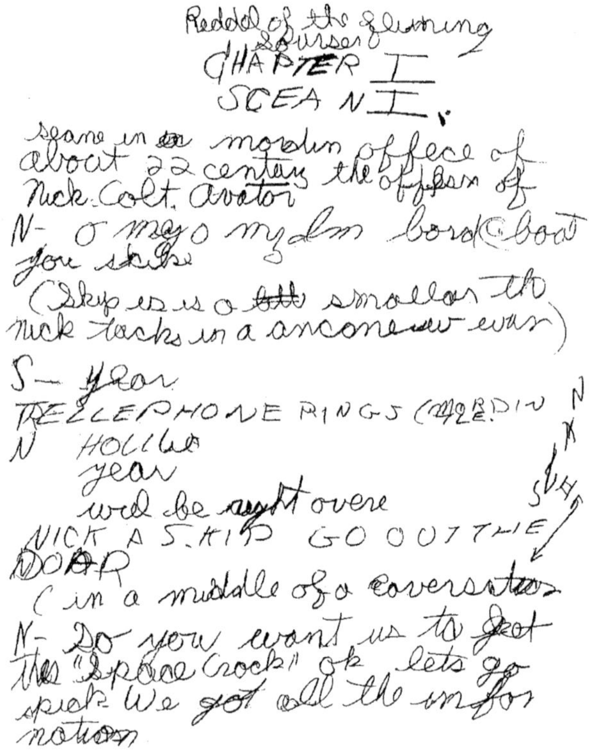

[handwritten draft]

Riddel of the glowing
Saucer
CHAPTER I
SCEA N I.

seane in the modern offece of
about 22 centery the offefin of
Nick Colt. Avator
N- o myo my dm bord bout
you skips
(Skip is is a th smaller th
nick tacks in a anconew evan)

S— Year
TELLEPHONE RINGS (MORDIN N
N HOLLE
year
wed be ayt overe SH
NICK A S.KIP GO OUTTHE
DOAR
(in a midale of a coversttos
N- Do you want us to get
the "Spooe Crock" ok lets go
skick We got all the infor
nation

RIDDLE OF THE FLYING SAUCER

Chapter 1
Scene I

Scene in modern office of about the 22nd century; the office of Nick Colt, Aviator
NICK: *Oh my, oh my, I'm bored. How about you, Skippy?*
(Skip is a smaller th---- Nick talks in a ----(intercom?) even.)
SKIP: *Yeah.*
TELEPHONE RINGS (MODERN TELEPHONE).
NICK: *Hello.*
   Yeah.
   We'll be right over.
Nick and Skip go out the door —SLAM—
(in the middle of a conversation).

Scene II

NICK: *So you want us to get this "Space Crook?" OK. Let's go.*
SKIP: *We got all the information.*

FIGURE 1–2 *Avi's play, written at age 9 or 10*

SCEANN III

JET ROCKET GOING THROGH SPACE

SCEANIV

IN JET

N— HAVING FUN

S— You bet cleang this gun of yours (scacasterly)

SCENN V

IN SPACE CROCKS PLANE

SC.— IVE GOT THOS' POLISE ALL BAUFULD THER 12 NAYER GE7 ME HA HA AND I GOT THE NFATUST HIDEOUT DON7 I BOY

(MURMUS FROM OTHED MEN)

IN SEANN VI

IN NICKS PLAIN

Scene III
JET ROCKET GOING THROUGH SPACE

Scene IV
IN JET

NICK: *Having fun!*
SKIP: *You bet, cleaning this gun of yours (sarcastically).*

Scene V
IN SPACE CROOK'S PLANE

SPACE CROOK: *I've got those police all baffled. They'll never get me. Ha, ha! And I got the nearest hideout, don't I, boy.*
(Murmurs from the other men.)

Scene VI
IN NICK'S PLANE

FIGURE 1–2, *continued*

determine which model of portfolio assessment is most consistent with your own assumptions and practices, complete the survey in Figure 1–3, and reflect on the results.

Are the majority of your checks in the Teacher column? If they are, you have adopted a stance to the portfolio process that places assessment primarily in your hands (Figure 1–4). You assume all responsibility for the selection and analyses of the children's work. Or, are your check-marks clustered at the left side of the continuum (Figure 1–4)? If so, you probably believe that the child should be in charge of the assessment process. The children in your classroom create showcase portfolios by choosing their best work, by assembling their portfolios, and by assessing their work. Or, are your checkmarks concentrated in the middle column? If they are, you view assessment as a joint endeavor, one that merges the child's insights and your informed judgment. You work with the writers in your classroom to build collaborative portfolios.

The continuum of portfolio models (Figure 1–4) acknowledges fundamental differences among educators about the nature and purpose of portfolio assessment. Central to these differences is this question: "Who assumes responsibility for the child's learning?" In the sections that follow, each of these portfolio models is examined with respect to their underlying assumptions, potential strengths and areas of concerns, and classroom implications. This overview is followed by a discussion of my belief that the collaborative portfolio best fulfills the mission of helping children learn to write well.

The Benchmark Portfolio

The benchmark portfolio is the most teacher-centered of the portfolio models. It was conceived to bridge the chasm between standardized tests and the current theory and practice of literacy. While teachers acknowledged the serious constraints of formal assessment, they felt unprepared to tackle the formidable task of assessing children's literacy. Literacy experts—such as Cambourne (1988), Cambourne and Turbill (1994), and Au (1990a, 1990b; 1994)—sought to ease the transition to portfolio assessment by urging that developmental benchmarks for literacy progress be established. According to Cambourne, teachers have a responsibility to observe children in formal ways and to analyze their products in order to build "a store of knowledge" about literacy development (1988, p. 122). With this knowledge, teachers create benchmarks or "markers" of progress which they use to analyze children's writing products and their processes. Markers are "overt forms of language behavior which mark or give evidence of the presence of some kind of linguistic knowledge, or skill, or attitude" (Cambourne, 1988, p. 124). Cambourne

PORTFOLIO SURVEY: WHO'S IN CHARGE?

Please read each question and check the appropriate column.	Child	Child & Teacher	Teacher
1. Who selects the pieces that go into the child's writing portfolio?	___	___	___
2. Who has ongoing access to/ ownership of the writing portfolio?	___	___	___
3. Who decides on the range of writing that is to be represented in the portfolio?	___	___	___
4. Who assesses each of the selected pieces and writes a reflective piece?	___	___	___
5. Who analyzes the portfolio for patterns of growth over time?	___	___	___
6. Who takes the lead in the student/teacher portfolio conference?	___	___	___
7. Who sets the goals for future learning?	___	___	___
8. Who shares the portfolio at the parent-teacher conference?	___	___	___

FIGURE 1–3 *Survey of portfolio stance*

provides a range of sample markers that teachers might devise. For example, in assessing a young writer's sense of audience, markers such as the following could be used:

a) Recognition of audience's degree of background information.
b) Recognition of the presence or lack of shared knowledge/values in audience through choice of words or forms of language.
c) Use of pronouns, e.g. explanations of who "he," "she," etc. is in retelling or sharing an experience (Cambourne, 1988, p. 125).

Cambourne stresses, however, that teachers should not adopt markers blindly; they must work to create markers that are consistent with their understanding of literacy and with the goals they have set for student learning.

Au, however, takes a more directive approach to the design of benchmarks by determining not only what aspects of literacy teachers should assess, but how they should assess them. For example, because one of the primary goals of literacy development is the ability to respond to literature, Au suggests that teachers ask children to read a story as part of their regular classroom activity and to complete a story frame (1990a). Then the teacher assesses each story frame for inclusion of the story grammar elements. The benchmark for second graders, for example, is that they accurately identify all of the story grammar elements. A second grader who does not meet all the criteria is judged to be functioning below grade level. In Au's assessment model, teachers collect: 1) questionnaires on reading and writing attitudes, 2) a response to literature, 3) a writing sample, 4) a running record (Clay, 1979) and 5) a list of books read voluntarily. These data, collected during the fall and the spring, are included in each child's portfolio. Au believes that if all teachers collect the same range of data and use the same benchmarks, children's progress can be monitored longitudinally. Furthermore,

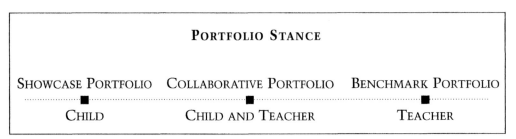

FIGURE 1–4 *Three portfolio models*

schools can strive to meet the goal of systemwide accountability (1990a, 1994).

The Benchmark Portfolio: What It Addresses

The benchmark portfolio recognizes that assessment and instruction are linked inextricably. Its fundamental goal is to inform instruction—we assess so that we know what to teach. In order for this assessment to be viable, it must be anchored in genuine literate activity, in the purposeful reading and writing endeavors of children. It also must tap affective, cognitive, and metacognitive (the ability to monitor and regulate one's own learning) dimensions of literacy. Essentially, then, assessment in the benchmark portfolio model is an integral part of instruction; that is, it is occurring continuously for the purposes of monitoring and acknowledging the learner's development.

Another prominent strength of the benchmark portfolio is its commitment to teacher knowledge. The benchmark portfolio is based on the conviction that teachers must know a great deal about literacy development in order to judge children's products and processes. It is not enough simply to collect pieces for the portfolio. What we collect is tied to what we know. However, there is disagreement about how teacher knowledge is acquired.

The Benchmark Portfolio: What It Doesn't Address

Much rests on the benchmarks. The quality of our benchmarks, and hence the quality of our assessment decisions, hinge on the quality of our teacher knowledge. The more we know, the more viable our benchmarks.

What, though, is the best way to acquire this knowledge? The two prominent benchmark models differ significantly in their approach to the acquisition of teacher knowledge. Cambourne insists that we must design our own "markers" of growth in accordance with our individual observations of children and our analyses of their work. He believes that literacy knowledge has to be constructed solely by the teacher; it cannot be passed on (1988). Au, on the other hand, suggests that the benchmarks should be designed by knowledgeable experts. She appears to believe that there is a core of objective knowledge that exists outside of the teacher's mind—a core that needs to be transmitted to and mastered by the teacher (1994). Epistemologists, scholars who examine conceptions of knowledge, would characterize Cambourne's perspective as endogenous and Au's perspective as exogenous (Fitzgerald, 1993). Not surprisingly, these philosophical orientations translate into different classroom practices. One model results in a laissez-faire approach to portfolios, with the potential for a wide range of portfolio variability among teachers. Decisions about what to collect and to analyze are idiosyncratic.

Theoretically, as teachers continue to learn from children, their understanding about assessment increases and their portfolios improve. But inevitably, questions about accountability surface. The other model takes portfolios out of the hands of the teachers and, in effect, leads to the standardization of portfolios. Teachers are told what to collect, when to collect it, and how to analyze it. Some experts have expressed concern about this trend toward portfolio standardization, cautioning that standardization will jeopardize the fundamental nature of the portfolio process (Fisher, 1995; Graves, 1994; O'Neil, 1993). Schools that adopt a benchmark model must grapple with the issue of the source of the benchmarks.

Also, somewhat problematic in the benchmark portfolio are the constraints that assessment checklists and standard forms place on our ability to observe and to reflect about children's performances. While checklists give us—especially those of us new to alternative assessment—"something to look for" in a child's writing sample, they limit what we "see." Checklists can cause us to pigeonhole some literacy responses and to miss others that are not on the checklist (Taylor, 1989).

But, the overarching reservation about the benchmark portfolio arises because the child has little, if any, involvement in the assessment process. Because benchmark portfolios exist primarily for the purpose of informing instruction, minimal, if any, attention is given to the students' self-evaluation. In this portfolio model, students generally are not asked to choose their favorite piece of writing or to write a reflective piece about their choice. Nor are they asked to consider how much reading/writing they do outside of school, or of what significance these endeavors are. Instead, assessment remains the province of the teacher. "The teachers we work with rely on observations to assess students' ownership of literacy" (Au, 1990b, p. 155).

It is no surprise, then, that concern about the exclusion of the child from the assessment process has triggered a reordering of priorities with regard to the fundamental purpose of portfolios. This reordering, which places the child's self-assessment ahead of the teacher's instructional decision-making, prompted the creation of the showcase portfolio.

The Showcase Portfolio

If the majority of your checkmarks filled the Child column in Figure 1–3, you probably agree with Jane Hansen that "evaluation is primarily an act performed by the student" (1994, p. 27). In contrast to the benchmark portfolio, where the teacher primarily is responsible for assessment and where the fundamental goal is to inform teacher instruction, the showcase portfolio essentially begins and ends with the student. Its mission is student self-assessment, followed by student goal-creation and attainment. In classrooms where showcase portfolios are used, students take charge of assessment. First, they select pieces from their working folders which they believe mark their progress as readers, writers, and individuals. Not only do students select a best piece and a favorite piece—one that holds personal significance as their best work, but they also are encouraged to choose writing in which they "learned something new" (Graves, 1994, p. 175). Children then justify their selections with written reflections. Selected items, whether written at school or at home, become part of the students' showcase portfolios. Once these generic guidelines are met, children are given complete control of their portfolios. They can choose to include the literacy biography they wrote or pictures of a special project they completed. They can include the "good news telegrams" that peers wrote about a piece they shared during Author's Chair. They can include a graph of the genres with which they experimented over the course of a term. They can include surveys they completed and so forth. As the name implies, writers create portfolios that showcase their strengths as learners and as individuals.

Goal-setting by the student is central to this model. With the support of the teacher, students set literacy goals and specify steps they intend to take to meet them. For example, in a portfolio conference, Hansen asked one sixth grader, "What would you like to learn next in order to become a better reader?" (1994, p. 37). The student replied that she wanted to read "bigger words." When asked how she might achieve this goal, the student said she would read books that were more challenging than the *Baby Sitter Club* books she had been reading. The showcase portfolio is based on the belief that students must be trusted to assess their strengths and to chart their own learning. As Rief points out:

> I have discovered that students knew themselves as learners better than anyone else. They set goals for themselves and judged how well they had reached these goals. They thoughtfully and honestly evaluated their own learning with far more detail and introspection than I thought possible . . . I don't have to be the sole evaluator of Nahanni's writing and reading. She's far better at it than I am. (1990, pp. 25–27)

The Showcase Portfolio: What It Addresses

Like the benchmark portfolio, the showcase portfolio has its origins in genuine literacy tasks in which children engage daily. It, too, taps various dimensions of literacy but does so by asking the children to collect and to reflect on their affective, cognitive, and metacognitive understandings. The principle advocates of the showcase portfolio make a compelling case for involving students in the assessment and advancement of their own learning (Graves, 1994; Hansen, 1994). They remind us that since literacy is a life event—one that encompasses both home and school—portfolios need to reflect the breadth of home and school endeavors. They point to the anecdotal data on the assessment insights of young learners and remind us that children often are perceptive about their strengths and weaknesses (Hansen, 1994; Rief, 1990; Stowell & Tierney, 1995; Tierney, Carter, & Desai, 1991). In addition, showcase advocates demonstrate the link between self-assessment and personal goal-setting; learning in its truest form results when we set our sights on a worthy goal and work diligently until we have achieved it.

The Showcase Portfolio: What It Doesn't Address

But the showcase portfolio is not without its challenges, as the following scenarios illustrate:

> Ted has selected a story about a dog as his best piece for his portfolio. In the portfolio conference, Ted explains that he chose this piece because it was "neat, and not too messy." You smile as you recall Graves's developmental research on what children's concept of good writing entails (1983). Ted, like most primary (and some older) children, has chosen his piece because it is aesthetically pleasing (neat, good handwriting and so forth). It appears that content of his piece did not factor into his decision. You jot down Ted's comment, and your own insight. You compliment Ted on his neat work. You then ask him to pull out his story about the grandfather and the young boy. This story surpasses the dog story in terms of story grammar elements and characterization. In an effort to show him how he has grown as a writer (Graves, 1994; Hansen, 1994), you explain to Ted that you think this grandfather story is his best piece because the characters' actions and dialogue show how much they care about each other. However, since the showcase portfolio gives total ownership to Ted, you respect his selection of the dog story and do not ask him to include his grandfather piece. His grandfather piece is tucked back into his writing folder.

> Maureen, grade 5, has a talent for writing mystery stories. Not surprisingly, at the end of the school term, she chooses two mysteries (the original and the sequel) to showcase in her portfolio. She states that her goal for the next term is to write the sequel to the sequel. As you look through her writing folder, you note that Maureen has written only fictional pieces (mysteries) over the first three terms and has not experimented with any other genres. Since goal-setting in the showcase portfolio is the purview of the child, you are reluctant to ask her to redesign her goal. Yet, you feel that she is not stretching herself as a writer. You plan to do a better job at immersing the class in poetry and nonfiction, with the hope that Maureen will broaden her genre experimentation over the course of the next term.

When our selections, assessments, and goals differ from the selections, assessments, and goals of the child, what do we do? What happens to our insights about the child's literacy progress? How and where are they recorded? Should the portfolio, which will stand as the evaluative instrument, represent only the child's thinking? Or do our thoughts also have a place in the record?

As valuable as children's insights are, we must recognize that they are new to the process of self-assessment. When children reflect on their writing samples, we can anticipate perceptions that range from remarkably insightful to developmentally bound. Graves's research, cited in the Ted scenario above, illuminates this point (1983). If asked what makes a piece of writing "good," a young child will explain that pieces with accurate spelling are "good." Soon, pieces with neat handwriting take precedence. Only after children gain some control of these aspects of composition does concern for writing conventions (punctuation, capitalization . . .), followed by concern for the quality of their ideas, begin to emerge. Graves's research corroborates other preliminary findings which suggest that children's ability to self-assess develops slowly. Only gradually do children learn to make more sophisticated judgments about their learning (Hansen, 1994; Snider, Lima, & DeVito, 1994). This research suggest two pivotal questions: Do we wait for children's assessment understandings to develop naturally? Or do we enter Vygotsky's "zone of proximal development" (1978, p. 86) and work side-by-side with children to extend their understandings in developmentally responsive ways? Vygotsky makes it clear that children cannot operate within this "zone of proximal development" without a more knowledgeable other. If we expect to bring children to the "cutting edge of learning" (Schickedanz, 1995), or in this particular case, the cutting edge of self-assessment, we have to enter the "zone" to determine what they do when they assess their work, and what they are ready to learn. Vygotskian theory suggests that we should not expect children to look at their learning with the same breadth and depth as we look at it. Nor should we ignore our responsibility to engage them in new learning.

It is for these reasons that a third kind of portfolio, the collaborative portfolio, has emerged.

The Collaborative Portfolio

If, in responding to the who's-in-charge survey items in Figure 1–3, you found yourself gravitating toward the middle of the continuum, you probably use a collaborative model of portfolio assessment. This model attempts to merge what is best about the benchmark and showcase portfolios. The collaborative portfolio allows us to "hear the voices of the child, the teacher, and the parent. . . ." through the creation of two portfolios (Paratore, 1993). In the collaborative portfolio model, the child retains responsibility for her showcase portfolio and takes it home at the end of the year. But, in addition, we create the collaborative portfolio by merging copies of the child's selections and reflections with our choices and analyses (and those of parents). The collaborative portfolio remains in school and moves with the child from grade to grade. The goals of the collaborative portfolio are threefold: 1) to engage children in self-assessment and literacy goal-setting, 2) to assess children's progress as well as their self-assessments and goals, and 3) to pool this data base of information for the purpose of guiding instructional interactions.

Tierney, Carter, and Desai's early work in the area of portfolios set the groundwork for the collaborative portfolio, although the authors refer to their portfolios as showcase portfolios (1991). In fact, Tierney et al. are cited for advocating the showcase portfolio (Valencia & Place, 1994). But thorough review of their work reveals a commitment to collaboration between child and teacher in the creation of portfolios that goes beyond the showcase portfolio profiled above. They advocate that the child and the teacher work together to collect and to analyze contributions to the portfolio.

With regard to the "who's-in-charge" question, the child takes the lead both in preparing and in analyzing the portfolio. Kyle, for example, decides initially which writing samples and so on will go into his showcase portfolio. He writes a reflective piece about each selection. During the portfolio conference, he shares these selections and rationales. I follow his lead, praising, questioning, and teaching, when appropriate. I also share my judgment about which writing samples mark his progress over the course of the school term, and, eventually, the school year. Copies of both of our selections/reflections are placed in the collaborative portfolio. During the portfolio conference, Kyle also shares his writing goals for the next term. I assess these goals, provide positive feedback, and discuss additional or alternative goals, if necessary. A record of these agreed-upon goals is placed in the collaborative portfolio. During the parent conference, he leads the session by sharing his work and progress. I buttress his observations with additional layers of assessment data and analysis. Thus, at each point in the portfolio process, collaboration prevails between the child and the teacher.

What exactly is included in Kyle's collaborative portfolio? While Kyle is responsible for the contents of his showcase portfolio (see generic guidelines, pages 14–15), I am responsible for the contents of his collaborative portfolio. As already mentioned, Kyle's collaborative portfolio includes copies of the pieces he selected for his showcase portfolio as well as his reflections along with copies (or originals) of my selections and reflections. It is important to note, though, that not every selection made each term by either Kyle or me remains in the collaborative portfolio. Portfolios are *selective* collections. It is my job to weigh the evidence at the end of each term and to select the pieces that mark growth. For example, if Kyle chooses a bed-to-bed personal narrative (see Chapter 4, p. 61) at the end of both the first and second term, I keep only his first term piece in the collaborative portfolio. When Kyle shifts from writing bed-to-bed narratives to writing a personal narrative that includes an affective or reflective component during the fourth term, I include this piece in his collaborative portfolio (with a reflection). It is also my job to ensure that his collaborative portfolio profiles his abilities as a writer. While Kyle chooses only stories for his showcase portfolio, I make sure that his collaborative portfolio contains examples of his work across the genres. While Kyle chooses only final drafts for his showcase portfolio, I include the evolution of at least one piece of work. I also include his writing record and his statement of goals for each term along with his assessment of meeting these goals. In addition, I select one or two of Kyle's early September pieces to use as baseline data. For example, I choose one of Kyle's earliest stories to which I can compare later stories. (Note: Some teachers also collect baseline data on the conventions of written language through use of a dictation at the beginning of the year. For example, some teachers dictate a nursery rhyme such as "Jack and Jill" to young writers or an excerpt from a chapter book to older children. These dictations are repeated in January and May. Children are asked to note progress over time; we also assess progress.) Kyle's collaborative portfolio also includes the portfolio retrospectives which I complete each term. These retrospectives, examples of which are included in Chapter 10, summarize his writing development each term (and across terms).

Kyle's collaborative portfolio also can include other documents. For example, if I have asked Kyle and his peers to write literacy biographies, I include these biographies. If I have asked parents to write letters about their child, I include these letters. If I have asked them to complete the "writing survey" (Atwell, 1987), I include these forms. If I have asked to complete other checklists and/or rating scales, I may include these also. Again, while I try to include only pieces of evidence that contribute to Kyle's profile as a writer and that mark his progress, I do work to ensure that the contents of his portfolio captures his understandings across the three primary dimensions:

Affective Development: How Kyle feels about the act of writing and about himself as a writer impinges upon his ability to write. The more positive his attitude about and interest in writing is, the greater his potential as a writer. As Piaget concludes, ". . . there is no behavior pattern, however intellectual, which does not involve affective factors such as motives. . . . The two aspects, affective and cognitive, are at the same time inseparable and irreducible" (1969, p. 158). Therefore, I need to collect data concerning his attitude about and interest in writing as well as his views of himself as a writer. While a number of data collection options are available to me, I want to ensure that I can corroborate one piece of evidence with supporting evidence. For example, I might ask Kyle (and his peers) to complete the writing survey and/or the Denver writing attitude survey (Rhodes, 1993) at the beginning of the year. I note that Kyle writes on his survey that he likes to write. As I look for other data to support Kyle's perception, I note that in his literacy biography he talks about the plays and stories that he wrote voluntarily over the summer. In addition, my anecdotal notes from conferences and from Author's Chair sessions corroborate his eagerness to write. Confident that Kyle's perceptions match his actions at the beginning of the school year, I continue to collect these affective data at the midpoint and end of year.

Cognitive Development: When writers write, they engage a multitude of thought processes. They activate prior knowledge of a topic and/or an experience, decide whom their audience will be and what literary form their knowledge will take, analyze the content of the piece in order to add, delete, or reorganize information, and so forth. Each of these and other cognitive activities is tied to specific packages of knowledge—cognitive structures known as schemata—that the writer has constructed. For example, if Kyle's schema (singular for schemata) for story is one in which the main characters are tumbled through a string of action-packed events, he probably will write what Applebee calls a focused chain (1978). If, on the other hand, Kyle's schema story is one in which characters and theme are interwoven, he probably will write a true narrative (Applebee, 1978). Thus, as I assemble Kyle's collaborative portfolio, I ask myself three essential questions: What knowledge does he have? How does he use this knowledge to construct meaning? How does this knowledge change over time? I ask these questions with regard to his understandings of specific genres (personal narratives, story, nonfiction, poetry), of the writing process, of the written conventions, and so forth. Answers to these questions are found by analyzing Kyle's writing samples, by talking with Kyle, by asking him to "think-aloud," and by observing Kyle and recording significant observations. As with assessment of affective development, I am collecting layers of corroborating evidence and drawing conclusions across these layers of data. I am also marking his progress over time.

Metacognitive Development: Kyle has just written a draft of a story about a lost dog. As he rereads his draft, he checks to see that he has included a story problem, attempts to solve the problem, and a resolution. He notices that his original problem hasn't been solved and decides that he needs to rewrite his ending. Kyle is engaging in metacognitive activity—in essence, thinking about his own thinking (Brown, 1980). Metacognition refers to the degree of self-awareness and of self-regulation that a writer brings to the act of writing. Good writers set purposes for their writing, know when they run into difficulty, know what corrective action to take, reread pieces to check the degree of correspondence between intended meaning and actual meaning, and so forth. Essentially, good writers distance themselves from their work in order to assess and rework what they have written. In order to collect evidence of Kyle's metacognitive understandings for his collaborative portfolio, I primarily rely on my anecdotal notes from conversations with Kyle during conferences and on the reflections Kyle writes for each piece he selects for his showcase portfolio. For example, I notice one day during writing workshop that Kyle is having trouble getting something on paper. I stop at his desk and ask how he's doing. When he explains that he can't think of anything to write, I ask what he can do to solve this problem. When he tells me that he can't think of anything to do, I have important data for an anecdotal note, and a teaching opportunity at hand. As with the other dimensions of literacy, I work to corroborate evidence across layers of data. I also watch for increased metacognitive understandings over time.

In the chapters that follow, numerous examples of the assessment of these literacy dimensions are provided. In addition, Chapter 10 offers further elaboration on the collaborative portfolio—how it is introduced to children, how it is used during the portfolio conference, and so forth.

The Collaborative Portfolio: What It Addresses

As already noted, the collaborative portfolio capitalizes on the strengths of both the showcase and benchmark portfolios to ensure that assessment:

1. Is grounded in genuine literacy endeavors and in a variety of social contexts (Cambourne, 1988; Graves, 1994; Valencia, 1990).

2. Is an integral part of instruction, occurring continuously for the purposes of monitoring and acknowledging the learner's development (Au, 1994; Tierney, Carter, & Desai, 1991; Valencia, 1990).

3. Taps the student's affective, cognitive, and metacognitive understandings of text (Au, 1990b, 1994; Valencia, 1990).

4. Encourages self-evaluation of both the learner and the teacher (Goodman, 1989; Graves, 1994).

5. Is process-oriented (Cambourne, 1988; Harp, 1991; Paratore & Indrisano, 1987).

6. Values the professional judgment of *informed* teachers (Goodman, 1989; Johnston, 1987).

In addition, the collaborative portfolio model is consistent with Vygotsky's "zone of proximal development" (1978, p. 86). It expects children to take on as much responsibility for their own assessment as they can handle. It expects children to reflect on their achievements and progress. It also expects these reflections to range from insightful to developmentally predictable. Because children's perceptions often differ from adult perceptions, the collaborative portfolio model also expects us to assess the quality of children's self-reflections and to extend or redirect their thinking. In addition, it expects us to teach children how to assess their own learning. As De Fina notes, students need "to develop criteria for judging their work by observing and internalizing standards and models presented to them" (1992, p. 32). Ultimately, though, we are responsible for providing a comprehensive profile of what the child is able to do and for establishing with the child suitable goals for future learning. In the collaborative model, the child takes the lead in exploring his literacy strengths and weaknesses, but we assess the child's level of reflection, as well as the portfolio as a whole.

The Collaborative Portfolio: What It Doesn't Address

Like the previous models, the collaborative portfolio is not free of problems. Like the benchmark portfolio, successful implementation of the collaborative portfolio requires considerable teacher knowledge. If we are to understand children's assessment comments, and if we are to analyze children's writing, we need to adopt a teacher-researcher stance in our classrooms and we need to know the research on writing development. We turn now to a fuller examination of this concern about teacher knowledge.

Teacher Knowledge and the Collaborative Portfolio

Make no mistake. In the final analysis, it is the teacher's knowledge that will make or break the promise of portfolio assessment. Holistic assessment is a complex and intellectually demanding undertaking, one for which many teachers have not been adequately prepared. In a recent study, Au found that while teachers were supportive of the whole literacy curriculum adopted by their school system, they were less than enthusiastic about the portfolio assessment component of the program. Teachers found it difficult to shift from reliance on the results of criterion-referenced tests to reliance on their own judgment of children's work. They also had difficulty linking assessment and instruction (Au, 1994).

When teachers are tossed into a sea of children's writing samples without a compass, they tend to bob aimlessly on the surface of the children's work. One team of researchers found that "teachers' assessments of genre-mixed collections of writing were superficial at best . . . teachers focused more on convention than communication, organization rather than originality, and generalizations rather than genre-appropriate comments" (Gearhart, Wolf, Burkey, & Whittaker, 1994, p. 426). Other researchers have found great variability in teachers' ratings of children's best pieces and have attributed such results, at least in part, to the teachers' lack of understanding (Koretz, McCaffrey, Klein, Bell, and Stecher, 1992).

Fortunately, other preliminary research suggests a brighter picture. Valencia and Place report positive findings on the part of both students and teachers after one year of experimentation (1994). The researchers stress, though, that these results depend on the presence of certain conditions: 1) a five-year implementation plan that has philosophical and fiscal support from the school district, 2) interest and commitment of a core group of representative teachers, and 3) monthly sessions during which participants discussed underlying assumptions about assessment, agreed upon the components of the portfolios, debated implementation plans, and so forth. During these monthly sessions, discussions about the theory and practice of literacy inevitably surfaced, enabling teachers to consolidate their knowledge.

Would that all of us could participate in a portfolio project of the calibre designed by Valencia and Place (1994). But, in reality, many of us venture into portfolio assessment as brave warriors, armed with solid convictions and boundless energy, but without essential support. Often, we enter without much depth and breadth of knowledge. As previously noted, conceptions of what constitutes knowledge and how it is acquired vary (Fitzgerald, 1993). Endogenicists, such as Cambourne, believe that knowledge about literacy and its assessment must be constructed by the individual (1988). Knowledge cannot be poured into our heads, it has to be created. Exogenicists, such as Au, on the other hand, believe that there is an objective knowledge base about literacy that needs to be mastered and applied (1994).

At a glance, these two perspectives appear so far apart that a middle ground cannot be achieved. However, in all likelihood, the acquisition of new knowledge is not an either-or situation but rather a continual interplay of endogenism and exogenism. Learning to assess children's literacy requires the recurring cycles of both periods of focused observation of children (along with conversation) and their work and the study of the literary research. For decades, educators "looked at" young children's scribbling and pretend writing and "saw" scribbling and pretend writing. It took one teacher-researcher to "look at" the same episodes of early writing in a focused and analytical way to "see" the range of hypotheses that young writers bring to the act of early writing (Clay, 1975). However, once we understand Clay's findings, it is our responsibility to make them our own and to use them to analyze what young writers do. While we use this knowledge to inform our assessment, we remain vigilant in our efforts to "see" things in new ways. Thus, the acquisition of new knowledge comes from both high levels of "kidwatching" (Goodman, 1989) and a working knowledge of the research. We need to check our observations against the accumulated knowledge. We owe it to ourselves to seek opportunities for quality professional development, to enlist the help of mentors and teacher study groups, and to engage in self-study. "Systematic, rigorous, informed intelligence, ordered and coherent grasp of subject matter, and deliberate application of thought to specific issues depends heavily on planned study" (Delattre, 1988, p. 17).

What we need to know about children's writing development is just beginning to find its way into the portfolio literature. Tierney et al. (1991) offer broad guidelines on what we might look for when we review a child's writing portfolio: 1) the range of writing included, 2) the child's attitude toward writing, 3) the presence of voice in the child's writing, and so on. However, what is needed, in addition to the broad strokes, are the finer strokes that capture the richness and the depth of children's writing. This book paints these "finer strokes."

About This Book

This book advocates the adoption of the collaborative portfolio model because I believe that insights of both the child and the teacher are necessary to illuminate the child's tapestry of learning—past, present, and future. This book illustrates the principles and practices of the collaborative portfolio model.

Organization

In the chapters that follow, important research findings about children's writing development are discussed. These findings are woven into the fabric of children's writing in order to focus on what children do before, during, and after the act of composing.

The first half of the book concentrates on the assessment of the content (ideas) of young writers' pieces. Research about what writers do when they choose topics, rehearse, draft and revise across the genres of personal narratives, story writing, and expository writing are discussed. The second half of the book focuses on the importance of assessing the writing conventions, including spelling, handwriting, punctuation, and capitalization. While the organizational framework of this book parallels the process of assessing writing—content first, mechanics second—the importance of connecting assessment data across the phases of writing is emphasized. Good assessment requires that we zoom in on a specific aspect of a child's writing, while placing this aspect in the context of the whole. A child's reluctance to revise may have more to do with his/her topic choice than with the actual process of revision. Just as writing is recursive in nature, so too must be our assessment.

To bring a sense of coherence and life to this book, the portfolio of a delightful third grader, Shane, is profiled throughout. Research findings are used to provide insights about Shane's writing record, his writing samples, excerpts from his interviews and surveys, and so on. In addition to Shane's third-grade writing, examples of his work from grades 4 and 5, as well as interviews and surveys collected at the end of fifth grade, are highlighted. To illustrate the development of writing across a broad age range, writing samples from both younger and older children are integrated into each chapter. Finally, writing samples from home, as well as from school, are included to emphasize the expansive nature of literacy and to strengthen the assessment tapestry.

Recurring Themes

Before moving into the next chapter to meet Shane and to become acquainted with the classroom context that supported his journey into writing, I want to highlight the recurring themes you will find in this book, because they are essential for effective portfolio assessment:

Teacher as Instrument

What the standardized test was to evaluation is what the teacher is to portfolio assessment. The teacher, girded by extensive knowledge, in effect, becomes the instrument of assessment. Rather than comparing children with other children on decontextualized test items as norm-referenced tests do, and rather than comparing children against cut-off scores on skills tests as criterion-referenced tests do, portfolio assessment examines the child's performances across time. This more powerful form of referencing is known as self-referencing (Johnston, 1992). The adoption of self-referenced evaluation insists that for ". . . teachers to be effective agents of assessment, they must have a deep knowledge of the disciplines of reading and writing. . . . The more knowledgeable teachers are about reading and writing, the more observant they are of students' literacy behavior, the more productive will be their assessments and their interactions with students" (IRA/NCTE, 1994, pp. 28–29).

Writer's Self-Assessment

According to Jeanne Paratore, "The collection of work samples doesn't become a portfolio until the child engages in self-assessment" (1993, p. 4). The centrality of this principle has already been emphasized earlier in this chapter. More importantly, it will be woven into each chapter under the subheading titled *Shane on Shane*, in which Shane will share with us his insights, musings, and the like.

Corroborating Evidence

In James's kindergarten, children are given fifteen minutes of free time each morning. Free choice options include: the book corner, the block area, the dress-up/drama area, puzzles, and the art center. During free time, I observe the four to five kindergartners, including James, and log their choices on an observational checklist. After three weeks, I note that James spends his time either in the block area or playing with the puzzles but has not gravitated to the book center. Wondering about the reliability of my observations with regard to his interest in books (since I rotate observations and tend only to watch James on Mondays), I decide to watch James on five consecutive days. His student teacher also keeps an independent log. The results, consistent across time and observers, render reliable (stable) data: James does not go to the book center. The temptation is strong to draw the conclusion that James is not interested in books. However, reliability is only one facet of the assessment data that must be taken into account; the other is validity. The fact that the observational log yielded reliable data does not ensure that it yields accurate or valid information. Assessment of the construct—interest in books—must be based on broader data than observation during free time. Anecdotal notes (Figure 1–5) taken during storytime reveal not only that James is highly attentive to stories read but that he is also very responsive to literature. For example, he readily makes connections between story events and his own life. A conversation with James's mother corroborates the fact that James adores books and spends a significant amount of time at home in book activity (Figure 1–6). A check of the library books signed out by James reveals a steady weekly flow of books from school to home. In a conference with James, the assessment puzzle falls into place:

CAROL: Your mom tells me that you are reading lots of books at home.

JAMES: Yeah, I read *More Spaghetti I Say,* and *Once There was a Dark, Dark Path*, and *More Spaghetti I Say* and some more.

CAROL: That's great, James. I haven't noticed you reading books during free time. Why is that?

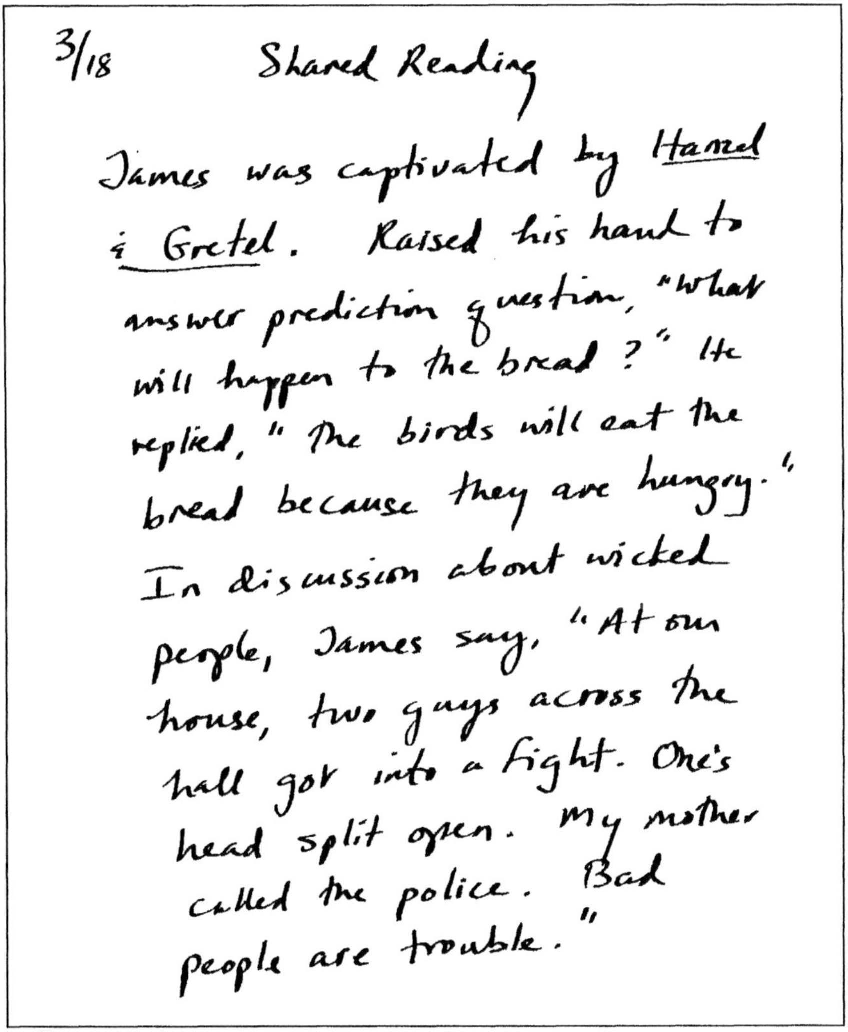

> 3/18   Shared Reading
>
> James was captivated by Hansel & Gretel. Raised his hand to answer prediction question, "What will happen to the bread?" He replied, "The birds will eat the bread because they are hungry." In discussion about wicked people, James say, "At our house, two guys across the hall got into a fight. One's head split open. My mother called the police. Bad people are trouble."

FIGURE 1–5   *Anecdotal notes on personal response to literature*

JAMES: I have. You didn't see me. Mrs. Leach gave me a B on my report card 'cause I didn't get a book but I did but she didn't see.

CAROL: Oh, my. Next time you're in the book center let me know. Do you play with puzzles at home?

JAMES: No, 'cuz my brother lost all the things. But Mrs. Leach has all the things and I play with them.

Without James's mother's corroborating evidence, and without layers of other important data, we risk making an erroneous classroom-bound decision about a literacy phenomenon (interest in books). Teachers who engage in portfolio assessment must approach the analysis of children's writing with the same investigatory spirit as defense lawyers approach their cases. We need to fortify our initial judgments with the "triangulating observations" of the child and the parents (Anthony, Johnson, Mickelson, & Preece, 1991, p. 52). We must record this anecdotal information

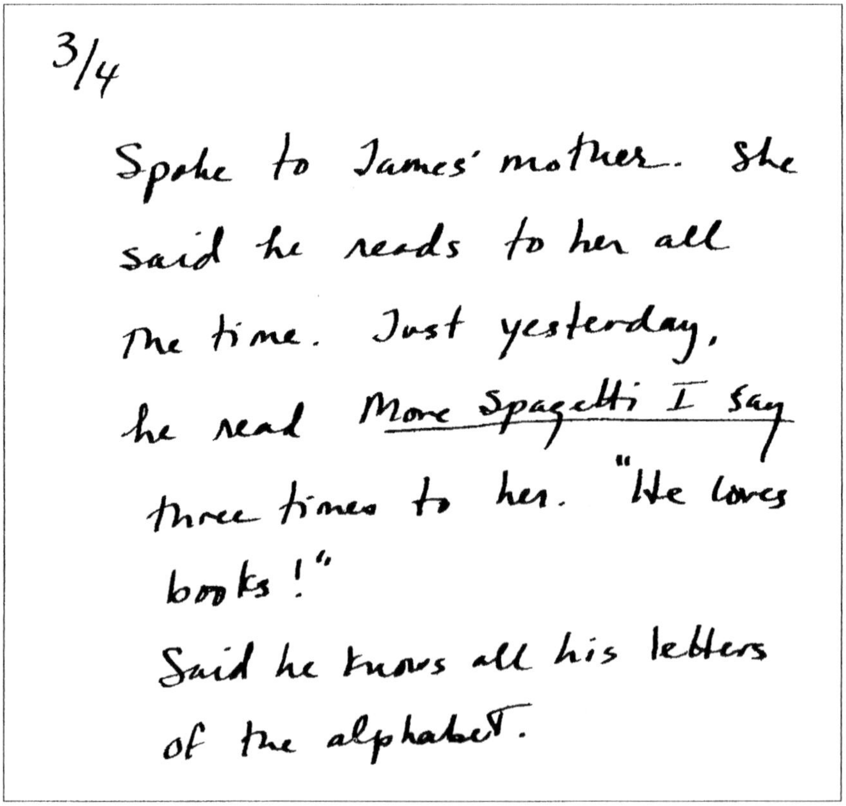

> 3/4
>
> Spoke to James' mother. She said he reads to her all the time. Just yesterday, he read *More Spagetti I say* three times to her. "He loves books!"
> Said he knows all his letters of the alphabet.

FIGURE 1–6   *Notes on conversation with James's mom*

in order to complete as much of the assessment puzzle as we can. It is the corroborating evidence that helps to strengthen our assessment decisions in terms of reliability and validity.

Teacher Self-Assessment

Before focusing our reflective lens on children's literacy activity, we need to turn that lens inward and assess ourselves, our curriculum, and our learning environment. It makes little sense to examine a child's writing folder for pieces of nonfiction if we first haven't asked ourselves, "What have I done to foster interest and knowledge in nonfiction literature?" It makes little sense to assess children's willingness to revise pieces they write, if we have not established a commitment to publishing/sharing final drafts. Our own self-assessment heightens awareness about our teaching as well as our learning, and often yields a level of inner dissonance that spurs us to redesign or refine our instructional focus.

Onward

We turn now to a key chapter in this book—the classroom context in which Shane, in his words, "learned to be a good writer." In the next chapter, Alice Earle, Shane's third-grade teacher, will describe the literacy milieu in which Shane and his peers blossomed as readers and writers. Shane, now a fifth grader, describes Alice as "awesome. She was just amazing with reading and writing. We got to have conferences every other day, and pick our own stuff to read and write."

Shane's Classroom

The Context for Portfolio Assessment

2

by Alice Earle

Shane

A scattering of freckles, a mischievous grin, and the twinkle in his hazel eyes are some of the memories that float back when I think of Shane. I also see sandy brown hair growing out from a flat top cut and starting to curl around the nape of his neck, his standard baggy sweat suit and his untied black Reeboks with white tube socks that have gathered themselves in a pile around his ankles. But this picture is only a glimpse of the Shane I came to know through my year with him as his third-grade teacher and in particular through the reading and writing workshops in which he participated as part of my language arts program.

During the first week of school I was approached by our Chapter I teacher who came to work out a schedule to provide tutoring for students who had been identified by the end of second grade as performing weakly in their use of language skills. Imagine my surprise when Shane's name was brought up as a potential candidate for these services. For after only a few days in the classroom, he had already distinguished himself as an enthusiastic participant in class discussions, sharing his insight, empathy, and quick wit. I probed further about why Shane had been referred, considering his competency in expressive language. I was told that he had performed poorly in some of the language sections on standardized tests which were given as a screening measure. In addition, his written assignments, which contained numerous misspellings and were difficult to read because of his handwriting, were often incomplete. I was reluctant to have him participate in a pull-out program because of the valuable time he would miss in class. Fortunately I worked out a compromise that allowed Shane to stay in my classroom during the regular writing and reading workshop times, with the in-class support of our special needs teacher and reading teacher. In addition he attended a fifteen-minute small-group tutoring session with the Chapter I teacher after lunch four days a week while his peers were working on individual spelling activities in the classroom.

In the final months of Shane's year in third grade it became obvious that Chapter I services were no longer needed and they were discontinued. Shane had shown progress in every area of his literacy learning and exhibited a confidence in his own abilities that was growing daily. Our time together had come to an end, but his commitment to reading and writing was just beginning to flourish.

Shane and the Writing Workshop

Let's go back in time to that September when Shane started participating in writing workshop in my third-grade classroom to get a sense of what was happening as he moved through his days in that program.

Shane is entering a classroom where he is given the opportunity to experience a model for literacy learning based on Atwell's principles of reading and writing workshops that I have adapted for my third graders. These principles—*time, choice, response, skills and strategies taught in context, adults model reading/writing, writers read/readers write,* and t*eachers become learners*—will be explained within the context of the writing workshop.

Shane's workshop begins each day with a ten- to fifteen-minute minilesson that can expand or contract to suit the needs of the topic being addressed. Early in the school year the minilesson focus is primarily

FIGURE 2–1   *Writers read*

on workshop procedures, dealing with topics like introducing and generating rules for using writing workshop time, demonstrating the procedure known as status of class which is used at the beginning of every workshop, introducing the file station for writing folders, demonstrating the use of forms, and explaining the format for weekly whole-group sharing. As the year progresses Shane's minilessons will focus more on the writing process and strategies of good writers and will include my sharing of books and authors I love, along with sharing my own writing and that of my students as we explore a variety of genres. During these minilessons, the principles of teaching skills in context, adults modeling, writers reading, and students receiving helpful response from peers and teachers are interacting as vital elements.

Following the opening minilesson, the organizational scheme of Shane's writing workshop each day includes sustained silent writing for everyone. I move around the room to take the status of class—recording what each child is doing—then I and any specialist who might be available that day confer with students. Shane writes every day for at least thirty minutes, and often longer, in accordance with the principle of providing regular chunks of time for students to think, write, confer, and read. Shane's workshop operates under the principle of choice, with Shane choosing his own topics and genres. Toward the end of the first

FIGURE 2–2   *Sharing books and authors I love*

term, Shane also chooses which piece he wants to take through the process of revision and editing for publication. Through the individual conferences with a teacher, Shane is provided another opportunity for helpful response and skills to be taught in context. The use of strategies, rules, and forms are made meaningful as they relate to his own needs for writing. Another principle of Shane's writing workshop—that teachers become learners—is evident when I observe and learn from Shane what skills he has acquired, what support he may need, and what goals we can set in our conferences. Several times a week Shane also sees me writing at some point before or after individual conferences, reinforcing the principle that adults model writing for their students.

At the end of each workshop session Shane shares his writing with a partner of his choice or in a group of three. If he can't find a partner, I or any of the other teachers who are in the classroom may be a listener. Again, time to confer and the opportunity to receive helpful response from peers and/or teachers—integral principles of the workshop model—are provided for Shane.

Additionally, whole-group sharing of writing run by a student leader is scheduled weekly, with three or four students reading their pieces to the class and then receiving comments or questions concerning what was heard. This expanded forum for sharing provides more chances for helpful response and for skills and strategies to be taught in context. Shane and his classmates model for each other strategies for successful writing as well as give appropriate feedback concerning what is working and what might be a solution for a particular problem the writer is having. As always, I participate in the sharing too, either having my turn to read to the class, or raising my hand to be called upon to tell what I heard and offer a comment or ask a question. I am modeling reading and writing, giving response, and observing and learning from Shane and all of the other students in my classroom.

At the same time these principles are being incorporated into Shane's writing workshops I'm constantly asking myself questions. "Is there ample opportunity for the social processes of demonstration, participation, role playing or practicing, and performance, that Holdaway considers critical to acquisition learning, to occur?" "Are Cambourne's conditions for literacy learning (immersion, demonstration, expectation, responsibility, use, approximation, and response) present within this setting?"

Shane and Some Specifics

Questions about spelling, punctuation, grammar, and handwriting are frequently raised by those not familiar with a writing-workshop model. Explanations have been given for how skills are taught in context and how helpful response is offered through minilessons, individual confer-ences, and whole-group sharing. Providing time for the practice and use of these skills during sustained silent writing is essential. However, I would like to elaborate on three aspects of Shane's classroom program that cover these areas in more detail.

First of all, Shane learns and practices cursive writing in short daily whole-class instruction periods that are separate from the writing-workshop sessions. Once all the cursive letters are introduced, he con-tinues to practice independently, using cursive during these periods and for particular activities. However, when Shane is participating in writing workshop he does not write in cursive, unless he is making a final copy of a piece that has gone through all the stages of the writing process and he is able to write in cursive legibly. It's essential that first drafts not be encumbered by concentration on formation of letters at the expense of expressing thoughts fluently. Occasionally, some students may beg to use cursive in all their writing, and I let them try it out but will ask them to return to printing for their workshop pieces if it hinders their ability to write easily and legibly. Naturally, producing legible handwriting, whether cursive or printing, can be difficult for some children, and in Shane's case this has been a problem in the past. The use of computers for composing writing, as well as for making final copies, is an option available to Shane on a rotating basis and serves to keep the excitement in the writing process alive.

Another avenue for providing a shared activity of teaching that uses spelling, punctuation, and grammar skills in context are daily whole-class oral language sessions. Two students a day are chosen from the class to serve as secretaries who write sentences with errors from the teacher's edition of a language book on a large chart in the morning. Shane gathers with the class later in the day to correct these sentences. The secretaries call on student volunteers to tell what might be changed to make the sentences look right and sound right; then they edit the sen-tences. I guide and monitor the activity, making suggestions about what might be considered, redirecting attention to anything that has been overlooked, or offering further explanation of rules or examples of forms when necessary. During this time I keep a tally of participation and ap-propriateness of suggestions for Shane and other class members, jotting down any notes for future minilesson topics that would be relevant. Through the helpful response from peers and myself modeling the use of skills in context, students are teaching and learning from each other.

Finally, Shane and the other members of his class participate weekly in a spelling program which focuses on their own individual lists of spe-cific words; this is adapted from a model shared with me by Janis Bailey of Stratham Memorial School. These individual lists are generated after an initial class list of words for the week is constructed. Each student contributes a word that he has heard or seen, understands, and wants to learn to spell, and it is written next to his name on a chart which is also used for classroom job assignments (see Figure 2–3). The only requirement for a class list word is that it can't be a name. Students may choose a word that is a name of anything for a bonus word when making individual lists later if they wish. After I review the list, I select two words that have particular spelling patterns, variant endings and forms, or prefixes/suffixes. These become the focus of a word study session that serves as a brief minilesson where I elicit from the students further examples of words that have word parts or groups of letters like those being examined. The students are then asked to choose two words with portions spelled like each of the two class list words, in addition to their original class list word, and add a bonus word that has no stipulation other than being a word they understand. This forms an individual list of four words. The lists are turned in to me, and I add the final two words, making a total of six words that will be studied for the week. These last two words are taken from an inventory quiz that I give students during the first week of school. It is made up of high frequency words that are generally used by children at the third-grade level. If students are unfamiliar with the spellings of any of these words, I give two words a week until they have been learned. After that, I take two words each week from their writing that they have not learned to spell conventionally for the

FIGURE 2–3   *Constructing class spelling list*

last two words on their lists. Shane then practices his words using a pre-scribed method for writing and self-correcting as well as self-selected methods of study throughout the week. He is quizzed by a partner whom he quizzes in turn at the end of the week. I have students check their quiz against the correct spellings on their lists, circling any letters that don't agree before they turn in their quizzes for me to analyze. I keep track of words that have been learned and add those missed back onto a list of words that can be studied again on a new list another week. The combination of words which they have had choice in selecting, along with a few that are useful for them to know how to spell seems to give them a balance that is manageable and motivating. In addition, when Shane is self-editing a piece for publication, he will be asked to circle any misspellings and correct at least three, checking with his own lists as well as using a dictionary when necessary. Shane and his classmates gain not only from studying words that they have selected, but they also enlarge their vocabularies with words even their parents regard with amazement.

Shane and Self-Assessment

Shane is encouraged to assess himself; to help in this process a number of activities take place. During the first week of school, he completed a writing survey (Atwell, 1987) which he will complete again at the end of the year and will compare with the first (see Appendices A and B). It asks him to reflect on what he thinks about the purposes for writing and his attitudes toward his own writing. As mentioned already, toward the end of the first term he selects a favorite piece of writing he deems worthy to revise, edit, and publish for sharing with others. A copy of this will become part of his portfolio along with the surveys and later favorite pieces that he selects as samples of his best work.

Shane also is introduced to a self-assessment scale (see Appendix C) via a writing-workshop minilesson toward the end of the first term. He continues to rate himself at the end of each term for the rest of the school year. At the start of the second term I confer with Shane about his self-assessment and my assessments of his writing; together we review goals he has set for himself and those I have constructed for him. When the second and successive terms draw to an end, he reviews the goals that had been set for that term and writes a reflection on skills he uses and goals he has met. At the start of each successive term he once again confers with me; we share assessments and goals for that term. At the end of the final term for the school year Shane writes about what he has enjoyed, what he thought was the best part of writing workshop, and his goals for the coming year. These reflections are kept with his portfolio and passed on to his teacher for the following year.

Life After Shane

In the years since Shane was my student, I have continued to add layers to my reading/writing workshop model. As my program has evolved some things have remained the same while others have changed. Inspired by Calkins's and Harwayne's work I have begun having students choose their own writer's notebook to use for all their "seed ideas" instead of using folders (see Figure 2–4). I encourage them to take their notebooks wherever they go and reflect upon what they have written in search of possible projects to take through the writing process. In addition to the welcome letter I send students before school starts in which I ask them to bring a writer's notebook, I enclose a letter for the family introducing myself and explaining the kinds of activities that go on in my classroom. I also send a letter asking parents to write to me of insights about their child as a learner.

During the first weeks of school I now ask students to write autobiographical sketches of themselves as readers, writers, mathematicians, and learners; later in the school year, I ask them to reflect and write about how they have changed in each of these respects. In addition to the surveys, interviews, student and teacher assessment scales, and se-

FIGURE 2–4   *Students write in their notebooks*

lected writing that I previously included in the collaborative portfolios, I now keep copies of the parent letters, autobiographical sketches, and reflections. Although in the past I never excluded students from parent conferences, I now invite their presence in order to share and explain their portfolios. Just recently I invited all the parents to visit on a day near the end of school when they could explore the classroom displays and view portfolios with their children. In our school district, a new format for progress reports that I have helped develop is sent to all parents of students in first through third grade. It lists descriptors for content area, literacy, and social skills in a checklist format, rating behaviors on a five-scale continuum ranging from not yet to consistently observed, and comments on each child as a learner. I have been having students fill out their own copy several weeks before I do and I use their self-evaluation as a reference when I make out the report for parents.

Because of my belief that children should have the opportunity to become literate in modes beyond reading, writing, listening, and speaking, I now offer more choices for artistic and dramatic expression in the content areas. I have begun to experiment with simulations and with extended theme studies involving multimodal learning (that includes role plays) which end with a whole-class event. Students create diary entries, write dialogue and make lists for props needed in the production of minidramas, and take notes during research for the creation of displays. I am also striving to open up the possibilities for children to create what Fisher and Cordeiro call "personal paths of inquiry" in which they formulate their own questions to pursue and answer and utilize all their literacy skills in that quest (1994). In a similar vein, I am encouraging students to use the "tools" of reading, writing, and mathematics for real purposes, resulting in what some describe as "authentic" activities, which have a value that lasts beyond the actual event.

Influenced by Doris's *Doing What Scientists Do*, I have also provided many experiences for children to make observations as scientists do and then encourage them to take those observations through the same processes as any other piece of writing before going public (1991). With all these endeavors I have been very conscious of the necessity of helping students develop the social skills of working together as a community and with each other. We work with the importance of language literacy in expressing feelings, in empathizing with others, and in helping resolve conflicts. Consequently, I encourage students to write about and discuss behavior problems while brainstorming possible solutions. Teaching students to care is essential for all. I agree with Ruth Charney that "My best teaching comes from my deepest convictions" (1991). My deepest conviction is that nothing matters unless we care about one another.

Not So Final Reflections

Earning a degree in education was only the beginning of what has been and continues to be a complex and exhilarating career. At the heart of all that I and all teachers must do to teach our students well is the principle that teachers become learners. I read, attend conferences, take courses, observe, and learn from my colleagues. In order for each and every student to become a successful learner, teachers need to recognize that there are different ways in which each child can succeed. We must seek out resources and research, observe and learn from our students, while enlisting the aid and support of their families as well. Together we will make a difference.

What the Writing Record Tells Us 3

CAROL: Shane, tell me about your writing record (Figure 3–1).

SHANE: This is my, well, (pause) it's like my index. It tells everything. You know how books have a page like this. (Shane opens to the index in the informational book, *Chief Joseph*, about which he had talked earlier in our conference.) Well, this is like that. It tells things I've written in Mrs. Earle's class—pages, all my stories, and stuff.

CAROL: Tell me what you write in each column.

SHANE: Well, the number (#) means what number the story is, like the first or the fifth. And under the Title or Topic, you write what it's called. For Date Started, you put the date here (pointing). And Fiction or Nonfiction means if it's real, like something that's really happened, I put NF for nonfiction. If it's not real, then F. The last one (the Conferences column) is when Mrs. Earle meets with me, and she writes down advice.

CAROL: What are these question marks here (pointing to column: Date Started)?

SHANE: Oh, that. Well, sometimes, it's hard to remember everything. I forget the date sometimes. There's a lot to remember in writing workshop.

A sense of accomplishment and pride accompanies Shane's excursion through his three-page writing record. It is clear that he perceives himself as a writer, one who chooses his own topics, genres, and timelines. He understands the purpose and the components of the writing record, and he acknowledges that record-keeping is a challenging skill. Entries 8 through 12, in Figure 3–1, in fact, were logged by Alice. When cross-checking his writing record with actual entries in his writing folder, Alice discovered that Shane had forgotten to log a number of pieces each month. Alice confirmed that managing the writing record continued to challenge Shane throughout the school year. Shane shows his awareness of these logistical challenges in the self-assessment of his goals for the first term, which are presented in Figure 3–2. Indeed, Shane had a lot to remember!

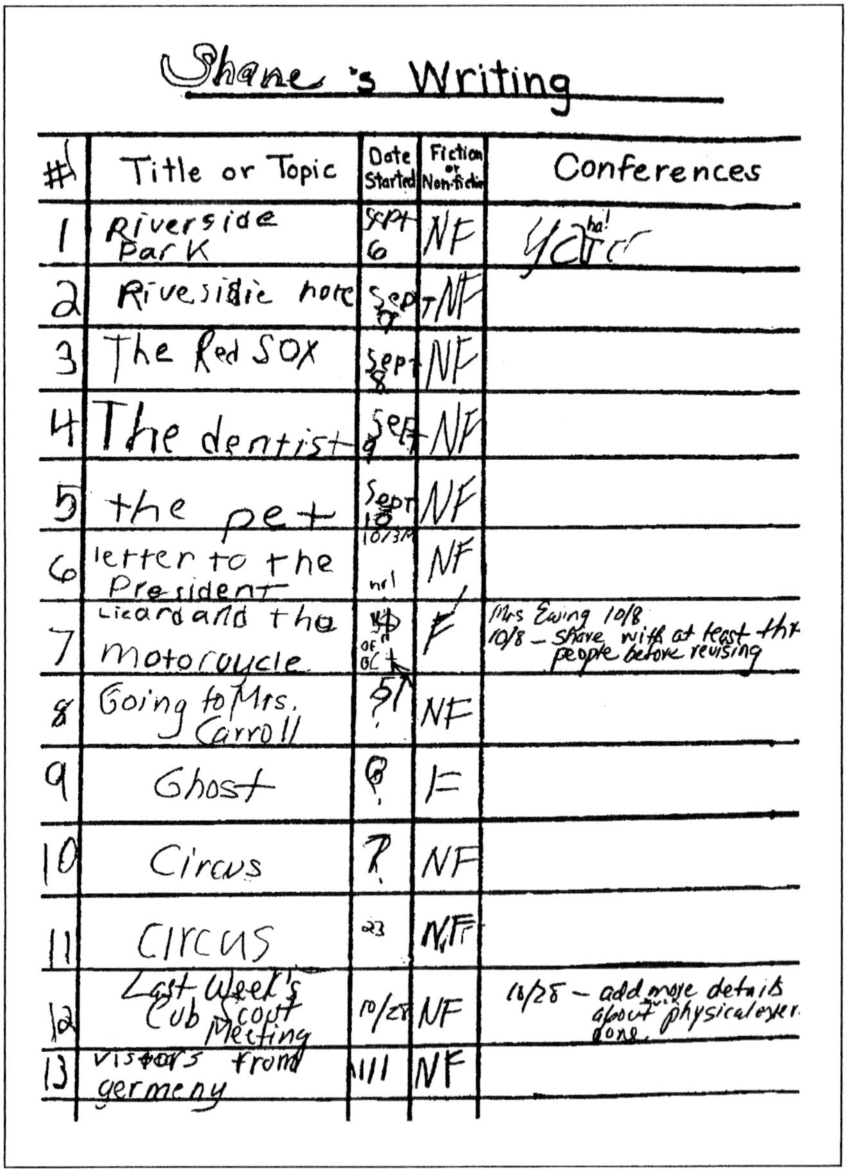
Shane's Writing

#	Title or Topic	Date Started	Fiction or Non-fiction	Conferences
1	Riverside Park	Sept 6	NF	ha!
2	Rivesidie note	Sept 7	NF	
3	The Red SOX	Sept 8	NF	
4	The dentist	Sept 9	NF	
5	the pet	Sept 10	NF	
6	letter to the President	10/3	NF	
7	Licard and the motorcycle	of OCt	F	Mrs Ewing 10/8 10/8 – Share with at least thr people before revising
8	Going to Mrs. Carroll	?	NF	
9	Ghost	?	F	
10	Circus	?	NF	
11	CIRCUS	23	NF	
12	Last Week's Cub Scout Meeting	10/28	NF	10/28 – add more details about physical exer. done.
13	visitors from germeny	11/1	NF	

FIGURE 3–1 *Shane's writing record*

This chapter demonstrates how an analysis of children's writing records, in conjunction with their writing folders, yields valuable data concerning children's topic choice, the length and duration of their pieces, and their experimentation with different genres.

Topic Choice

Graves notes that "the data show that writers who learn to choose topics well make the most significant growth in both information and skills at the point of best topic. With best topic the child exercises strongest control, establishes ownership, and with ownership, pride in the piece" (1983, p. 21). In asking Shane to share his strategies for selecting topics during writing workshop, the following conversation ensued:

CAROL: Now, how do you decide what to write about when it's writing workshop?

SHANE: Well, sometimes, when something is gonna happen that I like, I sometimes write about that. But sometimes, I like, I feel like writing a fiction story, 'cuz I have two fiction stories in here.

CAROL: Oh you do. Tell me about your fiction stories.

SHANE: It's sort of a series. One's called, um, "The Lizard and the Motorcycle" and one's called, um, "Lizard and the Caribbean."

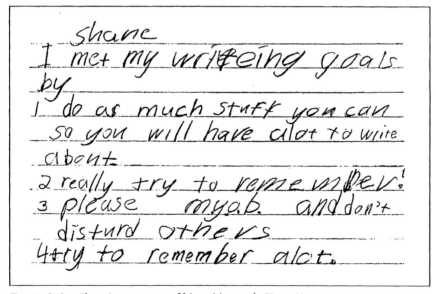

FIGURE 3–2 *Shane's assessment of his writing goals (Term 1)*

CAROL: Oh, what do you mean by a series?

SHANE: Well, I've written two stories about one person.

CAROL: I see. Where did you get the idea to write a series?

SHANE: Well, there's this book called *The Mouse and the Motorcycle* and so I wrote something and I changed it, the title, to the "Lizard and the Motorcycle." So then there's three books about the mouse and the motorcycle. One's called *The Mouse and the Motorcycle*, um, The Mouse—wait—Ralph *Runaway Ralph* and one's called *Ralph S. Mouse*.

CAROL: So how many Lizard stories have you written?

SHANE: Two . . . the "Lizard and the Motorcycle" and—oh and I also wrote another book—it wasn't about Lizard but it was sort like Lizard. I called it the "Mouse and the Bike"—the only problem is that it's one page long.

CAROL: Are you finding that you write longer stories now?

SHANE: Yeah.

CAROL: Why is that?

SHANE: Because in the beginning of the school year, I didn't know what to write about because I didn't know much about writing. Now I do. But then I saw that everybody was having so many pages of getting writing done so then I tried to write a lot.

CAROL: And did it work?

SHANE: Yeah.

This transcript illustrates the importance of talking to children about their literacy understandings. Children's insights and perceptions, captured in snippets of conversations during conferences, minilessons, and so forth, deepen our understanding of their literacy development and fortify our assessment decisions. By using both Shane's comments and his writing record and folder, we can assess Shane's facility in choosing writing topics.

At the beginning of our conversation (see transcript above), Shane briefly mentions his personal narratives: "Well, sometimes when something is gonna happen that I like, I sometimes I write about that." Children's personal narratives tend to be chronological retellings of personal events or experiences (see Figure 3–5). Children typically write narratives about what they did yesterday, during or after school, or they write about an upcoming event. (Personal narratives constitute so much of children's journal writing that the terms *personal narratives* and *journal writing* or *journal entries* are used interchangeably in this book.) Shane's writing folder reveals his penchant for the personal narrative genre. Uncertain about what to write in September ("Because in the beginning of the school year, I didn't know what to write about because I didn't know much about writing."), Shane taps his repertoire of life experiences. The vast majority (forty-one) of his September-to-March entries are retellings of daily experiences. Topping his list are school-related events (thirteen entries): What he did at PE, in art class, and in his Chapter I class. Sporting events (ten entries) also populate his writing folder: games he attended with his Dad or played with his teams. Home events (nine entries)—particularly trips taken for fun—are followed by cub scout activities (four). Shane seemed to rely on one key criterion when choosing a topic, namely, "fun." With the exception of five journal entries for the September-to-March period, Shane ended each piece with "I had fun" (or the equivalent). In narratives about upcoming events (of which there were only ten), he faithfully ends each piece with some version of "I hope I have fun."

The previous transcript also reveals Shane's excitement about his fictional pieces. After a quick mention of his personal narratives, he directs my attention to his story writing. He delights in the fact that he has created a "series" of lizard stories. Alice confirmed that whole-class conversations had occurred at the beginning of the school year about how and why some authors write a series of books or sequels. Shane absorbed and acted upon this information when he moved to this mode of writing.

Shane's acknowledgment of the influence of Beverly Cleary's books on his story construction is intriguing. He patterned his story title, "Lizard and the Motorcycle," after Cleary's *The Mouse and the Motorcycle.* As we will see in Chapter 5, Shane also paralleled (but does not copy) a number of Cleary's story events in his own story. This phenomenon, known as *intertextuality*, highlights the connections that readers and/or writers forge as they move from one text to another. While the construct of intertextuality is multidimensional (Bloome & Egan-Robertson, 1993; Cairney, 1990), for our purposes it can be defined as the influence of a text, previously read or heard, on the act of composing. Had Shane not read *The Mouse and the Motorcycle* at the beginning of the school year, his lizard series probably would not have been written. His reading record for the month of September reveals that although he read a number of picture storybooks, none infiltrated his writing. Yet, Beverly Cleary's books sparked a string of action-packed stories. Hypotheses about this literary eruption, and a closer look at Shane's intertextual experimentation, will be shared in Chapter 5.

All in all, Shane is successful in bringing his life and literature experiences to his writing. Although he started to make a list in September of potential writing topics, he did not continue with this strategy. Topics, for the most part, came readily to him because, early on, he recognized that writing springs from life experiences. As Shane put it: ". . . do as much stuff you can so you will have alot to write about" (see Figure 3–2). In addition, as noted in the last chapter, Shane was in a classroom where peers shared their topic choices on a regular basis, and where literature permeated all aspects of the school day. On occasion, entries revealed a false or undeveloped start. In only one early September entry did Shane acknowledge a dry period (Figure 3–3).

Length and Duration of Writing

Although they are difficult to decipher, the first five September entries on Shane's writing record indicate that he wrote a piece a day. Each personal narrative was started and completed within a thirty to forty minute writing workshop. Shane's September entries range in length from two to eleven sentences, with an average length of 6.2 sentences. Not surprisingly, his shortest personal narratives were those that were future-based. Not knowing what was to happen at the upcoming soccer game, he had little to say. These pieces averaged three sentences in length. It is not until his second story attempt ("Lizard and the Motorcycle"), which was five pages long, that Shane carried his writing from one day to the next. Shane's activity here is strikingly similar to that of Susie, the third grader, whom Lucy Calkins observed for two years. Susie wrote one-shot pieces (started and finished the same day) during the month of September until she began a story that took a week to write. "Each day she would reread the last lines from her previous entry and then add on and on . . . (Calkins, 1983, p. 43).

Beginning to write stories over an extended period of time marks an important step in the evolution of a young writer. Portfolios of strong writers show that they stay with a piece long enough to consider new and better alternatives, and to act upon their insights (Simmons, 1990, 1992). Both Shane and Susie increase the length of their pieces by "adding on," specifically within the context of story writing. Addition

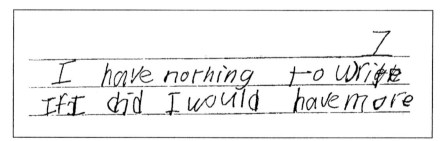

FIGURE 3–3   *Shane acknowledges he's out of writing ideas*

is the first revision strategy younger writers tend to use (Graves, 1994).

Assessing the length of Shane's pieces over time requires that we look at his writing folder (because of his difficulty with record keeping). Compared with the one-pagers of September, a number of Shane's personal narratives, in November and December, are two pages long (although not full pages). It is hard to know if each of these was written at one time or if they were written over a period of two days. Because the number of sentences tends to be under ten, it would be reasonable to guess that many continue to be written as one-shot pieces. His stories, on the other hand, average three pages, which suggests that he had some ability for sustained writing. But as we will discover in Chapters 4 and 5, even after the process of revision has been introduced and practiced, Shane revises pieces only when directed to do so. He does not return to earlier pieces to take another look. Shane illustrates what Graves has pointed put: "Children don't suddenly begin to revise during writing time. They need guidance" (1994, p. 226).

Experimentation with Genres and Writer's Stance

Shane's experimentation with genres over the first three terms of school are summarized in Figure 3–4. This graph shows this experimentation more vividly than does his writing record because of the missing entries. Note: Writers can be encouraged to create their own graphs during or at the end of each marking period—after instruction in graph making. Advantages include:

- The graph gives young writers a visual record of their writing preferences and allows them to self-assess the range of their genre experimentation.
- During the portfolio conference, the child can use the graph to summarize her writing activity and to set goals for future activity.

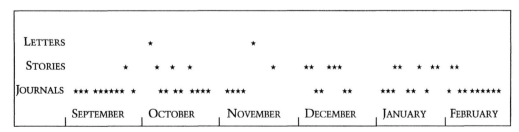

FIGURE 3–4   *Shane's experimentation with genres*

- A collective look across students, by the teacher, can signal the need for greater exposure to a particular genre during whole class meetings.

The graph (Figure 3–4) highlights Shane's propensity for personal narratives, especially during September and February. Concentrated efforts at story creation began in October and accelerated during the holiday period. One thank-you letter and one letter to the President also was written in this time period. But no nonfiction, with the exception of two lists, was attempted.

Research on the development of children's writing sheds some light on Shane's genre choices. Researchers who asked children "Why are you writing?" have unraveled some of the intricacies of writer's stance (Britton, Burgess, Martin, McLeod, & Rosen, 1975, p. 74). According to Britton, the functions of writing are threefold (1970, 1993).

Expressive Writing

Just as a young child's oral language is highly fluid, informal, egocentric in viewpoint, and produced in a shared, familiar context, so, too, often is a young child's writing. Young children write about what they know, what they have experienced. Such writing is highly expressive. It is as Britton et al. have said, "the language close to the self" (1975, p. 90). Because young, expressive writers assume that their readers know what they know, they make few allowances for their audience. They write primarily for themselves, not for readers. One of Shane's earliest personal narratives (Figure 3–5) tells of his experience at the dentist. No affective dimensions are included. This entry was not written for the entertainment or edification of readers. It was written to preserve a memory.

This early expressive writing, which is so prevalent among young writers, does not disappear over time. Rather, it matures. Journals, diaries, friendly letters—places in which personal exploration, speculation, and reflection continue to percolate—remain an essential form of written expression.

Poetic Writing

But, of course, not all of young children's earliest writing is of an expressive nature (Britton et al., 1975). Some children, especially those who have been immersed in literature from their earliest years, are drawn to the poetic mode of written discourse. These writers attempt to entertain, to delight, and to intrigue their audience with stories, poems, songs. Later they transition to literary forms such as memoirs and autobiographies. Unlike the fluid, loosely organized language of expressive writing,

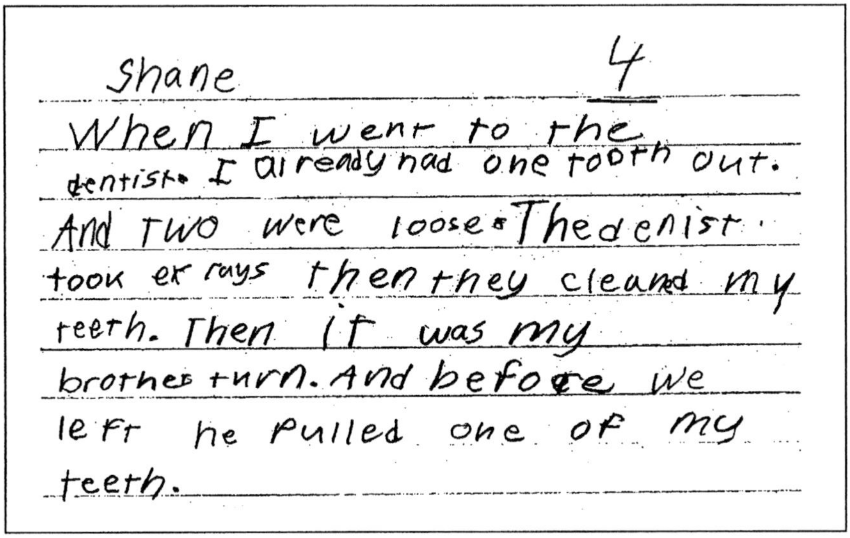

Shane   4

When I went to the dentist. I already had one tooth out. And Two were loose. The denist. took er rays then they cleaned my teeth. Then it was my brother turn. And before we left he pulled one of my teeth.

FIGURE 3–5   *Shane's personal narrative*

poetic writing requires a young writer to adopt a form of written discourse that has clearly defined structures. The language of stories differs in significant ways from the language of poetry. Poetic writers must begin to negotiate these literary boundaries as they arrange sounds, images, and ideas in deliberate ways.

Transactional Writing

Writers also write in order to complete a transaction. When expressive writers are faced with the challenge of describing, explaining, instructing, or persuading, they must shift "self" to the background in order to attend to audience needs in explicit ways. Each form of transactional writing—the business letter, the recipe, the shopping list, the experiment, the report, the newspaper article—has its own specific text structure. Transactional writers gradually learn to remove themselves from the expository and persuasive modes of writing because it is the transaction that now must be at the forefront.

Are the Functions of Writing Developmentally Ordered?

According to Britton, these functions do occur in a particular developmental sequence (1970, 1993). While acknowledging that "It is certainly not the case that every child's first attempts at writing are expressive . . ." (p. 82), Britton et al. argue that expressive writing stands at "the matrix from which differentiated forms of mature writing are developed" (1975, p. 83). These researchers believe that children's earliest writing represents "speech written down," and that it is centered in the children's personal experiences and feelings. It is only when children develop an awareness of audience—an audience they would like to entertain or inform—that they begin to use the more advanced forms of poetic and transactional writing. Children do not write expressively one day, and transactionally the next. Rather, they gradually make the transition over a period of time. Thus, transitional writing evidences an interplay of expressive and poetic, or expressive and transactional.

Interestingly, both case studies and classroom-based research have not borne out Britton's claim of fixed writing stages. Bissex found that the earliest writings of her son, Paul, (age five) spanned the genres: signs, labels, cards, messages, stories, facts, directions, and so on (1980). He created cards, typed five-page stories, made a gameboard, wrote a newspaper and so forth. Bissex noted, however, that the first birthday card Paul created wasn't made for anyone in particular, but simply for the sake of making a card. "To some extent he seemed to be practicing the forms rather than using them for their intended purpose" (Bissex, 1980, p. 16). However, by age five and one-half, Paul's experimentation with a range of literary forms shifted to include both form and function. For example, he wrote valentine cards for real people; he wrote signs for his door (DO NAT DSTRB GYNS AT WRK) and his block area. Transactional and poetic writing predominated in this young writer's home.

Other research findings, too, have challenged the notion of fixed stages. Susan Sowers found that first graders' earliest form of writing was transactional ("all-about books") (1985). Children wrote books in which they told everything they knew about a particular topic, such as dinosaurs. Hipple (1985) found that kindergartners who made their own choice of topics, and who shared their writing with peers utilized all three of Britton's modes. Children wrote about events in their lives (expressive). They wrote stories about rainbows, the stars, and animals (poetic); they drew objects and wrote or stated a fact about them (early transactional).

These three researchers provide three different windows on the communicative powers of children. Why didn't Hipple's kindergartners write signs, birthday cards, and so on in their journals? Why didn't Paul experiment with diaries/personal narratives until he was eight years old? Why were Sowers's first graders the only ones to write "all-about books"?

The answers to these questions hinge on the literacy contexts in which these children participated. The children in each context responded differently, propelled by varying social interactions and by varying literacy demonstrations. The children in Hipple's classroom were handed a journal (five pages stapled together) each Monday morning and instructed "to write on only one page a day" (1985, p. 256). Given these constraints, it is not surprising that birthday cards, signs, and so forth did not emerge. Paul, on the other hand, was writing at home, when he chose to, with paper and writing utensils (including a typewriter) of his choice. He watched, and he participated in the literate activities of his parents. His excursion into writing was not confounded by the physical, temporal, and interactional constraints, operating in Hipple's kindergarten. However, if Hipple's kindergartners had had access to paper of all sizes, to a variety of writing utensils, and had been given opportunities to write throughout the day, wondrous creations might have emerged. And what of Sowers's "all-about books?" The popularity of "all-about books" among Sowers's first graders was related to the literacy demonstrations provided in this classroom. An "all-about book" was shared with the class, and presto—ten "all-about books"—were underway the next day. The influence of children's writing on other children is another potent example of intertextuality at work.

We must never underestimate the power of the literacy context on the young writer. Nor should we underestimate their sensibilities. One afternoon, after watching live coverage of the Gulf War on TV, Vanessa sat down to create a news broadcast of her own. Vanessa read her piece (Figure 3–6) at the dinner table to her astonished parents and siblings. Vanessa was in first grade at the time.

Jeffrey, too, brought the world to his writing (see Figure 7–5 in Chapter 7). When President Bush's campaign pledge ("Read my lips. No new taxes.") came back to haunt him in 1992, Jeffrey was listening. When Peg, his teacher, read a story about Abraham Lincoln, Jeffrey was listening. Jeffrey concluded that Presidents have the power to undo a perceived wrong. So he set forth to create Lincoln's pledge to the nation. Vanessa and Jeffrey remind us that children too can "read the world" (Freire, 1985, p. 19).

In sum, then, "All language settings are not equal. To continue to collect developmental data with blatant disregard for context can in the end only confuse us and do a disservice to children" (Harste, Woodward, & Burke, 1984, p.159). Harste et al.'s warning brings us back full circle to Britton's hypothesis about the developmental stages of writing. It seems fairly evident that when one goes directly to the source—the child—there is little support for the notion of fixed writing stages. However, this doesn't minimize the contribution that Britton has made with regard to the functions of writing and to the understanding that personal narrative is an important form of written discourse.

A working knowledge of Britton's expressive, poetic, and transactional categories facilitates our analysis of Shane's writing record. The

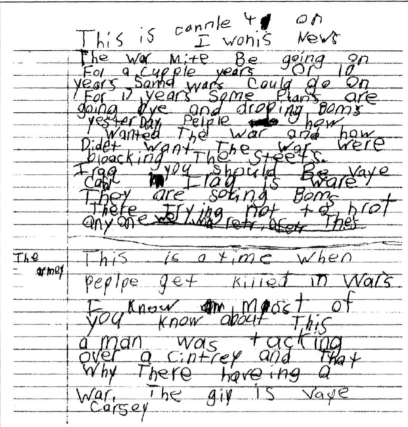

This is Channel 4
Eye Witness News.

The war might be going on
for a couple years or 10
years. Some wars go on
for 17 years. Some planes are
going by and dropping bombs.
Yesterday, people who
wanted the war and who
didn't want the war were
blocking the streets.
Iraq, you should be very
careful. Iraq is where

they are sending bombs.
They are trying not to hurt
anyone. We will be right back
    after this.

This is a time when
people get killed in wars.
I know most of
you know about this.
A man was taking
over a country and that's
why they're having a
war. The guy is very
crazy.

FIGURE 3–6   *Vanessa's news broadcast of the Gulf War*

graphic organizer in Figure 3–7 is a reconceptualion of Britton et al.'s hypothesis about the acquisition of functions (1975). Britton et al. depict their notion of stage theory by situating expressive writing at the nadir, and by shooting arrows diagonally from this point to represent the later developing modes of the poetic and the transactional. Figure 3–7, however, places the writer in the center of his social context and suggests that she will choose to explore any of the three functions of written language, depending on the extent and quality of the literacy demonstrations occurring around her, on the degree to which writing is shared with others, and on the availability of materials.

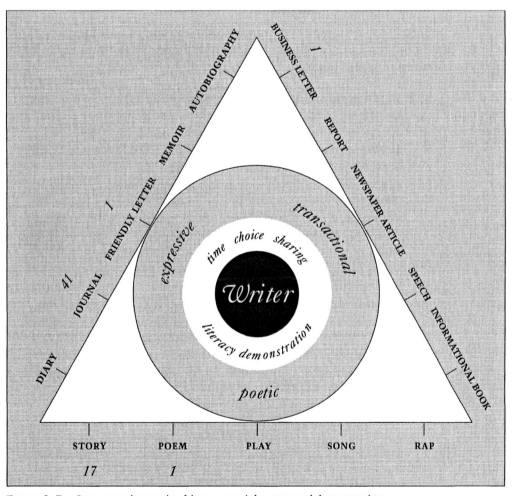

FIGURE 3–7   *Genre experimentation hinges on social context and demonstrations*

The tallies placed next to each particular genre represent the number of pieces written by Shane over the first three marking periods (September to March). The preponderance of personal narratives (journal entries) highlights Shane's comfort with expressive writing. His impressive tally of stories signals his enjoyment in entertaining his readers. Shane's limited experimentation with transactional writing (two Christmas lists and a persuasive letter) during writing workshop may be attributed to the fact that he wrote observations, experiments, predictions, and so on in the Investigation Notebook he used during science and social studies. In the chapters that follow, we will examine his progress in each of these writing modes.

Concluding Comments

A number of tentative conclusions can be drawn about Shane as a writer from an analysis of the data found in his writing record, accompanying writing folder, and interviews:

- Topics about which to write appear to come easily to Shane. Talk of school, family, and sports fill the pages of his writing folder. Topic lists are tried at the beginning of the year but abandoned.

- Expressive writing, in the form of personal narratives, constitutes much of his written discourse.

- Poetic writing in the form of stories blossoms in October and intensifies in December and January. Shane immerses himself in story writing for extended periods of time and, then, may not write another story for a month. One rhyming poem of six lines is drafted; no other experimentation with poetry is undertaken.

- Shane's journey into the story genre is launched and sustained by the works of Beverly Cleary.

- Duration of Shane's pieces is tied to his choice of genres. When Shane writes stories, he allows the story's momentum to carry him from one day to the next. By adding on new plot episodes each day, he is able to stay with one piece over a two–three day stretch. Duration of personal narratives, however, are time-bound. All of his personal narratives are started and finished on the same day.

- Record keeping challenges his organizational skills. Shane's earliest entries are his most successful. Since he writes a piece a day, it is easy to record numbers, titles, and dates of each piece. As he begins to sustain his story writing over a few days, it becomes more difficult to log information.

Assessing Personal Narratives

4

When children first write they focus on themselves. This is as it should be. The child will make no greater progress in his entire school career than in the first year of school simply because self-centeredness makes him fearless. The world must bend to his will. This child screens out audience. He is fascinated with his own marks on paper.
(Graves, 1983, p. 239)

Children's journals, indeed, are one place where the self takes center stage. It is the place where the process of playful, unfettered creation—not production—takes precedence. Personal narratives, a form of expressive writing discussed in the last chapter, abound in children's journal writing. It is clear that Graves (1983) and Britton (1970, 1993) agree about the centrality of expressive writing in the literacy lives of children.

Personal narratives (journal entries) are described by those who have studied them as safe havens—havens in which writers are free to record observations and experiences, to invent, to debate, to explore inner thoughts, to daydream, to vent emotions, to heighten understandings, and so forth, without the trappings of literary form or structure. In identifying the language features of journal entries, Fulwiler notes the following characteristics: informal, fluid conversation; experimentation with form and voice; first person pronouns; and unconventional punctuation (1987).

At its best, journal writing forces a personal reckoning, a private dialogue with oneself on a significant matter. We write to discover our thoughts without attention to a critical audience. As the celebrated journal writer Henry David Thoreau said:

A journal is a record of experiences and growth, not a preserve of things well done or said . . . the charm of the journal must consist in certain greenness, though freshness, and not in maturity. Here I cannot

afford to be remembering what I said or did . . . , but what I am and aspire to be. (January 24, 1856)

Such writing "invites solitude" and disciplined engagement. Once we
have found our voice, issues of audience fall into place (Elbow & Clarke,
1987, p. 32). In this chapter, we enter the world of children's journals
for the purpose of understanding why they are drawn to this kind of
writing, and how they frame their personal narratives within and across
time.

What We Know About Personal Narratives of Emerging Writers

While scholars such as Britton, Elbow, Graves, and Moffett have established the theoretical importance of expressive writing, little research has been done on children's personal narratives. This is due, in
part, to the fact journal writing only recently has been reintroduced
in classrooms (Fulwiler, 1987). Thanks to the efforts of many researchers, a baseline of data is beginning to emerge (Calkins, 1986,
1994; Graves, 1983, 1994; Giacobbe, 1988; Hipple, 1985; Karelitz,
1988). Both Calkins and Graves have found personal narratives of
young writers to be chronological retellings of life events. Calkins
notes that speech, like drawing, often accompanies the act of narrative
writing (1986). First graders often "talk" their way through their
pieces. They begin with detailed illustrations and finish with a line or
two of text. While drawing, children rehearse potential ideas for their
text. Calkins speculates that children are drawn to personal narratives
because their experiences have a beginning, middle, and end, thereby
providing "both the propulsion to continue and an organizational
framework" (1986, p. 59).

Assessing Philip's Personal Narratives (Grade 1)

Philip's first grade journal contains one personal narrative after another—expressive writing from the beginning of the year to the end.
When it's time to write in his journal, he taps into his memory bank, re-
trieves yesterday's events, and plays them out chronologically. Philip's
competence and confidence increases throughout the year. Peruse his
journal entries from September (Figure 4–1), January (Figure 4–2), and
April (Figure 4–3), and jot down your thoughts about the content and
development of these narratives. (Analyzing these samples with a colleague can be highly instructive.)

Because all holistic assessment has an element of subjectivity, our

I hDChRIS OFR AnD ꟼE PL BSCB.

FIGURE 4–1   *Philip's personal narrative: September*

observations are not likely to match one for one, but I suspect that much commonality of thought will surface. My observations are as follows:

- Philip's choice of topic is anchored in his daily experiences with friends and family. These entries, which are representative of the other entries in his yearlong journal, center on Philip's family experiences, trips in particular. Family events are followed in frequency by activities with friends, such as playing basketball

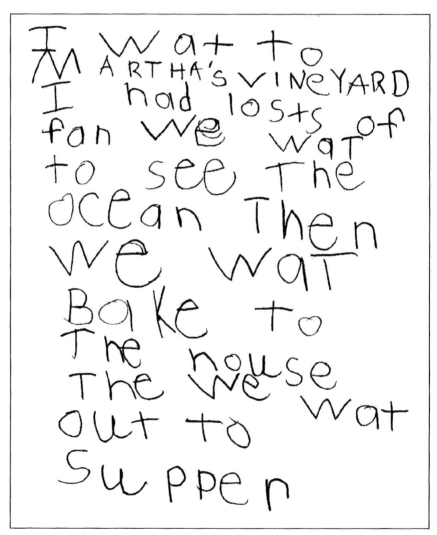

FIGURE 4–2   *Philip's personal narrative: January*

(Figure 4–1) and "NALKIG OFF THE SNOWMAN'S HEAD," in another entry.

• In the September entry (Figure 4–1), Philip gives us a precise synopsis of a recent event. Because it takes great concentration and effort for an emerging writer to produce a meaningful text, Philip uses a picture to round out his message. It is Philip's picture that carries the action. It tells the reader how exciting this basketball game is, how happy the players are to be shooting baskets, and what it's like to have a friend. Text and picture work together to create the whole. In all likelihood, Philip drew his picture before attempting the text. As noted earlier, illustrations are a prominent rehearsal strategy (Calkins, 1986; Graves, 1994).

• In three short months, Philip has gained enough command of written conventions to tell his message through print, rather than through illustrations (Figure 4–2). (This is not to suggest that illustrations disappear from his journal; they do not. Illustrations continue to accompany and support some journal entries throughout the year. But when they appear, they are much smaller and more limited in detail. As Philip's facility with invented spelling increases, his need to communicate via pictures diminishes (Bissex, 1980)). The volume of print in his January piece is striking in comparison to his September piece. So is Philip's ability to capture some of the individual events of his

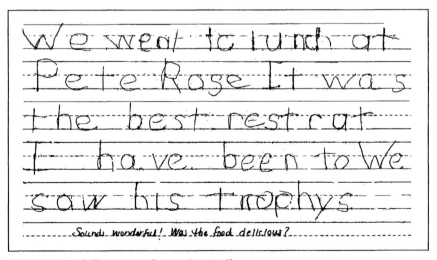

FIGURE 4–3 *Philip's personal narrative: April*

trip to Martha's Vineyard. His "and then . . . and then . . . and then" sequence, known as a chain narrative, is an important marker of growth. Moving beyond the one-sentence synopsis of his September entry, Philip now attempts to record the events within the event. In chain narratives, children give equal weight to all events. No one event is given extra details; no event is given any commentary. Philip sees his task as one of recreating the sequence of events—no more, no less—with one exception: "I had losts of fan (fun)." In this case, Philip steps back from the experience long enough for momentary reflection. Philip is moving forward as a writer.

- Philip's April entry (Figure 4–3) is actually part of a journal that he was asked to keep while he was on a two-week vacation in Florida. (Three cheers for his teacher for seeing the writing potential in his trip and for refraining from sending a packet of worksheets to complete!) The entries in this journal continue to remain faithful to the chronology of Philip's day. Each of the first five entries begin with "We went swimming," and chain through the day from there. No response to any of the events is recorded. The April narrative is the only entry that deviates from this pattern and marks another leap forward. In this entry, Philip distances himself from the day's events long enough to settle on the day's most important happening—eating at Pete Rose's restaurant. Philip not only singles out this event from his busy day but also sizes up the event ("It was the best restrat I have been to."). He leaves us with the feeling that this restaurant rated top billing not because of the food which isn't even mentioned, but because of the ambiance. This experience held such significance that, on this one day, he was able to leave his chain narrative behind and do what mature writers do—linger on the event that carries personal meaning.

In Philip's subsequent entries about Florida, he returns to the daily chronology. It is important to reemphasize that writing development often spurts ahead, then returns to a stable plateau until greater control of the genre occurs, or teacher/peer feedback spurs new activity. It is evident that Philip has found his niche in chronology writing. Its structure is predictable and focused. If he continues to write journal entries and receive feedback from peers and teachers, he will move in time to the essence of his experiences and explore their significance. In the meantime, Graves reminds us that, "Repetition, a centering of its own kind, is important for growth. It can be a kind of marking time and can fulfill many of the needs of the learner-writer" (1983, p. 241).

As you read through Philip's entries, some of the following questions probably occurred to you:

- How did Philip arrive at the concept of a journal as "the place to write down what I did yesterday"? Is he merely following the teacher's directions/demonstrations of what constitutes a journal entry, or is he truly drawn to the expressive mode?
- Has he been allowed/encouraged to experiment with varying topics and genres in his journal?
- Are journals in his classroom shared? Does he have a chance to learn what his peers are writing about in their journals?
- Does he write at home? If so, with what modes of writing does he experiment?

As was emphasized in the previous chapter, answers to these questions and others cannot be surmised from the writing samples themselves. We must have the benefit of a series of conversations—conversations with Philip, with his teacher, with his peers, with his parents. If we are to paint an accurate profile of Philip as an emerging writer, we need to probe the specifics of the literacy context in which he participates.

What We Know About Personal Narratives of Older Writers

With the exception of Graves's and Calkins's work, research on the journal writing of older children is virtually nonexistent. Calkins found personal narratives firmly entrenched in the writing of the third graders she studied. She speculated that they are popular for two reasons: a) teachers prompted children to write about their experiences and b) children are drawn to this form of expressive writing because of their developmental needs. Calkins found that third graders' narratives tend to be "tightly structured pieces that proceed step by step through a chain of events . . . the narrative, like time itself, marches steadily on" (1986, p. 82). Graves notes the popularity of "bed-to-bed narratives" among writers in grades 3–8 who record every event of their day—eventful or otherwise—from the time they awake until they go to bed (1983, 1994). The stellar example of a "bed-to-bed narrative" in Figure 4–4 was penned by me at the age of 12. My Dad "asked" my sister and me to keep a daily journal of our Ireland trip. Every entry in my journal mirrors the one in Figure 4–4, with the substitution of different people and places. Dreadful sameness plagues this journal.

Calkins is quick to point to the idiosyncratic nature of writing devel-

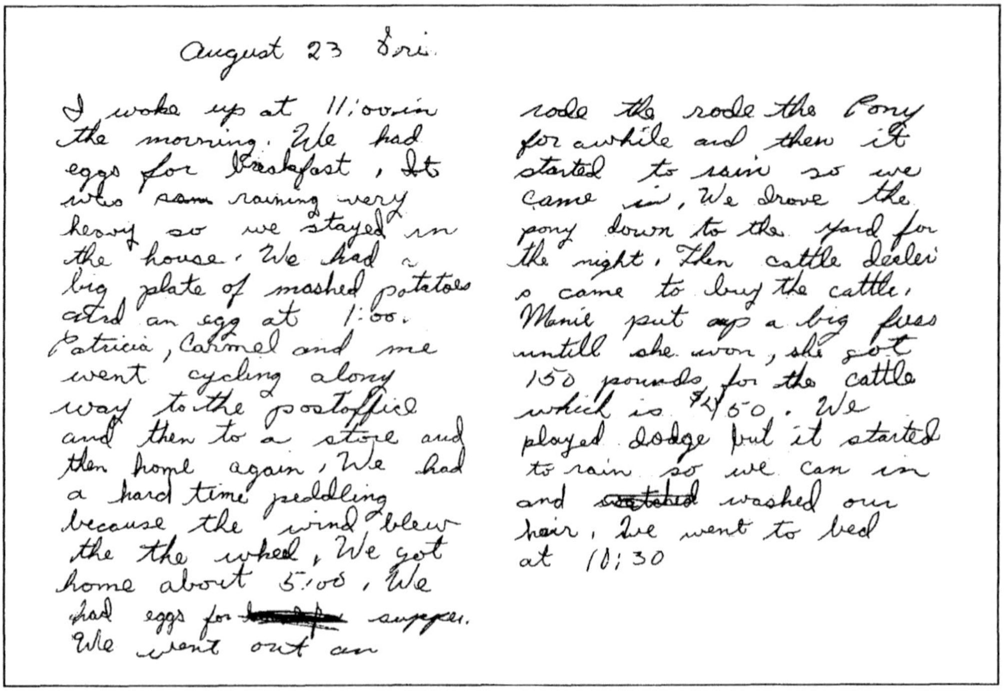

August 23 Fri.

I woke up at 11:00 in the morning. We had eggs for breakfast, It was ram raining very heavy so we stayed in the house. We had a big plate of mashed potatoes and an egg at 1:00. Patricia, Carmel and me went cycling a long way to the postoffice and then to a store and then home again, We had a hard time peddling because the wind blew the the wheel, We got home about 5:00, We had eggs for ~~breakfast~~ supper. We went out an

rode the rode the Pony for awhile and then it started to rain so we came in, We drove the pony down to the yard for the night, Then cattle dealer s came to buy the cattle, Manie put up a big fuss until she won, she got 150 pounds for the cattle which is $450. We played dodge but it started to rain so we can in and ~~watched~~ washed our hair, We went to bed at 10:30

FIGURE 4–4 *My bed-to-bed narrative, age 12*

opment and to stress that some third graders are able to control their pieces rather than be controlled by them. Some children are able to slow down their chronology in order to explore one event more fully or to share a response to an event. She found that most third graders rarely reread or reflected on their pieces; for the most part, entries were logged and forgotten.

In the previous chapter we surveyed Shane's writing record and writing folder, and established his partiality for personal narratives. Given Calkins's and Graves's insights, we expect Shane's third-grade journal entries to reveal chain narratives which are tighter and more detailed than Philip's entries. We begin with Shane's assessment of his favorite personal narrative during the first term.

Shane on Shane: Self-Assessment of His Personal Narratives

It is the end of the first marking period. Shane and his classmates have been asked to review their writing folders to locate, among their many pieces, their favorite and best pieces (not always one and the same for some writers) for placement in their portfolios. Not surprisingly, Shane chooses as his favorite piece his story, "Lizard and the Motorcycle" (Appendix D), explaining that "awesome things happen to Owl and Lizard . . ." For his best piece, Shane chooses a personal narrative entitled, "The Visitors" (see Figure 4–5). He explains his choice during our portfolio conference.

CAROL: Shane, why is this your best piece?

SHANE: 'Cuz I had to keep going over it to make it better, the periods and stuff. I had to put in all the capitals in the right place.

CAROL: So because you used capitals and periods, you chose this piece as your best.

SHANE: Yeah. I know it's right.

CAROL: Why did you chose this piece ("The Visitors") instead of the piece (pulling out his earlier Red Sox piece [Chapter 9, Figure 9–8]) you wrote about the Red Sox game that you went to with your Dad?

SHANE: Well, that story is . . . you see, this is just about me (pointing to the Red Sox narrative) but this one (pointing to "The Visitors") is about real people and real places. They traveled all over the place.

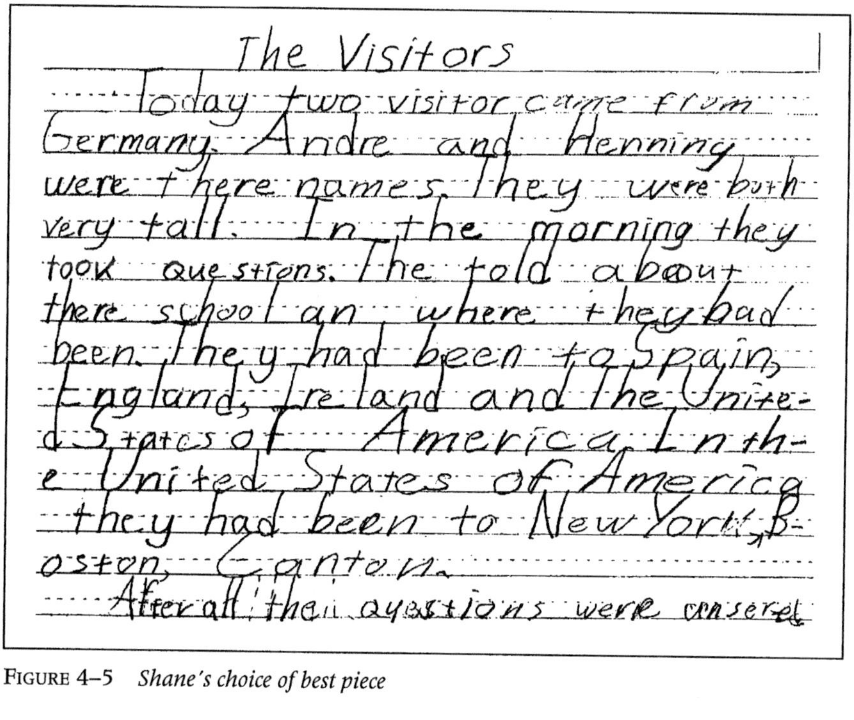

The Visitors

Today two visitor came from
Germany. Andre and Henning
were there names. They were both
very tall. In the morning they
took questons. The told about
there school an where they had
been. They had been to Spain,
England, Ireland and The Unite-
d States of America. In th-
e United States of America
they had been to New York, B-
oston, Canton.
After all the questions were ansered

FIGURE 4–5 *Shane's choice of best piece*

Involving children in self-analysis is critical to portfolio assessment. It takes us inside the writers' thought processes—inside the criteria that the children use to make decisions about what constitutes good writing. Shane tells us that the written conventions of punctuation and capitalization are the primary criteria he uses to select his best writing. Capitals and periods are important to him. Our ability to draw conclusions about Shane's assessment of his work is advanced greatly by the knowledge that most second and third graders equate good writing with proper usage of the conventions. Graves's research, which is summarized in Figure 4–6, indicates that children do not use the same criteria in judging their work that we use (1983). His work also shows that the criteria children use become increasingly more sophisticated over time.

We can use Graves's developmental scheme to understand Shane's concept of what constitutes good writing. We have evidence (from the previous transcript) that conventions are a major concern. Corroborating evidence about the importance of conventions is found in Shane's response to the question about "what a good writer needs to do well to write" on the Writing Survey, completed at the beginning of the school year (Atwell, 1987). (See Appendix A.) Shane writes that good writers "use captial and peereids." In addition, his conversation about the Lizard story in Chapter 3, pages 43–44, suggests that composition length is important to Shane. In his mind, the longer the piece, the better it must be.

It is also likely that his decision to select "The Visitors" was influenced by the fact that he was required to revise and edit this piece. Because this was the only piece he had to rework during the first term, it stands to reason that it would be selected as his "best" piece.

Is Shane aware of the relationship between content and good writing? Yes. The case can be made that it was the content of this piece on the visitors that intrigued Shane in the first place and resulted in its selection. Remember, he was asked to look through his writing folder and find the piece that he liked and wanted to revise. Out of all of his pieces, he chose this one because, as my probe uncovered, it was "about real people and real places." This was the only personal narrative during the first term in which other people were the "main characters," so to speak. In all of Shane's other journal entries, he was the key player. From Shane's perspective, other people's lives are intrinsically more interesting than his life. These young men had traveled the world; he had only been to Riverside Park and to a Red Sox game. Readers certainly would be more interested in the travelers' lives than in his life. In time, Shane will learn that the everyday experience is grist for the writing mill. He will learn that it is not the experience, per se, that contributes to powerful writing, but the level of insight that the experience triggers. We need to praise Shane for his new level of reflection and then watch to see if he

What "Good" Writing Means to Children

When Graves asked children what makes a piece of writing "good," they responded with the criterion that posed the greatest challenge for them at their point of development:

SPELLING:
> Emerging writers view a "good" piece of writing as one in which the words are spelled correctly. When some control of spelling has occurred, the emerging writer shifts to a concern about handwriting.

HANDWRITING:
> "Good" writing to many young writers is equivalent to good handwriting. A concern for the aesthetic appearance of the piece predominates; cross-outs, erasures constitute "bad" writing. With increased control over handwriting, children begin to equate good writing with proper usage of the conventions.

CONVENTIONS:
> Capitals, periods, quotation marks...become the key criteria in judging good writing. It is not until children put the mechanical aspects of writing in proper perspective that concern for topic is exhibited.

TOPIC:
> Young writers eventually equate good writing with topic chosen and information shared. With further writing experience, the shift to a concern for revision takes precedence.

REVISION:
> Finally, writers demonstrate an understanding that "good" writing is linked to the process of revision.

Graves describes this general ordering of spelling, aesthetics, conventions, information and finally revision, as children's "consciousness of problem solving" (p. 237). He notes that exceptions certainly exist, and makes the point that all five aspects come into play for writers of all ages, every time they write. It's the preoccupation with what's perceived as important by the younger writer that shifts over time.

FIGURE 4–6   *Graves's (1983) findings concerning children's concepts of "good" writing*

brings this new knowledge to bear in selecting future pieces for his port-folio.

In summary, Graves's work gives us a lens through which we can examine children's thinking about the assessment of their writing. It suggests that we need to: a) encourage children to assess, b) use our knowledge base to assess their assessments, and c) scaffold their thinking both by acknowledging their point of view concerning what constitutes good writing, and by introducing them to more advanced markers of growth. This new knowledge, as the following section illustrates, re-quires repeated demonstration and conversation on our part.

Bringing Shane Inside the Assessment Process

Shane has just shared why he has selected "The Visitors" for his show-case portfolio. Now, it is my turn during our portfolio conference to ac-knowledge his insights and to extend his thinking. I remark: "Shane, I am so pleased to see that you thought about two things when you chose 'The Visitors' as your best piece. You thought about punctuation and capitalization, and you thought about the ideas in your piece. Let's talk first about your ideas because good writers chose their best pieces based on the importance of their ideas. You said you chose 'The Visitors' be-cause it was about real people and real places. What an interesting ob-servation! It tells me that you were thinking about your audience and what they would find interesting. Guess what—I chose a different piece for our collaborative portfolio for the same reason. I chose 'Stickers' be-cause it was about a real person too—you. I think your life is just as in-teresting as Andre's and Henning's. I thought 'Stickers' was even more interesting than 'The Visitors' because you told me not only what you did during the sticker game, but also how you felt. The best journal en-tries are the ones in which we share our thoughts and feelings. In a minute, I'm going to show you how much I think you've improved as a journal writer this term. But first, I don't want to forget to thank you for paying attention to capitals and periods. When writers edit their final draft, they need to fix as many capitalization and punctuation mistakes as they can find. You did a good job here."

I then share my selection of best piece, the narrative "Stickers" (see Figure 4–7), which was written a few days before "The Visitors," and about two weeks before the end of the term.

In order to help Shane see the progress he is making in journal writ-ing, I show him how I compare and contrast "The Dentist" and "Stick-ers." The dentist entry, written the third day of the school year (Chapter 3, Figure 3–5), serves as my baseline piece. A summary of the observa-tions I share with Shane includes:

<u>21</u>

Today when I went to Mrs.
caroll we did something
where you would see to
words and name two ma
things that go with those
two things. Then we tried
it with another friend
if you tricked your friend
you could get a sticker
But I diden't trick my friend
but he did not trick me. so we
both got a prize. I had
alot of a fun time. fBut
it theres something werid
because I forget alot. But I'm
still happy I got a
sticker.
                theend.

FIGURE 4–7 *My choice of Shane's best personal narrative*

- The dentist piece is a straight chronology of events. While the experience must have had its trying moments, Shane reports the facts as they happened, with no elaboration on key events or any personal response.

- In "Stickers," however, Shane steps out of the chain narrative long enough to place some emphasis on the game. Rather than just telling us the sequence—he went to the room, then he played a game, then he got a sticker—he stays with one event long enough to help the reader recreate the episode. He has chosen the important event within the event and elaborated on some of the details.

- In addition to this beginning sense of elaboration, Shane brings the reader inside his piece by sharing his feelings ("I had a lot of fun . . . But I'm still happy I got a sticker.") about the event. Even more significant is his self-evaluation of the event ("But theres something weirid because I forgot a lot."). Shane stands back from the event and evaluates his performance as a learner. Fulwiler notes that "self-awareness" is one of the important cognitive activities of journal writing (1987). Journals are places where writers can come to terms with their strengths and weaknesses—academic and otherwise. Shane's observation is also an invitation to talk about his concern about forgetting. Shane's goal of "really try to remember!" reinforces the notion that strategies to facilitate his memory may be helpful. (See Chapter 3, Figure 3–2)

Assessing Shane's Personal Narratives Over Time

One conversation with Shane in a portfolio conference about what constitutes a good personal narrative will not result in qualitatively better journal entries right away. Helping children refine their concept about good writing takes time. It also takes repeated instructional episodes in the form of minilessons, conferences, and so on. As Atwell reminds us, "My students and my own writing have taught me that writing growth is seldom a linear progress, each piece presenting an improvement over the last. I know it's hard to write well when trying new genres and chancing complex topics" (1987, p. 114). I expect Shane's journal entries over the next term to vacillate between chain narratives and more reflective pieces. I also expect that at some point in the school year reflective pieces will outweigh the chain narratives. I expect that Shane will sharpen his ability to assess personal narratives.

I am not disappointed. At the end of the third term, we independently choose "The Children Muesam" (Figure 4–8) as our favorite personal narrative.

I am struck by Shane's presence in this piece. He guides us through this museum adventure with energy and humor. Shane uses the chronology of the event to frame the piece, but he does so in much looser fashion. He no longer seems to be marching to the tempo of the "and then . . . and then . . . and then" beat. Rather, for example, he takes

Shane Forsyth   the Children muesam   93

When I went to the Childrens muesam,

I did alot of fun things like they had these Special telaphones you could press a button and you could talk about something personal. they had a machine with a tv and there was a girl and you would go places on the tv When a girl said I can I put my coat I said no So She Said if that is the way you feel this show is over and So I put down Alright then the machine went backon. I really liked Sticking my hand up the fake nostral I also liked the Mole path where you Climb up diffrent Spaces, ((you really had to watch your head)). I liked how they had a base ment that you could pretend you were using different tools for working I had a really fun time !!!

the end

FIGURE 4–8   *Shane's best piece (Term 3): Unanimous decision*

us inside the opening event—"the special telaphones" (an interactive video)—by offering elaboration on how this video system works, and by incorporating dialogue that reveals some affective content ("If that is the way you feel this show is over . . ."). Greater attention to details that a reader might like to know is also noted with the inclusion of his double parentheses "((you really had to watch your head))." Shane is moving ahead as a writer and self-assessor.

To support students' efforts at reflection, we can ask them to reread the personal narrative they have chosen as "best piece" and to complete the survey in Figure 4–9 prior to the portfolio conference. During the conference, the writer can explain the survey results. The survey enables

---

WHAT I WROTE ABOUT IN MY JOURNAL ENTRY

IN THIS JOURNAL ENTRY,   YES   NO

I wrote about what I did on a certain day

I told everything that happened to me from
the time I got up until I went to bed.

I picked one important thing that happened
during the day and I wrote only about that event.

When I told what happened, I included important
details to help the reader "see" the event.

When I told what happened, I included how
I felt about it. I shared my thoughts and feelings.

I chose a topic that is really important to me and
I included my thoughts and feelings.

I took some ideas from this journal entry and used
them to write a story, or a poem, or a report.

FIGURE 4–9   *Self-assessment checklist for personal journal entries*

us to enter the "zone of proximal development . . . What the child can do in cooperation today he can do alone tomorrow. Therefore the only good kind of instruction is that which marches ahead of development and leads it . . ." (Vygotsky, 1978, p. 86). The survey, also, helps us explain to students why our choice of personal narrative may different from their choices.

Assessing Shane's First Attempt at Revision

As noted earlier, in Shane's classroom, writers are asked each term to choose one piece from their writing folder for publication. The children, then, revise and edit their pieces, prior to final edit and formal publication. Before taking a look at Shane's first effort, let's highlight the parameters of the revision process and what researchers have found children do when they revise.

Mem Fox, acclaimed children's author, understands firsthand what Roald Dahl means when he tells us that "Good writing is essentially rewriting" (Murray, 1990, p. 182). It took Mem five years to perfect *Koala Lou* (1988)—five years and forty-nine drafts. In her delightful autobiography, Mem writes, ". . . my shoulders ache with tension in trying to chose the right words to put in the right places" (1990, p. 151).

Revision, in effect, requires the equivalent of an "out-of-body" experience—a psychological distancing from the words that represent our search for meaning. Only from a distance can we "re-see" our message, weigh its significance, consider its audience, and confirm, rediscover, or reject that message. Mem Fox and others make it clear that revision is a social process, one in which others must participate if we are to arrive at the essence of our thoughts (Calkins, 1991; Graves, 1983, 1994).

Given the complexity of this process, it is not surprising that most children tend not to engage in revision of their own volition (Calkins, 1986; Fitzgerald, 1988). Graves speculates that "Revision, or reseeing, is not necessarily a natural act" (1983, p. 160) until writers outgrow their egocentricity and anticipate the needs of the reader. Scardamalia and Bereiter, however, found that elementary age children can distance themselves from their texts and assess the quality of individual sentences (1983). But they cannot negotiate successful revisions. Scardamalia et al. speculate that children have yet to develop the "executive function" which allows writers to shuttle back and forth between writing and critiquing.

When children revise, they do so primarily at the word, phrase, or sentence level rather than at the text level (Hillocks, 1986; Applebee et al., 1990). These findings corroborate Graves's general ordering of problem-solving strategies used during writing (see Figure 4–6).

WHAT STRATEGIES DO YOUNG WRITERS USE WHEN THEY REVISE?

Lucy Calkins noted four increasingly sophisticated strategies that third graders used:

RANDOM DRAFTING:
When faced with the decision to rewrite, a small number of third graders engaged in random drafting. These writers handled the challenge of rewriting by simply starting a new draft, often on the same topic. Random drafters basically ignored their first drafts in favor of new related or unrelated pieces.

REFINING:
A number of the third graders, however, were attentive to their first drafts as they approached the task of rewriting. These refiners saw rewriting as a process of fixing surface features (spelling, handwriting...), and of inserting a line or two on occasion. They rarely used proofreading symbols (caret, arrow, paragraph symbol...). Refiners essentially edited for mechanics, and did little or no reenvisioning.

TRANSITION:
Other third graders waffled between random drafting and refining, adopting a strategy that Calkins calls transition. They experimented both with looking back at drafts in order to fix as well as looking forward in order to try out new ideas but seemed unable to integrate the two processes.

INTERACTING:
This final strategy, acting, which some third graders adopted, involved revision in its truest form—the reconstruction of meaning.

FIGURE 4–10   *Calkins's (1980a) findings on children's revision strategies*

Young writers hold spelling as their top revision priority. With increasing control over spelling, their attention shifts to aesthetic aspects (handwriting primarily). Mechanics replace aesthetics, but in time attention to topic information prevails. Finally, attention shifts to content revision. Graves makes it clear that all writers grapple with all of these areas of "consciousness" as they draft and revise, but that some writers never get beyond the concern for spelling and the mechanics (1983).

Calkins's investigation into what third graders in a writing-process classroom actually do during the rewriting process sheds important light on the strategies adopted by young writers (1980a). Calkins's four tentative strategies of revision—random drafting, refining, transition, and interacting—are summarized in Figure 4–10.

Calkins's work provides a lens through which we can inspect Shane's first revision attempt. Figure 4–11 presents the piece that Shane chose to revise during the first term. As you examine this piece, keep Calkins's strategies in mind. (Please note that the following changes in "The Visitors" piece were made by Alice, Shane's teacher, in her final edit: *Andrae* to *Andre*, *have* to *had*, *there* to *their*, *finished* to

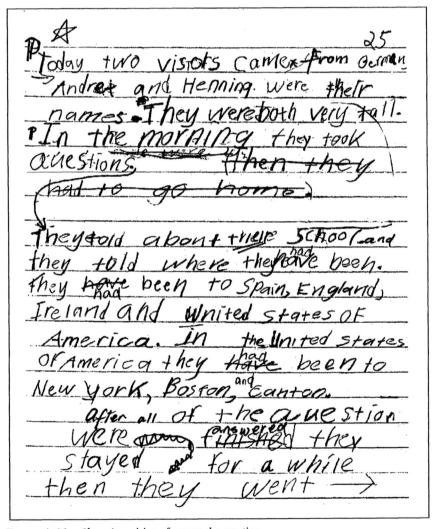

FIGURE 4–11 *Shane's revision of personal narrative*

answered, the insertion of *after all*, and the insertion of *and* in the fifth sentence.)

The opening section of Shane's personal narrative in Figure 4–11 reveals his propensity for a tight chronology: The visitors came, asked questions, and left. Realizing that he had more to say, though, Shane adds additional information about where the visitors traveled. Addition is the most popular revision strategy of young writers (Calkins, 1983; Graves, 1983, 1994). Shane's addition of information, however, results in a disorderly chain of events. To rectify this, Shane erases the sentence, "They were both very tall," which originally occurred after "Then they had to go home," and moves it into the lead. He then crosses off "Then they had to go home," and inserts an arrow to indicate the continuation of text. Hence, Shane's revision efforts encompass one or more rereadings of his original text, the recognition that meaning has been disrupted (sequence violated), and the adoption of revision code (arrows, paragraph code) to fix the incongruities. These data suggest that Shane is transitioning toward Calkins's interactive stage. However, revision at the macro level is not entertained by Shane. Learning to stand back from the piece as a whole to discover why it was written in the first place, to rethink the personal significance of the event, and to rework the piece from that standpoint is an intellectual feat that many high school and college students have yet to master (Emig, 1971; Bridwell, 1980; Perl, 1979).

Concluding Comments and a Word About Teacher Self-Assessment

Shane's concept of what writers do in personal narratives has begun to shift in five short months. His entries have progressed from voiceless replays of daily experiences to narratives that are beginning to resonate with voice, that evidence a growing awareness of audience, and that incorporate brief moments of personal response and self-reflection. While Shane has yet to view his journal from Thoreau's vantage point: "I cannot afford to be remembering what I said or did . . . , but what I am and aspire," he has the potential to do so if he continues to keep a journal, and if he reads and discusses the journal entries of talented writers.

One way to pull together what I have learned about Shane's development in personal narratives is to graph his progress (Figure 4–12). I order the categories on the Y-axis according to what Calkins and Graves have found to be characteristic of young writers' personal narrative writing over time. I plot only the pieces that have been chosen each term for Shane's collaborative portfolio. I understand that some samples will fall between the categories on the axis, that some pieces may not even find representation, and that the graph will need ongoing revision. In essence, I am adopting the teacher-researcher stance. This stance urges teachers to build a working knowledge of the literacy research, to test these findings against our daily observation of children's thought and work, and to continue to refine our thinking about literacy development.

In the final analysis, however, I cannot stand in judgment of writers' work, if I have not created a classroom environment that supports children's efforts in journal writing. Prior to assessing children's personal narratives, I need to assess the quality of my own teaching and the calibre of my classroom environment. I need to be able to answer affirmatively to the following questions:

- Have I written journal entries and shared them with the children? Have I demonstrated how I select topics for my entries?
- Have I shared journal entries from authentic journals (Thoreau, Anne Frank, Zlata Filupovic, Laura Wilder . . .) with children?

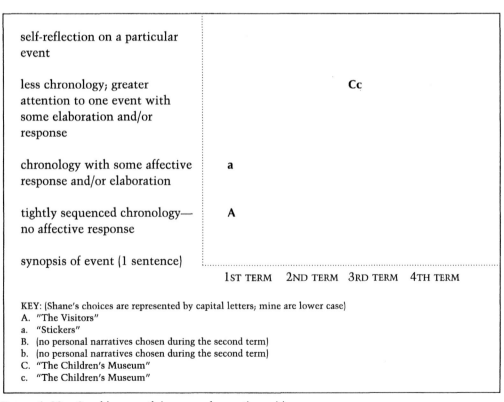

FIGURE 4–12   *Graphing growth in personal narrative writing*

Have I, for example, taken excerpts from Thoreau, placed them on the overhead, read them with the children, and savored their messages? Have I engaged the children in a discussion about what Thoreau does in his entries, and why he does so? Have we compared his entries to others?

- Have I shared journal entries from quality literature with children? (e.g. *A Gathering of Days: A New England Girl's Journal, 1830–1832* (Blos, 1979); *Dear Mr. Henshaw* (Cleary, 1983))

- Have I asked permission of children whose entries include personal reflection, opinion and so forth to share their work on the overhead?

- Have I used quality journal entries to engage children in a series of conversations about what constitutes a good journal entry?

If I can respond affirmatively to these questions, I am ready to assess students' personal narratives.

Assessing Story Writing

5

The call of story. Caitlyn, my godchild, age three-and-a-half, greets me at the door with a doll in hand and says, "This is for the baby." Caitlyn is awaiting the arrival of "her baby," who is "in the hospital and in mommy's belly." When asked if she'd like to write a story for the baby, she races for the paper, composes the first line of text (Figure 5–1) with great concentration, and then pauses. I ask her to tell me the story. Since this is the first time Caitlyn has been asked to tell a story, she smiles, unsure about how to respond, looks around the room, and says, "Kristen [her younger sister] put two holes in the chair [pointing to the damaged goods]."

"Is that your story?" I ask.

Caitlyn smiles again, not sure what to say, and returns to the paper, writing the second line of text. Half way through, she says, "The baby don't cry. She to play with the dinosaur."

"And what happened?" I ask.

Caitlyn rattles off the remainder of the "story," complete with head-shaking, and with pointing to her finger to show a pretend "booboo." She ends by requesting one of her favorite books, *It's Much too Hot* (Graham, 1986). While I rummage through her bookshelf, Caitlyn continues to work on her story, and proudly shows me the picture she had drawn of "her baby."

What does Caitlyn understand about story? She understands tacitly that story is rooted in her own life experiences—the new baby, the booboo that her sister Kristen had recently incurred while on the swing, and Barney the Dinosaur. She understands unconsciously that in telling a story she can recreate these moments, and thereby make sense of her world. In addition, according to the research of Arthur Applebee, she has developed "a sense of story" because of her ability to use two critical processes: centering and chaining (1978, 1980). Centering is a process of holding a central element constant across the story. Caitlyn chooses to center her story on the baby, tying each event directly to her main

The baby don't cry.
She to play with the dinosaur.
("And what happened?")
Not on the big swing.
She too little.
She hurt her hand on the swing.
Booboo. Baby crying.

Read Jenny (her favorite book).

FIGURE 5–1 *Caitlyn's (age three and a half) concept of story*

character. Caitlyn recognizes that characters alone do not make a story. Rather, a story must have a chain of events. So she strings one event to the next, creating an implied, rudimentary sequence of sorts. With continued exposure to stories, Caitlyn, over time, will interweave the processes of centering and chaining with increasing sophistication.

This chapter explores the development of children's stories and the knowledge we need to assess these stories. The research on story development is extensive. It covers aspects such as developmental stages, story grammar, intertextuality, character development, theme development, and story revision. In order to keep our mission of assessment at the forefront, this chapter weaves important research findings through various children's stories. We turn now to Applebee's seminal work on young children's concept of story.

Concept of Story: Applebee's Developmental Stages

Applebee examined how young children (ages two to five) manipulate the structural principles of centering and chaining during the telling of a story and delineated six developmental stages to describe children's concept of story (1978). These hierarchical stages are summarized in Figure 5–2. As you read the stages, decide which category describes Caitlyn's story.

As you reread Caitlyn's story, you probably decided it fell somewhere between the categories of sequence and primitive narrative. Since her story events remain centered on the baby, and relate to each other fairly directly ("She hurt her hand on the swing. Booboo.") or inferen-

YOUNG CHILDREN'S CONCEPTS OF STORIES

HEAPS:

When young children tell stories containing only strings of unrelated statements/ objects, a heap results. Children who create heaps have no sense of centering or chaining. Only five of Applebee's thirty two-year-olds generated this most basic structure (similar to a free association of items).

SEQUENCES:

Sequences were more prevalent among two-year-olds. Sequences are story structures in which the process of centering takes hold. Children tell stories in which events occur one after another, although they aren't linked to each other. Rather, each event is tied only to a center attribute (a character or a repeated action) of the story.

PRIMITIVE NARRATIVES:

Centering also characterizes the primitive narratives with which the two- and three-year-olds experiment. With a character or an event at the center, children create a string of events, some of which may relate to and complement each other but which do not add up to a story.

UNFOCUSED CHAIN:

With the advent of this stage, centering loses prominence as the child rushes head-long into a chain of events—events that lead directly from one to another but which have no focal point. As Applebee notes "characters pass in and out of the story, the type of action changes, the setting blurs" (1978, p. 64). Relatively few children in Applebee's study used unfocused chains.

FOCUSED CHAINS:

Focused chains featured prominently in over half of the five-year-olds' stories. Children are able to hold both centering and chaining in mind while creating a story. Stories now have a main character who is thrust into an action-oriented string of events, reminiscent of Saturday morning cartoons or movies like *Batman*. But focused chains are not true narratives because character and theme development are not woven into the action. There is only the action.

NARRATIVES:

A few of the five-year-olds created true narratives in which "Each incident not only develops out of the previous one, but at the same time elaborates a new aspect of the theme or situation...stories begin to have a theme or a moral" (1978, p. 65).

FIGURE 5–2   *Applebee's developmental stages of young children's concept of story*

tially ("Not on the swing. She too little."), I'd probably categorize her story as primitive narrative.

To appreciate Applebee's findings that children as young as two years old have internalized the concept of story (from stories read or told to them) and that the complexity of their story structures increases with time, we can examine the story in Figure 5–3 that Caitlyn wrote one year after the baby story (Figure 5–1). The lead of Caitlyn's monster story seems to fit Applebee's category of unfocused chain, with characters floating in and out her "and then" chain of events, although her story certainly comes into clearer focus at the end (1978, 1980)!

While Applebee's work focused on children's sense of story through their storytelling, others have used Applebee's developmental story categories to analyze children's writing (Giacobbe, 1988; Golden, 1984; Temple & Gillet, 1984; Temple, Nathan, Temple, & Burris, 1993). Temple

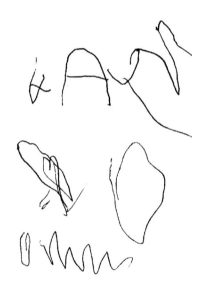

A little monster, only one. The boys ran over the little monster. He had to go and see his mother, so now he feels better. And then a little girl was outside in the woods and then what happened she got lost. And then three monsters came and ranned over—no—and the bikes ranned over three more monsters. And then they had to go back home and see them mother.
And the mother said "Don't go out in the woods without mommy."
And then they ran out with the mommy. Then the mommy went to work and then they ran out all by theirself.
The mother came back home and said, "Why did my monsters run outside by themselves again? I should stay home with them."
But the daddy was home with them and told them to run outside and don't come back until mommy comes home.
"Honey, what did you let them outside by themself?"
And the daddy said, "I want to make you yell."

FIGURE 5–3   *Caitlyn's (age four and a half) concept of story*

et al., for example, provided examples of kindergartners' and first graders' stories which range from heaps to narratives (1993). We turn now to the assessment of a first grader's story writing and to the degree to which Applebee's work is applicable.

Assessing Philip's (Grade 1) Concept of Story

Recall that Philip showed a strong propensity for personal narratives during first grade (Chapter 4). In addition to journal writing, Philip's class occasionally wrote stories which were edited by the teacher or parent volunteers, typed and spiral-bound. Figure 5–4 presents the contents of Philip's January story. Each line represents the text Philip placed on one page. As you read his story, use Applebee's categories to assess Philip's concept of story.

In terms of Applebee's categories, it is easy to rule out the extremes of heaps and sequences on one end of the hierarchy, and focused chains and narratives on the other. Because Philip's piece has a clear center (his friend) we can eliminate the category, unfocused chain. "My Friend" then appears to meet the criteria of the primitive narrative. Philip centers his piece on his friend and creates a collection of events that relate in a general way to each other and to his center. The events could be reordered without affecting the integrity of the story. Philip even experiments with expanding his center from the concrete "my friend" to the more conceptual center of "friendship," by shifting between the pronouns "he" and "we." Taken as a whole, though, the events do not approximate a plot structure. When assigned to write a story, Philip writes a piece more along the lines of Sowers's "all-about" books—all about my friend (1985).

Philip's next story, a fairy tale called "The Three Wishes" (Figure 5–5), was written three months later. As you read this piece, ponder Applebee's story categories. (Philip's dialogue bubbles are unedited.)

"The Three Wishes" approximates Applebee's category of narrative.

My friend's name is Patrick. I like him because he is nice. He has brown hair and blue eyes.
We live near each other. His house number is 4.
We like to play basketball.
His favorite pet is a dog.
We go to the Davis School on Bus 3.
He likes to wrestle with me. He likes to spy with me. Mostly we like to spy on my sisters.
He has a brother named Christian. We like to play Nintendo.
Our favorite book is *Green Eggs and Ham*.

FIGURE 5–4   *Philip's primitive narrative: January*

The Three Wishes

Once upon a time, there was a mean King and Queen. They had a bad tree.
One day they did not want it. They were thinking about how to get rid of the
tree. They remembered the witch that had given them three wishes.
The first wish was to make the magic tree smaller.
   (Dialogue Bubble: "I want to make him smaller")
The second wish was to make the mean tree kind.
   (Dialogue Bubble: "well, I want to make him kind")
The third wish was to be happy always.
   (Dialogue Bubble: "well, I always want to be happy.)
The tree got smaller and smaller until it was only as big as an ant.
The tiny tree protected all of the insects.
   (Dialogue Bubble: "hey what do you think your doing")
The King and Queen became kind, and they lived happily ever after.

FIGURE 5–5   *Philip's narrative: April*

In addition to centering and chaining his story, Philip delights his readers
with his rather sophisticated, albeit tacit, knowledge about the characteristics of fairy tales. Charlotte Huck would give Philip high marks for
his inclusion of the following fairy tale characteristics: swift, action-
oriented plot that sustains a repetitive structure; motifs (pattern) including three wishes and wicked protagonists; unidimensional characters;
minimum description; use of dialogue (Philip's dialogue bubbles) to express emotions; a basic theme of goodness; and a happy ending (Huck,
Helper, & Hickman, 1987). Because Philip understands that fairy tale
characters undergo personal transformations, he reforms his "mean King
and Queen" and his "bad tree," over the course of his story. Although
we can't quite grasp why "mean" royalty would get rid of the tree by
making it smaller and kinder, or by giving the tree its own wish (see shift
in dialogue bubble), we cheer the noble transformation the tree has un-
dergone. The virtue of kindness is brought into clearer focus when the
tree fends off the intruder who is stepping on his ants, signaling Philip's
beginning awareness of the importance of themes in stories.

Do Children's Stories Move Through Fixed Stages?

According to Applebee's developmental stage theory, Philip should have
moved from the primitive narrative stage (his friend story) to an unfo-

cused chain. However, as we have just analyzed, Philip's "The Three Wishes" meets the requirements of a true narrative. Did Philip leap from primitive narrative to true narrative in three short months, skipping two levels (unfocused chain and focused chain) along the way? It's very doubtful that he did. My hunch is that Philip's creation of these two pieces has more to do with the story prototype he chose to write than with violating stage theory. Philip may well have been able to write a comparable fairy tale in January, because of his strong schema—his mental representation of how stories are structured—for this particular genre of story. (A fairy tale unit was enjoyed in school, and fairy tales were read at home.) Because he chose to write a story about his best friend rather than a fairy tale, he adopted the loosely structured mode of an "all-about" book, sharing one attribute of his friend after another. Many of us would approach the same task in a similar fashion. Biographical sketches have a text structure different from that of a story. That Philip interchanges story and biography is not at all unusual when we consider that, as teachers, we often preface a biography with a statement such as, "I'm going to read you a story about . . ."

What I am suggesting here is that children's schema for story may contain specific subschemata: a subschema for fairy tale, one for adventure story, one for fable and so forth. (A story schema is the child's mental representation of how stories are structured; a subschema is a mental representation of a specific kind of story.) If Philip had tapped his subschema of a cops-and-robbers story, he might have written a focused chain because children know that cops-and-robbers stories are action-packed, with events literally tumbling out one after the other. It is this knowledge of story subschemata, rather than fixed stages that may drive, in part, children's story creation. In other words, what children intuit about the particulars of fairy tales or of cops-and-robbers stories from their vast exposure to story through books, TV, movies, and so forth—a phenomenon called intertextuality—may account for the category of story they write (unfocused chain, focused chain, and so on).

Therefore, Applebee's stage theory, per se, should not inform our assessment in terms of stages. Applebee himself recognizes that what very young children do with oral narratives may or may not parallel what older children do with written narratives (1980). More importantly, since this research does not take into account the broad social context and the influence of intertextuality, it cannot begin to capture the complexity of what children do when they write. However, Applebee's finding that children's concept of story does mature over time should inform our assessment. In addition, his two key concepts of centering and chaining as well as his accompanying story categories are valuable because they give us useful language with which to describe children's stories.

Assessing the Story Grammar Elements in Children's Narratives

Assessing the extent to which children are able to create genuine stories requires us, at minimum, to analyze story grammar elements. All good stories contain key story grammar elements: a) characters who live in a particular place and at a particular time, b) a problem or tension point encountered by the main character, along with the character's response to the problem, c) the character's plan of action and attempt(s) to solve the problem, d) outcomes of attempts—successes or failures, e) a resolution to the problem and a reaction from the character (Stein & Glenn, 1979). A story grammar, then, is a set of rules that describes a story's structure.

Children as young as four have an intuitive understanding of some of these story grammar rules; they use these rules to write or tell stories (McKeough, 1984). We have already noted that this mental representation of story structure is known as story schema (Mandler, 1983). Philip's strong story schema is played out in his fairy tale, "The Three Wishes," which has been parsed to illustrate the story grammar elements:

> Setting: Once upon a time, there was a mean king and Queen. They had a bad tree.
> Episode:
> *Initiating event:* They were thinking about how to get rid of the tree.
> *Internal Response:* One day they did not want it. They remembered the witch that had given them three wishes.
> *Attempt(s):* The first wish was to make the magic tree smaller. The second wish was to make the mean tree kind. The third wish was to be happy always.
> *Outcome(s):* The tree got smaller and smaller until it was only as big as an ant. The tiny tree protected all of the insects.
> *Resolution:* The King and Queen became kind, and they lived happily ever after.
> *Reaction:* (omitted)

When we labeled Philip's story, "The Three Wishes," as "narrative," according to Applebee's scheme, we did so because it contained all of the primary story grammar elements. This is quite a feat for a first grader, especially in light of some of the research. Golden collected written stories from first, second, and third graders and analyzed children's inclusion of the story grammar elements (1984). She found that their stories increased in complexity over the grade levels. Stories written by first graders usually included brief settings and the main character's actions but omitted the initiating event, reactions, and resolution. Second graders' stories demonstrated better attention to plot development by including the setting, the initiating event, attempts, and a resolution. The third graders' stories contained more complex story grammars than the stories of first and second graders. For example, their stories included the characters' reactions. Different results, however, might have emerged if all groups had been asked to write, for example, fairy tales. Given first graders' familiarity with this story schema, many probably would not have omitted the initiating event or a resolution.

Stein and Glenn discovered that fifth graders generated complex story episodes which included characters' goals, motives, and emotions. About two thirds of the third graders included purposive behaviors; about half of the kindergartners in the study also were able to do so (1979). Whaley asked third, sixth, and eleventh graders to read stories in which varying story grammar elements were omitted and to supply the missing parts (1981). Whaley found that all students tended to expect certain story elements—with the exception of the reaction element—and that third graders were able to predict story elements less frequently than older students.

These studies impress upon us the fact that children bring an internalized story schema to their stories. They understand that stories are created according to a specific set of rules (story grammar elements), learned through listening to and reading specific story genres. They, then, use this schema knowledge to generate stories—both oral and written—with increasing levels of competence, complexity, and sophistication over time.

Intertextuality—What Is It?

Philip's ability to create "The Three Wishes" is tied unquestionably to the fairy tales he heard at home and in school. This dimension of literacy, known as intertextuality, was introduced in Chapter 3. To reiterate, intertextuality focuses on the connections that readers and/or writers forge as they move from one text to another. Jane Yolen vividly captures one essence of this construct:

> Stories lean on stories, art on art. And we who are the tellers and the artists do what has been done for all the centuries of tellings: We thieve (or more politely) borrow and then we make it our own. (1991, p.147)

Text is defined as either oral (including television, movies, radio) or written productions used in social interactions. While the construct of intertextuality has been the subject of extensive scrutiny in the literary world, it is a relative newcomer to education (Bloome & Egan-Robertson,

1993; Cairney, 1990). Attention to this phenomenon derives in part from the keen observations of classroom teachers, such as Ellen Blackburn (1985), June McConaghy (1985), and Wilde (1985). These kidwatchers noticed the power that children's literature had on children's story creations. Their classroom research has been corroborated by other investigators. A brief review of this research, and its implications for assessment, follows.

Cairney, in interviews with eighty sixth graders ranging in reading ability, asked students, "Do you ever think of stories you've read when you are writing a story?" (1990, p. 480). If the response was affirmative, additional probes followed: "Give me an example. Did your story end up like it in any way?" (1990, p. 480). Ninety percent of the students acknowledged an awareness of intertextuality. High percentages of high and low readers noted that they borrowed ideas from story plots they had read or heard, without directly copying the plots (although some students from both groups did borrow plots directly). Interestingly, thirty-three percent of the low readers used content from nonfiction books in their stories, while high readers did not. Genre and characterization, however, served as an impetus (at least at a conscious level) for relatively few students. In addition, very few students talked about merging two or more stories into their own pieces.

In an investigation of children's perceptions of intertextual links as well as their actual written stories, Bearse (1992) replicated and extended Cairney's work. After a six-week genre study of fairy tales, Bearse asked eighteen third graders to write their own fairy tales and then complete a questionnaire which asked about connections between stories they had heard and those they had written. She found that sixty-one percent of the children verbalized intertextual links, although analysis of actual stories revealed that all children had incorporated, in varying degrees, fairy tale leads, characters, or plot details into their own stories. Four children transferred elements of several fairy tales into their pieces. In addition, Bearse found that children captured intuitively the cadence and rhythm of fairy tale language, an aspect not specifically addressed in her genre study.

Cairney, in a subsequent study, attempted to determine the source of intertextuality by tracing the social dynamic in one first-grade classroom over a school year (1992). During the first month of school, the teacher read two books to the class from the series *Faraway Tree* (Blyton, 1939–1943). One child, Amanda, embarked on a written retelling of the first book. Her story was published for the class to read. Cairney traced the ripple effect that Amanda's undertaking had on the class. By the end of the year, ten budding authors had penned take-offs on the Blyton series. Integral to the creation process, however, were high levels of dramatic play, note writing, letter writing, and endless conversation. Social interaction among students, between teacher and students abounded, bolstering authorship efforts. Students talked spontaneously about story ideas and even sought informal advice of their peers. It is clear that intertextuality extends beyond personal connections readers and writers make between or among texts. It also is a process of "social construction, located in the social interactions that people have . . ." (Bloome et al., 1993, p. 308).

Assessing Intertextuality in Shane's Third Grade Stories

Shane's stories are a study in intertextuality. To assess this dimension in his stories, it is essential to juxtapose his writing record and his reading record, to find out what literature has been read to the class, and to recall Shane's discussion about the influence of Beverly Cleary on his Lizard "series" (Chapter 3).

Beverly Cleary, as Figure 5–6 indicates, was only one of the many scaffolds for Shane's story writing over the first four months of third grade. Figure 5–6 presents each of Shane's stories in the order they were produced, along with each story's intertextual link.

The impact of stories, heard or read, on Shane's story creations is pervasive. Shane borrows not only ideas for his stories from intertextual sources but also plot details. The extent to which Beverly Cleary's *The Mouse and the Motorcycle* infiltrated Shane's creation of "Lizard and the Motorcycle" is traced in the flow chart presented in Figure 5–7.

As Figure 5–7 reveals, Beverly Cleary's story served as a powerful demonstration for Shane. Frank Smith notes that one of the essential conditions of literacy learning is the demonstration (1982). Literacy demonstrations exist in two forms: the artifact (the text) and the action (the instruction). The artifact, in this case, *The Mouse and the Motorcycle*, stands as an instructional scaffold for Shane's story creation. While Shane leans heavily on Beverly Cleary's work during the first half of his story, he also explores the cops-and-robbers prototype (the intertextual link is most likely television). It is as if Beverly Cleary gives Shane the jump-start he needs to craft his own story.

Assessing Shane's Third Grade Stories Over Time

Focused Chain: "Lizard and the Motorcycle"

It is little wonder that Shane chose "Lizard and the Motorcycle" (Appendix D) as his favorite piece during the first term of school. For the first time, he wrote a story that in his words, "is awesome 'cuz exciting things

SHANE'S STORIES	INTERTEXTUAL LINKS
1. "The Mouse and the Bike"	*The Mouse and the Motorcycle* (Cleary, 1965)
2. "Lizard and the Motorcycle"	*The Mouse and the Motorcycle* (Cleary, 1965)
3. "Ghost"	(Matt Christopher - Sylvester/main character)
4. "Caribean Lizard"	*The Mouse and the Motorcycle* (Cleary, 1965) *The Lion, the Witch, and the Wardrobe* (Shane saw the play at school.)
	His father's stories about Vietnam
5. "The Bombing of Pearl Harbor"	*A Wall of Names: The Story of the Vietnam Veterans Memorial* (Donnelly, 1991; read to the class)
6. "Lizard Rocks" (abandoned)	*The Mouse and the Motorcycle* (Cleary, 1965)
7. "Jackpot Catcher"	*Jackrabbit Goalie* (Christopher)
8. "Santa's Nutcracker Fatiner"	*The Nutcracker* (T.V. show)
9. "Booker Saves Christmas"	*The Nutcracker* (T.V. show)
10. "World War Weird"	*Terminator II* (Movie)

FIGURE 5–6   *The influence of published works on Shane's stories*

happen to Lizard and Owl, and it's a really long story—five pages. I was gonna make it longer but Ms. Earle stopped me."

"Lizard and the Motorcycle" is a terrific example of Applebee's focused chain. The main protagonist, Lizard, is rocketed through a roller-coaster chain of events in an effort to thrill the reader and to sustain momentum. If we were to plot his story grammar elements, we would bump into three story problems (initiating events) on the first page alone. Lizard's first problem of "catching" a motorcycle is resolved immediately ("And then he found one.") without any explanation of attempts or of Lizard's motive for wanting a motorcycle. Then Shane states that "the problem was he couldn't resist the smell of cheese." (Shane may have substituted his Lizard for Cleary's mouse but Ralph, the mouse, is clearly present in this story!) This initiating event remains unresolved. Toward the end of the first page, we have the makings of a true problem (". . . And he had only had one friend his name was owl. But

"Lizard and the Motorcycle"	The Mouse and the Motorcycle
Lizard finds a motorcycle.	Ralph (the mouse) finds a toy motorcycle that comes to life.
Lizard gets into mischief.	Ralph gets into mischief.
Lizard can't resist the smell of cheese.	Ralph always hunting for food.
Lizard has a friend named Owl.	Ralph befriends Keith (a boy).
Other animals laugh at Lizard, except Owl.	....
Lizard zooms down the halls on motorcycle.	Ralph races down the hotel hallway on Keith's toy motorcycle.
Lizard crashes into open refrigerator and door shuts tight.	Ralph and motorcycle land in a pillow-case, and end up trapped in a clothes hamper.
Lizard escapes.	Ralph escapes.
Lizard finds his room ransacked.	....
Lizard hears men planning a bank robbery. and a kidnapping.	....
Robbers are caught; go to jail.	....

FIGURE 5–7   *The intertextual link in action*

whenever lizard went near any other animals they laughed at him and he did not no who they were talking about so he was laughing too and once they knew that they laughed some more but the only animal that did not laugh was owl . . .") . But it, too, is dismissed. After experimenting with various initiating events, Shane thrusts his characters into a fast-paced plot that jumps from one event to the next. Basically, Shane tries to do in two pages what Beverly Cleary has done in seven chapters and eighty-five pages. The result is that Shane packs three or four stories into one, without fully developing any one of them.

While not true narratives, focused chains allow writers to experiment with plot structure. Given his choice of an adventure story, Shane appropriately prioritizes plot structure over other elements of a good story and he remains faithful to this priority. While he dabbles a little with theme and character development, he is not able to juggle simultaneously all of these story attributes. The theme of friendship which he broaches touchingly at the beginning of the story and returns to at the end (". . . When they got out owl said to lizard i'll be a friend of you for the rest of my live. And they were friends for ever.") gets lost in the action. Characterization suffers the same fate. Poor Lizard doesn't even have any lizard attributes. Unlike Beverly Cleary's Ralph, who learns what it means to let a friend down and who resolves to risk his life to prove his friendship and trustworthiness, Shane's Lizard remains fairly unidimensional. He survives one crisis after another and does not grow as a character. Complex, indeed, is the task of spinning a well-developed story. As Graves points out, "Of all the genres, I think fiction is the most demanding" (1994, p. 287).

Focused Chain: "Caribean Lizard"

Pleased with his newly found talent as a story writer, Shane launches into the ultimate focused chain in his next story. "Caribean Lizard," created about a month after "Lizard and the Motorcycle," sends Lizard and Owl back into an even wilder eight-page story chain. A peaceful vacation on St. Martin takes a turn for the worse when Lizard is kidnapped by Lion (a new character) and is taken into the deep dark woods. With the introduction of a time machine, they end up in the middle of the Vietnam War. While plot structure remains Shane's priority, some additional story features surface. First, with the exception of characters and the plot prototype (adventure), Shane leaves Beverly Cleary behind. New intertextual links guide the creation of this story: a) *A Wall of Names* (Donnelly, 1991), b) a school play of *The Lion, the Witch and the Wardrobe*, c) the movie, *Back to the Future*), and d) the stories Shane's father shared with him about the Vietnam War. One marker of growth in this piece over the earlier lizard story is Shane's beginning attention to theme development. In his first lizard story, Shane directly tells us that friendship is important. In "Caribean Lizard," the theme of friendship appears again, but this time Shane is able to use one scene to "show" us what it means to be a friend. He allows the concept of friendship to emerge through the actions of the characters and their dialogue (text edited):

> . . . they stopped and had lunch. Then a lion came and picked up Lizard and ran in to the woods. Owl chased the lion but the lion got away in the woods. The lion turned at Lizard and said, "Hello my name is Lion. I

did not mean to pick you up." And Lizard said, "You scared the heck out me." Then lion said, "I'm sorry." Then Lion and Lizard lived together while Owl was scared if Lizard was dead or alive. Owl just hoped Lizard was alive. Every day they looked for each other for a month . . .

Narrative: "Jackpot Catcher"

Three stories later, Shane writes "Jackpot Catcher" and gives us another important marker of growth for his portfolio. This story was Shane's favorite piece of the year. As you read it (Appendix E), keep the story grammar elements in mind.

While remnants of the focused chain linger, "Jackpot Catcher" signals Shane's shift to a basic narrative. Rather than volleying his characters through a series of settings, Shane allows his main protagonist, Eric, to stay in the ballpark. He tries to create the story suspense through Eric's and the team's actions, rather than through wild events. Stronger control over the story grammar elements is evident, especially with regard to attempts. He keeps his chain of events within the context of the baseball game. His control over these story elements probably is attributable to the fact that he is writing a sports story, and not an adventure story. However, Shane has difficulty sustaining the story's momentum. For example, rather than having his characters play out the tension of the 5–5 tie, Shane simply reports it as fact.

Shuttling between "Caribean Lizard" and "Jackpot Catcher" alerts us to the tenuous nature of new learning. With "Jackpot Catcher," Shane takes two steps forward, one step back. In this story, he leaves behind wild episodes and fantasy characters and relies on an experience that is much closer to his own life. He keeps the storyline intact, evidencing good control of story grammar elements. His successful experimentation in "Caribean Lizard" with allowing the characters tell the story, however, is lost in the baseball story. We sense that Shane wrote "Jackpot Catcher" to share, at some level, his thoughts about the importance of being accepted by our peers, but he doesn't develop this theme. Nor does he bring us inside the heart and head of his main character, inside his thoughts, anxieties, and dreams. Indeed, the transition to true narrative does not happen overnight. Fiction writing is an art that take years of concerted effort. In time, Shane will come to understand that a well-written story is more than the sum of the story grammar parts.

What Happens When Shane, the Fifth Grader, Revises His Third Grade Story?

In the last chapter, we surveyed some of the research with regard to the challenge that the revision process presents to young writers. In the most recent National Assessment of Educational Progress (NAEP) study, fourth graders were asked what they do to make their "papers better" (Applebee, Langer, Mullis, & Jenkins, 1990). Seventy-five percent said they correct their spelling. Sixty-five percent said they correct punctuation, sixty-three percent add ideas and information, and sixty-two percent change words. Clearly, editing takes precedence over revision. Only thirty-nine percent of the fourth graders reported using the strategies of moving sentences or paragraphs, or of rewriting most of their paper (thirty-five percent). Interestingly, only thirty-nine percent of the eleventh graders surveyed reported rewriting their pieces. The NAEP findings corroborate Fitzgerald's conclusion that "Overwhelming evidence supports the belief that writers at various ages and various levels of competence mainly make surface and mechanical revisions, often revealing a view of revision as proofreading" (1987, p. 492).

Calkins (1980a) traced the development of one child over two years (third and fourth grade) as she moved from random drafting to refining to transition and finally to interacting (see Chapter 4, Figure 4–10). But she is careful to suggest that continued research into children's revision strategies is essential before any conclusions can be drawn about the developmental aspect of revision. Curious as to how Shane, now in fifth grade, would view his third grade story, "Lizard and the Motorcycle" (Appendix D), I asked him to reread it and comment.

SHANE: I remembered words from stories that had been read to me like *ransacked*. I heard that in *James and the Giant Peach*. I also noticed my penmanship and my spelling. No way is it as good as it is now.

CAROL: If you were to write this story today, would you write it the same way?

SHANE: I'd put in a couple of more details . . . like what the police car looked like on the inside.

CAROL: Is there anything you didn't like about the story?

SHANE: No.

Shane, then, to my delight, offered to rewrite this story on his computer.

Given the research cited earlier, it was not surprising to find that Shane's revision (Appendix F) of his third-grade story ("Lizard and the Motorcycle") primarily resulted in surface level changes. Examination of Shane's revision, completed two years after the original was written, revealed Shane's utilization of the four primary revision operations: additions, substitution, rearrangement, and deletion. Examples of each of these operations are underlined on the following pages. Notice that, at times, multiple operations exist within one sentence or section. Excerpts of Shane's text (Figure 5–8) are presented in unedited form.

These examples reveal Shane's attention to the semantic features of text (as well as to the syntactic and orthographic features). He uses the revision operations of addition, substitution, rearrangement, and deletion to clarify and to enhance the story's meaning. Revisions occur at the word, phrase, sentence, and paragraph level but they do not affect the overall story in terms of text level (story grammar, characterization, or theme development). The focused chain is tightened for sure, but it remains a focused chain. The lizard and owl remain static characters who exist to serve the plot. The theme of friendship opens and ends the story as it did in the original version; it doesn't find its way into the characters' thoughts and actions. Shane's revision strategies certainly improve the readability of the story but not the story's essence. Revision is a highly complex undertaking.

A Longitudinal Look at Shane's Story Writing: Grade 5

Shane on Shane: Self-Assessment of "The Missing Report Mystery"

When I contacted Shane for his permission to use his third-grade writing samples in this book, he was delighted but was quick to say, "I could write a much better story now because I just finished fifth grade." When I visited his home for his parents' signatures to release his work, Shane presented me with the story he had composed on his computer (Appendix G), and remarked, "I knew in third grade I was a good story writer but I didn't know I could get this far in writing a story." I then asked Shane to write a reflection piece on his story, telling me what he liked about it and what future goals he might have for story writing. His reflection is presented in Figure 5–9.

While Shane is no longer equating "good writing" with periods and capitals, his concern for the written conventions continues to prevail. In an effort to steer Shane away from the surface features of text to the deeper aspects, I ask:

CAROL: What do you like about the storyline itself?

SHANE: Sometimes, it wasn't a lot, but every now and then, I'd say a humorous phrase. Like I thought it would be funny if Bill Griffey's (the detective) number would be 999–9999, and it was funny how Eunice Monique, the sergeant would keep on going on and laughing and stuff . . .

EXCERPTS OF SHANE'S ORIGINAL
THIRD GRADE STORY

SHANE'S REVISIONS
AS A FIFTH GRADER

ADDITIONS
Used to clarify story meaning,
to add detail

Whenever a motorcycle went by it couldn't catch one (ride one). And then he found one.

Whenever a motorcycle went buy <u>Lizard wished he could</u> ride on one, and then he found one <u>abandoned in the wood.</u>

...but the only animal that did not laughing was owl. Then they stopped laughing and

The only animal that never laughed was Owl. <u>Owl came</u> and then they stopped.

And they drove of in a flash and when they got there sell at the police station. They were pushing and shoveing. Then owl flew

and he took of in a flash <u>(because the car was till running).</u> Owl was flying.

SUBSTITUTIONS
Used to strengthen story cohesion,
to clarify who is doing what

Then they stopped laughing and he got on his motorcycle and the owl said step on it. he lived in an apartment.

Owl came and then they stopped. <u>They</u> both got on the motorcycle and Owl said "Step on it." <u>Lizard</u> lived in an apartment.

REARRANGING
Used to create a stronger story sequence

...and then he heard the man said where are we going to rob tonigt a bank. The man who asked said lets kidnap somebody. They weren't lucky because the go caugt And they went to jail. For twenty years. Lizard called the police...

Then Lizard heard the man say, "Where are are we going to rob tonight, a bank?" the man who asked said, lets kidnap somebody!" <u>Lizard called the police.</u> They weren't lucky because they got.

FIGURE 5–8   *Shane's (Grade 5) revisions of his third grade story*

EXCERPTS OF SHANE'S ORIGINAL THIRD GRADE STORY	SHANE'S REVISIONS AS A FIFTH GRADER
Then owl flew over the police stashin and swoped on to the roof. And herd lizard call for help and then owl got to the building and saved lizard from a jeep that almost ran over lizard.	Owl was flying over the road leading to the police station and heard lizard calling for help. Owl <u>swooped down</u> and saved Lizard before a car accident with a jeep.

DELETIONS
Used primarily to eliminate redundancy and to enhance sentence structure

It looks like it's been live in by crockadiles! And then he said wow! That's imposable it's really been ransaked by animals by monkeys, tigers.	It looks like crocodiles have lived in it. Wow! It's been ransacked by monkeys, tigers...
...he went in the wrong room and crashed into the open refridgerator and it shut and locked he could not get out. And he stayed	...they went into an open refridgerator and it shut and locked. They stayed

FIGURE 5–8, *continued*

CAROL: Yes, Monique is quite a feisty character. If you had to think of a goal for future story writing, what would it be?

SHANE: Well if I had nothing to do, I'd probably take a notebook and write down the first page of a story and I might have three first pages of all different ones. I'd probably keep on reading them until I could plan more to add on, then I'd keep on adding on and adding on until I have a whole story.

Two years and twenty leagues of learning was my first reaction to Shane's story and to his self-assessment comments. Shane was right. At every level—from plot, theme, and characterization to organization—his story had come so "far." Curious as to what had transpired over the last two years, I asked Shane about his story writing in grades 4 and 5. He replied, "I really didn't write hardly any stories in fourth or fifth grade . . . We did a lot of reports (nonfiction) and book reports . . . In fourth grade, we communicated our feelings through talking instead of writing. We did

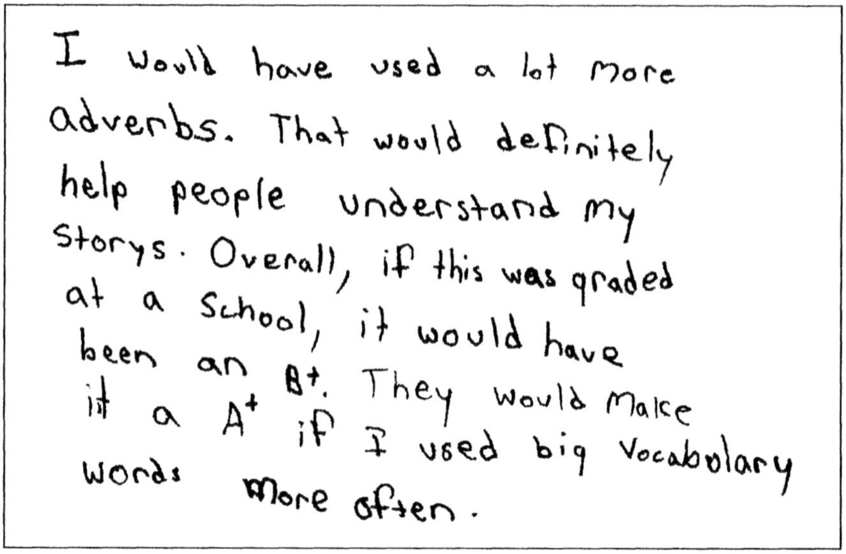

I would have used a lot more adverbs. That would definitely help people understand my storys. Overall, if this was graded at a school, it would have been an B+. They would make it a A+ if I used big vocabulary words more often.

FIGURE 5–9   *Shane's (Grade 5) reflection on his story*

plays and creative dramatics too." In order to corroborate Shane's recollection that he had written few stories, I spoke with Susan, his fourth-grade teacher. She expressed great surprise that Shane didn't recall his "bulging creative writing folder with incredible stories and poems." Shane had written four or five nonfiction reports that Susan recalls was a challenging, at times frustrating, experience. It appears that Shane's induction into exposition in fourth grade held such import for him that he dismissed the other genre writing in which he engaged. All of this points, once again, to the importance of corroborating evidence. Writer's perceptions need to be placed in a context of the whole. Shane's recollection, on the other hand, of little story writing in fifth grade was corroborated by his teacher. Content reports, book reports, and journals in science and math predominated in grade five. Hence, Shane's marked progress as a story writer can be attributed to his continued story writing in fourth grade and to his extensive reading, both in school, and at home (with John Grisham's books topping the list). Shane's schema for narrative had matured in pronounced ways.

In asking Shane about the origin of "The Mystery Report," he explained, "My brother wrote a 'Nate the Great' story for school, so that gave me the idea. Then I thought about what I was going to do. I thought about if you want to take my reports along with my story and how Nate the Great was finding stuff." The reports to which Shane refers were nonfiction reports (New Zealand, Andrew Carnegie . . .) that he wrote in fourth and fifth grade. Shane's comments evidence not only intertextual and personal links but also rehearsal strategies. As you will see from the following conversation, Shane did a significant amount of planning/rehearsing before sitting down at the computer to compose this first draft:

CAROL: When you turned on the computer, how much of the story was in your head?

SHANE: Only the beginning, 'cuz you know how they have those little things where you read the beginning stories and you have to finish them. It was kind of like that. I knew where I was going to start off and I knew I could build up and build up. 'Cuz it was a pretty good topic. See I got the idea of listing all my characters on my front page from Eric (his friend). See he had to do a book report for school and on the front page of his, he listed all his characters in the story and what they did.

CAROL: How interesting. I thought maybe you got that idea of listing your characters from John Grisham or another author.

SHANE: No.

CAROL: Did you do this list of characters before the story or after the story?

SHANE: I did it before the story. I had all my characters and jobs and what they do and, like, how I was going to put them in but I still didn't know the end story. I knew the beginning part of the story and what all the characters were supposed to do and I filled it in so all the characters did their job. Like the way I got Pele, I already thought of it in the beginning because we went to the World Cup games and there was this cardboard picture of Pele which looked real and so I went up and put my arm around it and my Dad took a picture and it looked like that was really Pele. So I was thinking about that and put Pele in the story.

CAROL: The idea of Pele and of accepting friends from different cultures, where did you get that idea?

SHANE: Well, my old teacher, the main thing she concentrated on was differences. She wanted to know about differences in different people and the cultures and where they come from.

CAROL: What were you trying to get across to readers by including Pele?

SHANE: That people can be friends no matter what their differences.

Before sitting down at the computer, Shane had worked out his title. He also had planned his cast of characters and their roles in the story, and his story lead. He had figured out one of his story tension points (acceptance). Noteworthy, also, is Shane's comment about trying out three leads as his next story-writing goal (see transcript on page 95). Murray tells us that rehearsal is essential to good writing: "I spend most of my time planning what I may write, making lists, making notes, talking to myself in my head and in my daybook . . . These days I plan more and rewrite less" (1989, p. 211).

Story Grammar Elements

While Shane may not have planned the specific elements of his story plot ahead of time, it is clear that his control of story grammar elements has increased markedly since third grade. In "The Missing Report Mystery," Shane not only creates a series of episodes that link one to the other (the lost report, the call to the police, the call to the detective agency . . .), with varying degrees of success, but also attends to story grammar elements within each episode. Recall that in his third-grade stories Shane tended to move the reader from one attempt to the next without explaining the subsequent consequences or the character reactions attached to each attempt. Shane, the fifth grader, is able to incorporate these elements into each of his primary episodes. For example, after the problem of the missing report is established in Chapter 4 of the story, Chapter 5, "Police," follows with an attempt (John calls the police), a consequence (the Sergeant laughs at John's request), and a reaction (frustration with police response and creation of new plan). With the exception of Chapter 3, "Pele," which we will discuss later, Shane does a fine job of centering and chaining his episodes.

His facility with episode generation seems strongest in his final four chapters; momentum gains as does an attempt to build the suspense. His first three chapters, however, wobble a bit. The reader expects John's reading problem to emerge when he goes to the library, and later when he attempts to read his book. Instead, Shane profiles a rather proficient reader. This is reminiscent of Lizard's problem ("he couldn't rezist cheese") in "Lizard and the Motorcycle." In both cases, Shane tells the reader directly what "problem" plagues his main protagonist but then seems to forget to weave the problem into the plot. I suspect that Shane isn't using the "problem" in the story grammar sense. Rather he is trying to build his character's profile by giving us more "details" about his characters.

Details are of great importance to Shane, as his response to question 2 in the story survey reveals (Figure 5–10). When asked what the most important thing an author needs to do to write a great story, he writes, "explain *all* the details." His allegiance to details is very strong as his elaboration on his written response shows: "Want to know something, see, I know I can make hundred page story on my own. But the key is just details. I'd probably just say that if John Grisham took all of his details out, he'd have only twenty pages. It could take off many pages." From where does his preoccupation with details come? In all likelihood, it comes from us, his teachers. In surveying the comments a teacher wrote on one upper elementary child's papers across the year and across genres, I found details mentioned on *every* paper: "The description of the story needs more information"; "Try to carry details throughout your work"; "Good descriptions of the characters"; and so on. Calkins reminds us that "The goal of writing is not to 'add description' but rather for writers to see the drama unfolding as they write it, and to write it in such a way that the readers can see that drama unfolding" (1986, p. 324).

This is not to say that details are inconsequential. In fact, Shane understands the place of details in narrative: "It (details) gives the person that's reading it as if they were there, watching it happen. See, like, it's as if they are watching a movie when they're reading a book. The movie is a visual so they get a visual idea, same while reading it. And even though the author explains it, they can put a different kind of person in their mind. So everyone might have their own character in their mind." Shane attends to "visual" language at times in his own piece: ". . . Mr. Cockroach" (Chapter 1); "John went parading around town" (Chapter 4); ". . . Monique burst out laughing" (Chapter 5). Recall also his comment about trying to invent humorous characters (see transcript on page 93). His effort to affect humor via characters' actions or story details without telling us directly is notable. At other times, though, he inserts details for the sake of inserting details: "So he was a typical, average, american boy" (Chapter 1); "Ralph (The Dog) came speeding into John's hot but tranquil room" (Chapter 2).

Character Development

In "The Missing Report Mystery," Shane inducts nine characters into his story, significantly more characters than in any of his third-grade stories. He, undoubtedly, is impressed with the menagerie of characters with which authors such as John Grisham flood their books. Weaving a large cast of characters through the plot is a sizable undertaking for a young writer. Shane manages his characters by manipulating his story settings. At school, we meet Mr. Cockroach, whose name needs no explanation. At home, we meet the nurturing parents; at the police station, the boisterous sergeant; at potential crime sites, the incompetent detective. All of these characters, perhaps with the exception of the sergeant, are unidimensional and predictable, in place to support the plot.

Pele, John's best friend, however, is a character without a setting and consequently a character without a role. In asking Shane about the purpose of Chapter 3 in his story, he replies, "that people can be friends no matter what their differences. Well, my old teacher, the main thing

Name _Shane Forsyth_   Date _9/1/94_

What Makes A Good Story?

1. Think of a great story that you have read lately. What makes that story great, in your opinion?

   I have read the Client by John Grisham. It was great because it showed people the Consiquences of Lying ~~writing~~.

2. What is the most important thing an author needs to do to in order to write a great story?

   I think an Author should use common words and explain All the details.

3. What is the next most important thing an author needs to do in order to write a great story?

   He should stop a chapter So the reader will say, "I wonder what will happen."

4. What does an author need to do to create an interesting character?

   He Should not make him the average - everyday person.

FIGURE 5–10   *Shane's responses to Story Survey*

5. Why do authors write stories?

Sometimes to express their feelings.

6. Are there any other reasons that authors might have for writing stories?

To do something during space time.

7. What 's the easiest part of writing a story of your own?

I can write with my own Ideas.

8. What's the hardest part of writing a story of your own?

Getting the story corrected

9. How do you feel about yourself as a storywriter?

I feel good that people notice me because of how well I write.

FIGURE 5–10, *continued*

she concentrated on was differences. She wanted to know about differences in different people and the cultures and where they come from." A noble subtheme—however, it is a subtheme that stands detached from the story. Shane is not able to fold this theme of tolerance into his characters' actions and thoughts. In asking Shane if Pele is important to the story, he replies, "Yes! Pele wanted to be John's friend no matter what. It showed that their friendship was so big. He wanted to help him find the report." It is only through this conversation with Shane that we understand the centrality of Pele to the story. Shane, in time, will learn to allow his characters' thoughts and actions to convey his themes. All in all, though, Shane's ability to manipulate a series of characters in believable ways is a credit to his burgeoning skill as a story writer, especially when we analyze Shane's portrayal of his main protagonist, John Borneo.

John Borneo receives the fullest attention in terms of character development. The fact that Shane "just made up" John Borneo marks an important departure from his third-grade penchant for generic characters (Figure 5–11). As Graves notes, "It is a very important moment when a child creates a character with a name no one else knows. A new name is the beginning of any dimension to a character" (1989, p. 778). Unlike Superman, for example, whose character portrayal is defined before any story even starts, a character such as John Borneo is free to evolve over the course of the story. John Borneo's actions and reactions are limited only by Shane's imagination. Shane introduces us to John Borneo through description, another notable departure from his third-grade characterizations. In the story lead, we learn about John Borneo's physical attributes, interests, and academic standing. Through dialogue, we learn that John is a friendly chap (interaction with Susan in library scene) and cooperative (conversation with father). Through John's actions, we learn about his virtues of self-discipline, hard work, and resourcefulness. Hence, Shane's understanding that characters are brought to life through actions, dialogue, description, and commentary of others has grown considerably since third grade. In addition, we marvel at another layer of his understanding, namely, character credibility. Just as the ancient poet, Homer, does not portray any human in *The Iliad* or *The Odyssey* as singularly heroic (Tigner, 1993), Shane does not portray John Borneo as singularly "good." John Borneo, with all his admirable traits, becomes too boastful for his own good. Shane intuitively realizes that believable characters are not unidimensional—neither all good nor all bad. Successful writers create characters that tap the range of our human complexity.

It is interesting to juxtapose Shane's story description of John Borneo as "a typical, average american boy" with his answer to question 4 in the story survey (Figure 5–10) concerning the creation of an interesting character. Shane writes that "He (an author) should not make him

WHEN CHILDREN WEAVE CHARACTERS INTO THEIR STORIES
(GRAVES, 1989, 1991, 1994)

GENERIC CHARACTERS:

> First and second graders pluck characters for their stories directly from their story world: TV/ movie characters, book characters, and so on. Characters are created to serve the plot. They are pawns to be tossed and tumbled as the action demands.

FRIEND CHARACTERS:

> Equally popular in grades one to three is the inclusion of characters who have names of the writer's friends. Children, in the early grades, also include themselves in their stories.

INVENTED CHARACTERS:

> A significant step forward occurs when children invent a "new" character, a character unknown to the writer and the reader. The introduction of a "new" character into a story can begin as early as grade two but is commonplace by grade four.

CHARACTERS THROUGH DIALOGUE:

> While younger writers allow bits of their characters' personalities to emerge through dialogue, older children (generally grade three and up) create character profiles through supporting dialogue.

CHARACTERS THROUGH DESCRIPTION:

> Physical description, in addition to dialogue, brings characters to life; generally grades five and up.

CHARACTERS THROUGH REACTIONS:

> The final developmental swing occurs as writers come to understand that characters' personalities are best revealed through their actions and their reactions. Fifth graders (and up) allow characters to share their inner thoughts. They also enjoy creating characters who are older than themselves, and who engage in adult activities (i.e. driving).

FIGURE 5–11   *Graves's research on children's use of characters*

an average-everyday person." In elaborating on this written response, Shane makes the intertextual link with Grisham's work, "Well, for *The Client*, Mark wasn't the average boy. He, um, got into trouble, he got into fights in school. He smoked; he taught his little brother to smoke. He does bad stuff but he is aware of the consequences . . ." Thus, part of Shane's thinking is still ensconced in story as high drama. Somehow his own "typical, average" life is not the stuff of story. And yet when he writes his own story, we feel Shane's presence in the character, John Borneo. (Shane verified that certain events in the story dovetailed with his life: He wrote a report on Andrew Carnegie, studied about George Washington, has a dog, outlines a report before writing it, is frequently complimented for his report writing by his parents, loves soccer. . . .) In probing this incongruity, Shane argues that his characters are not really "average because I made a few of the names really wild like John Borneo and Mr. Cockroach and Eunice Monique. See I wouldn't make all my characters John, Judy, Mike. I try to mix in some wild names and some wild things that they do." We notice that, in fact, the characters in "The Missing Report" may have "wild" names but they don't do wild things. Shane tacitly understands that in order for characters to work in stories, they must be believable to the reader.

Shane grapples with what challenges even the best of writers, namely, the harmonizing of character and action. For example, Shane short-circuits the pivotal part of the story in which John gets himself in trouble with his friends ("The Mystery Report," Chapter 4). Rather than showing us through dialogue, action, and reaction how bumptious John has become about his report, Shane, without any foreshadowing, chooses simply to tell us ("Kind of cocky . . . Don't you think?"). Nor is he able to create the degree of tension between John and his classmates that the reader expects in the story climax. As this scene draws to a close, we are "told" that John "panicked" but are not brought inside his main protagonist's head. What John thought and felt about the confrontation with his friends and the ensuing dilemma is not revealed. In time, Shane will understand Price's take on characterization: "Writing is like acting on paper. I don't try to transcend my people, rather to become them. If I can trance myself into becoming a character, I can load every gesture and interaction with enough information for a book in itself. It is a simple matter of show and tell. There is a way to 'show' every 'tell' . . ." (Price in Calkins, 1986, p. 325).

Theme Development

"Good fiction must be about something that matters to the writer" (Calkins, 1986, p. 322). This remark aptly captures Shane's strength as a storyteller. When he writes stories, whether as a third grader or a fifth grader, he works to infuse themes (especially friendship) that matter to him. But Shane's propensity for telling the story rather than showing it often overshadows his attempts at theme development. In "The Mystery Report," Shane creates John Borneo to send a message to his audience about the risks of self-aggrandizement. But, he can't quite synchronize John's thoughts and actions in a way that makes us believe John has learned "an important lesson." Shane, like all writers, is faced with the challenge of interweaving character development and theme development in subtle but significant ways. Just as John Grisham, in *The Client*, "showed people the consiquences of lying" (Figure 5–10), Shane, too, wants to show people the consequences of boasting. Shane, however, chooses to convey his theme in a explicit, didactic fashion rather than to allow it to emerge implicitly through the interaction of his characters and the force of their actions.

Little is known about the emergence of themes in children's writing. Research to this point has centered on children's ability to abstract themes from stories. One recent study (Lehr, 1988) was undertaken to probe children's sensitivity to story themes across three grade levels (K, 2, 4) and to ascertain the impact of literature on theme development. Children were asked to listen to three books (realistic fiction) and to chose the two books that "tell about the same idea." They then drew a picture of the shared theme. Children were also interviewed about their responses. The same procedure was repeated with three folktales on another day. Books varied by grade level. Lehr found that kindergartners could identify similar themes in eighty percent of the realistic books, and thirty-five percent of the folktales. In addition, kindergartners who had high exposure to books could generate concrete thematic statements about the matched books. Increasing levels of thematic abstraction was found for second and fourth graders, prompting Lehr to conclude that "thematic identification is a fairly early developmental strategy" (1988, p. 351) and that exposure to literature is highly correlated with thematic awareness.

Shane's responses (in grade five) to question five (Figure 5–10) about why authors write stories ("Sometimes to express their feelings") and to question one as to what makes a story great (. . . "It was great because it showed people the consiquences of lying.") attest to his growing thematic sensitivity. Shane understands that authors write stories in order to explore the complexity of the human condition. With further story writing and mediated instruction, Shane will merge character and theme development with increasing success (Au, 1992).

Shane on Shane: Self-Assessment of Story Revision (Grade 5)

CAROL: When you were writing the story ("The Missing Report"), did you write your first draft and then go back and make changes in your ideas, or did you make changes as you went along?

SHANE: Well, I went all the way through it and then I looked over it because, sometimes, on my Spellcheck I put two words together and it becomes a real word and the computer won't catch it.

CAROL: After you finished writing it, what did you do?

SHANE: I read it and thought it was OK, and then I gave it to my father and he said it was OK, and I gave it to my mother, and she said it was OK.

CAROL: What did you ask your parents to do?

SHANE: I asked what it sounds like so I can make it sound better, like if there's any run-on sentences like I had in my third-grade story.

CAROL: Did you reread it to see if you got all your ideas right?

SHANE: Yeah but I don't have to make changes in my ideas. I just have to make corrections.

Shane's comments corroborate researchers' findings which show that children do not revise voluntarily. Even when they are instructed to do so, they tinker minimally with the substance of their ideas and concentrate on the conventions (Fitzgerald, 1987). Researchers' speculations as to why children are reluctant to revise range from theories of egocentricity, to low levels of abstract thinking, to knowledge about what to revise but not how to revise (Graves, 1983; Scardamalia and Bereiter, 1983).

It is important to stress that research on children's revision is still in its infancy (Fitzgerald, 1987). Unfortunately, far too much of the research has been executed without attention to the social milieu in which children worked. In addition, most researchers ask children to revise for the sake of revising. Lucy Calkins argues, though, that successful revision can only occur when the piece is of significance to the writer:

> I realize now, in retrospect that I used to view writing as a process of producing and then repairing drafts. I talked about fixing leads, inserting details, strengthening weak sections, reworking endings. When the pieces were alive to begin with, these revisions strengthened the pieces. But quite often the children with whom I worked ended up fiddling with and fixing pieces of writing that weren't alive in the first place. (1994, p. 270)

According to Calkins, until children learn to write about slices of their lives that have true significance for them—the slices that force them to deal with some level of dissonance or puzzlement or wonderment in their lives—it makes little sense to ask them to revise (1991, 1994). There is nothing to revise. Furthermore, she notes that for many writers, drafting and revising occur simultaneously. They write a little, test out its integrity, and often rewrite on the spot. Researchers haven't begun to unravel the complexities of drafting and revising as unitary process for writers at any level.

Concluding Comments and a Word About Teacher Self-Assessment

At the end of grade 3, Shane, in response to the question, "Why do people write?" wrote: "To get people to read" (Appendix B). Asked the same question at the end of grade 5, Shane wrote, "Sometimes to express their feelings" (Figure 5–10). When asked to elaborate, he said, "The point I am trying to get to is that a lot of people write stuff about how they feel and stuff that's happened to them. They want to know what's happened to them so they write it down." Shane's wisdom rivals that of Pulitzer Prize–winning novelist John Cheever's, who when asked why he wrote, responded, "It seems to me that writing is a marvelous way of making sense of one's life, both for the writer and for the reader" (Murray, 1990, p. 4).

Shane's remarkable evolution as a story writer has not occurred in a vacuum. It has occurred because of the interplay of several essential conditions. Before we assess our children's story writing efforts, we need to judge our own efforts at ensuring that these essentials permeate our teaching. We need to answer affirmatively to the following questions:

- Have we flooded the classroom (whether grade 1 or grade 6) with quality stories—from picture books to chapter books—and encouraged aesthetic responses on a daily basis?

- Have we encouraged story writing during writer's workshop regardless of grade level?

- Have we written and shared our own stories and asked children to respond? Have we explained the significance of our stories, and how they came to be?

- Have we helped children understand that story writing begins not with topic lists but with an acute awareness of life's wonders and life's experiences?

- Have we showed them how many published authors record their observations, thoughts, memories in notebooks in order to find topics of significance?

- Have we showed children how to read across their collection of writings to discover connections, and to push for a level of new understanding/insight?

- Have we pulled up a chair beside each writer and asked how and why they created their stories? Have our conferences and mini-lessons kept the question of topic significance at the forefront of our discussions?

- Have we asked children to speculate on how authors use other authors' books (or other sources such as film and art) for ideas (intertextuality)?

- Have we taught children about the art of story creation? Using published and personal stories, have we conducted series of minilessons on character development, theme development, story grammar elements and so forth in a developmentally appropriate fashion?

- Have children had ample opportunity to share their story drafts formally and informally with different audiences, and to receive ongoing feedback?

- Have we provided ongoing demonstrations on how revision is a process of distancing ourselves from our stories, of reflecting on the level of congruity between our intended meaning and our actual meaning, of thinking about audience and voice, and of discovering deeper meaning?

- Have we asked children to bring to school stories they have written at home?

Assessing Nonfiction Writing 6

Stories and story writing hold a place of undeniable primacy in the elementary classroom. The most recent data from the National Assessment of Educational Progress (NAEP) reveals that when children were asked about the kinds of writing they had done the previous week, forty-three percent of the fourth graders sampled reported that they had written a story. Thirty-two percent of the fourth graders reported writing "other reports," not including the book report. Surprisingly, the same trend was found for eighth graders. Forty-eight percent reported writing stories the previous week—only twenty-nine percent writing "other reports" (Applebee, Langer, Mullis, & Jenkins, 1990). Langer's (1986) earlier work corroborates the thrust of the NAEP findings. In interviews with third, sixth, and ninth graders, Langer found that only twenty-five percent of the third graders said that they wrote reports often; seventy percent reported writing stories frequently. Sixth graders evidenced the same trends. While fifty-eight percent of the sixth graders reported that they wrote stories frequently, only thirty percent said they wrote reports.

Why is the pull of story so strong? A contributing factor, of great import, is the emergent literacy research which has demonstrated a critical link between story and literacy development (Durkin, 1966; Holdaway, 1979; Snow, 1983; Sulzby, 1985). Children who are steeped in books from the earliest years have stronger vocabularies (Burroughs, 1972; Snow, 1983), more advanced language development (Burroughs, 1972; Chomsky, 1972), and greater success in learning to read in school (Durkin, 1966, 1974–75; Heath, 1983; Snow, 1983). In addition, as we noted in Chapter 3, there is the belief that children must first experience fictional modes of writing before they can tackle the more distant, nonfictional modes of writing (Britton, Burgess, Martin, McLeod, & Rosen, 1975; Moffett, 1968). Transcending this research,

WHAT WE KNOW ABOUT THE EXPOSITORY GAP

PART A

- Children choose fiction over nonfiction. Langer found that while seventy-eight percent of third graders reported that they read stories often, only twenty-seven percent made such claims for nonfiction texts; very similar trends were found for sixth graders (1986).

- Children tell us that non-narrative texts are harder to process (Alverman and Boothby, 1982). Researchers have found that readers have more difficulty comprehending non-narrative writing than narrative writing (Chall and Jacobs, 1983; Kameenui, Carine and Freschi, 1982).

- Unlike the story grammar elements which children intuit from their extensive exposure to narrative, children in general have not had enough exposure to expository text to garner the prominent text structures (description, cause and effect, comparison...) underlying exposition. Their inability to recognize the particular organizational structure of an expository piece impacts negatively on their comprehension of that text (McGee, 1982; Taylor and Samuels, 1983).

- Children have greater difficulty writing nonfiction than they do fiction (Crowhurst, 1987); Langer, 1986; Britton et al., 1975). The *NAEP Writing Report Card* revealed that only thirty-seven percent of fourth graders in the sample could write an adequate business letter, and only twenty-four percent could write an adequate newspaper article (given a written prompt of notes about a haunted house) (Applebee et al., 1990).

PART B

- Young children are immersed in fiction to a much greater degree than they are nonfiction; parents choose story books over informational books during storytime (Sulzby and Teale, 1987).

- When children arrive at school and are placed in a basal reading program, they read a preponderance of fictional material with only a sprinkling of nonfiction pieces (Durkin, 1981; Flood and Lapp, 1984).

- Even as teachers transition away from basals toward literature-based reading programs, the narrative remains the focal point (Pappas, 1991). One survey of pre-K and kindergarten teachers revealed that of 236 books read to children, only seventeen percent were nonfiction (Putman, 1991).

FIGURE 6–1 *Why children are reluctant to read and write nonfiction*

PART C

- Sixty-five percent of the kindergartners in one study who had equal amounts of immersion in fiction and nonfiction said that they preferred nonfiction books during storytime (Pappas, 1991).

- When given the freedom to choose their own writing topics at home or at school, young children experiment with exposition (Bissex, 1980; Hipple, 1985; Sowers, 1985).

- When children receive instruction in expository text structures, comprehension increases (McGee, 1982; Taylor and Beach, 1984).

FIGURE 6–1, *continued*

though, is the belief that story is the "primary act of the mind" (Hardy, 1977) because

> stories have a role in education that goes far beyond their contribution to the acquisition of literacy. Constructing stories in the mind . . . is one of the fundamental means of making meaning; as such, it is an activity that pervades all aspects of learning . . . (Wells, 1986, p. 194)

Whatever its origins, the end result of this passion for story is what Daniels calls the "expository gap":

> Indeed, the writing curriculum experienced by many American students as they go through the grades is essentially: story, story, story, story, story, story, story, story, story, story, story, term paper. (1990, p. 107)

Research on the expository gap is fascinating and multifaceted. However, it challenges us to refrain from drawing preliminary conclusions until careful deliberation of all the data has occurred. You will notice that I have grouped the research findings into three parts in Figure 6–1. The findings in Part A of Figure 6–1 suggest that children choose not to read or to write nonfiction because exposition is too difficult for them to process. Some researchers speculate, for example, that the discrepancy between children's narrative and non-narrative writing is tied to limited levels of cognitive development. They believe that children need to write in the expressive mode before tackling exposition (Britton et al., 1975; Moffett, 1968). However, when the findings in Part A are placed in the context of what we do—or should I say fail to do—as parents and teachers (Part B of Figure 6–1), new questions emerge. Do children experience difficulty with nonfiction because they have little opportunity to listen to, read, and write it in our classrooms and their homes? What happens when children are given equal exposure to fictional and nonfictional texts? What happens to children's levels of comprehension when expository text structure is taught? As the preliminary findings in Part C of Figure 6–1 show, if we invite children into the genre of exposition, they respond with eagerness. Young children's fascination with the world around them appears to be as strong as their fascination with story. Figure 6–1 reminds us of the critical importance of the literacy context—what we do in our classrooms makes a difference. We can expect the same dismal findings reported in Part A of Figure 6–1 if we deprive children of opportunities to listen to, to read, and to write nonfiction and if we deprive them of instruction in exposition.

What Young Children Know About Nonfiction Writing

The discovery that young children are drawn to the genre of nonfiction (Part C in Figure 6–1) has led researchers to explore their intuitive understandings about exposition (Newkirk, 1987; Pappas, 1991). Intrigued as to whether children are sensitive to the differing linguistic patterns in fictional and nonfictional genres, Pappas conducted a case study with one kindergartner. After listening to a fictional book and an informational book, the child was asked to "read" (pretend read) each book to the researcher. (This procedure was repeated two more times with the same texts; the child produced a total of six reenactments.) Pappas found great sensitivity, on the child's part, to the distinctive features of these two genres at two major levels: patterns of global organization and patterns of language texture. In order to illustrate (and extrapolate to written text) Pappas's findings, let's take a look at two pieces, written by Danielle in grade 1. As you read "A Whale of a Tale" and "Stars" in Figure 6–2, think about the criteria you used to identify the fictional piece and the nonfictional piece.

. No doubt, you recognized some of the basic story grammar elements (see Chapter 5) in "A Whale of a Tale" and designated this piece as fiction. The main character appears to solve the problem of being sick by having a dream (although, there is a chance that the story has the more complex structure of a dream within a dream). "Stars," on the other hand, doesn't have a plot structure. It was created during a phonics lesson on r-controlled vowels. The teacher asked the children to create an "ar" pictionary, a booklet of "ar" words with corresponding pictures. (The teacher was prompting a labeling book of sorts.) Danielle, however, saw this as an opportunity to record everything she knew about one "ar" word, *star*.

As we examine the organizational and language patterns of "Stars," we see that Danielle intuitively knows a great deal about nonfiction. She knows that when writers share their knowledge about a subject like stars, they organize their information by: a) introducing the topic, b) describing the attributes of the topic, c) giving the characteristic events associated with the topic, and d) providing a summary (Pappas, 1991). This global organization is very different from the organization of her fictional text. Figure 6–3 demonstrates Danielle's attention to all of the obligatory elements of informational books (topic presentation, description of attributes, characteristic events, and final summary) as well as the optional element of category comparison.

A WHALE OF A TALE

Once there was a little girl named tracy
she was sick in bed she had a sorr
trout her eyes stinged she fell asleep
she had a dream all whales were
swimming they said wood you like to
come to the circus city there were seals
riding on bikes and they had fun but
when trasy woke up it was a dream
her trot dini't hurt hier eyes dini't sting
and she felt better
the End

STARS

Scars ar my faft tay ar sahl
I luc Tum Becus Tay liv up
in the scuy I luc yum Becus
tay do art and tay tay do art and
tay ar out at nut and Tey ar
spucle and scar mac desus
and Tey mac pess srs and
tey ar out ol nut log but Tey ar
not out dre the day becus the sun
ess up ol day log and Tay Tay
spucl ol nut log and yn The sun
sus up The scar go uya
The end.

(Translation: Stars are my favorite. They are special. I like them because they live up in the sky. I like them because they do art and they are out at night and they are special and stars make designs and they make pictures and they are out all night long but they are not out during the day because the sun is up all day long and that they sparkle all night long and the sun is up the stars go away.)

FIGURE 6–2   *Danielle's intuitive understanding of fiction and nonfiction text structures*

GLOBAL ELEMENTS OF INFORMATION BOOKS (Pappas, 1991)	EXAMPLES OF DANIELLE'S GLOBAL ELEMENTS
TOPIC PRESENTATION: the writer presents the topic	Stars are my favorite.
DESCRIPTION OF ATTRIBUTES: the writer describes/explains distinctive features associated with the topic.	...They live in the sky...they are out night long... they sparkle all night long.
CHARACTERISTIC EVENTS: the writer explains characteristic/prominent events associated with the topic.	...they do art ...stars make designs and they make pictures...
CATEGORY COMPARISON: the writer compares and/or contrasts attributes and characteristics of the topic with those of a different but associated topic. (Optional)	...but they are not out during the day because the sun is up all day long...
FINAL SUMMARY: the writer brings closure by summarizing some information about the topic.	...the sun is up the stars go away.
AFTERWARD: the writer provides additional information. (Optional)	

FIGURE 6–3   *Danielle's intuitive sensitivity to the language and organizational patterns of exposition*

In addition to global organization, Danielle demonstrates sensitivity to the three patterns of texture that are particular to informational texts: choice of pronouns, verb tense, and degree of description (Pappas, 1991). The first pattern of texture evident in Danielle's piece is her appropriate choice of pronouns. Notice that Danielle begins her piece, "Stars are my favorite." She does not begin this piece, "The stars . . . ," because she is referring to stars in a general sense. She, then, consistently refers to stars as "they" throughout the piece—stars as a class. She knows not to use pronouns which typically are reserved for reference to characters in stories (she, we, you . . .). A second pattern of texture that Danielle uses to distinguish her informational text from a narrative text is verb tense. Throughout her piece, the present tense prevails. Danielle uses present tense verbs, such as *are, make, sparkle*. Past tense, on the other hand, dominates her "Whale of a Tale" story (was, had, said, woke . . .). The final pattern of texture concerns the degree of description found in informational texts. While Danielle's narrative piece contains some description (whales swimming), it does so to a significantly lesser degree than her nonfiction piece. An analysis of Danielle's "Stars" indicates that primary attention has been given to description of the stars in terms of attributes, characteristics, and comparison.

The impressive array of knowledge that Danielle brings to the creation of nonfiction text and that Pappas's kindergartner brings to the reenactment of informational books help to refute the notion of cognitive limitations. If limitations exist, they, in all likelihood, reside with us:

> The problem is simply that schools and teachers have not capitalized upon students' manifest interest in the many nonstory forms of writing. We do not work explicitly and intentionally to invite kids into persuasion, exposition, and description. We have failed to show children the natural bridges from personal narratives to the more public modes of writing. (Daniels, 1990, p. 108)

Assessing the Nonfiction Writing of Young Writers

The most significant investigation of what young children do when they approach nonfiction writing was undertaken by Newkirk (1987). Intent upon using authentic writing rather than teacher-prompted pieces, Newkirk collected expository pieces from two classes of first, second, and third graders at the end of the school year. Newkirk, to his credit, describes the classroom contexts. The children in these classrooms wrote regularly, conferred with their teachers about their writing, and shared their writing with peers. They were not given any specific instruction in expository writing. Newkirk found ample evidence of exposition across the three grade levels, further disputing Britton's (1970, 1975) and Moffett's (1968) claims that children cannot handle modes of writing other than expressive. Newkirk found a general progression of eight non-narrative structures in their writing. As you read Newkirk's progression (Figure 6–4), decide which category describes Danielle's piece on stars (Figure 6–2).

When examining "Stars," you probably eliminated the extreme categories of Newkirk's continuum. Danielle's piece is more sophisticated than the *label* and *basic list* structures. Since she does not "chunk" related information, her piece does not fit the structures at the highest end of the continuum (*Attribute Series—Hierarchical* and up). Of the remaining categories, "Stars" seems to fit the *Reason List* category. Danielle is making a case for why she likes stars. Most of her statements tie to her assertion that she likes stars. Note that she does include a couplet: "they are not out during the day because the sun is up all day long." This couplet may signal her readiness to transition to a higher organizational structure.

Interestingly, none of Newkirk's first graders wrote a reason list (1987). Forty-one percent of the first graders labeled pictures; twenty-one percent wrote attribute lists; eighteen percent wrote couplets; fifteen percent wrote unordered paragraphs. Looking across the data, Newkirk found evidence for "general developmental progression" (1987, p. 126). While a high percentage of first graders labeled, none of the third graders labeled. First and second graders constructed a high percentage

---

How Young Children Grow as Nonfiction Writers

LABEL:
Writer draws a picture and labels it.

LIST:
Basic List: Writer creates a list of words, an inventory of what they know.

Attribute Series: Writer creates an unordered list of statements about a topic which may contain affective and informational statements.

Reason List: Writer lists reasons to support an idea, opinion, or attitude.

Couplet: Writer connects two statements together, e.g., a general statement followed by a specific statement; a statement followed by an example; a question by an answer...

ATTRIBUTE SERIES—HIERARCHICAL:
Writer includes some categories of information but statements within categories are fairly random.

PARAGRAPHS:
Unordered: Writer links three or more sentences to the topic of the paragraph; the paragraphs, however, are randomly ordered.

Ordered: Paragraphs are arranged logically and cannot be reordered without disruption of meaning.

FIGURE 6–4   *Newkirk's (1987) general progression of expository writing in grades 1–3*

of attribute lists, while only a small percentage of third graders did so. Couplets were evident across the grade levels with more prominence at the lower grades. Basic paragraphs also crossed the grades with higher percentages of third graders writing them. Only third graders wrote ordered paragraphs. Newkirk stipulates, though, with regard to the categories in his progression that "no claim is made that students must progress through them in this order or that every instance of an earlier type is 'developmentally below' instances of the later types" (1987, p. 126). Newkirk's work gives us a valuable framework for assessing young children's expository writing.

KOALA NEWS

Info About the Koala

Koalas have very sharp claws which are perfect for climbing trees. Most koalas have gray fur, but some have brown. Koalas only grow to be twenty four inches long. Both the male and the female have different weights. The male can weigh up to twenty-six pounds, and the female weighs up to seventeen pounds. The koalas are smaller in the northern part of Australia.

Habitat

Koalas live in the Southern part of Australia and coastal regions of Queensland. They are solitary tree-dwellers, so they live in trees. The trees that they live in are called eucalyptus trees. The eucalyptus trees have leaves. Koalas live in eucalyptus trees which is very convenient because they eat the leaves.

Why They are Endangered

Koalas are an endangered species. They don't really have any enemies except fires. Fires are why koalas are endangered. Their home catches on fire and burns down. Even though they are now protected, their habitat can still get burnt down by seasonal brush fires. One other thing that kills koalas, is cutting down eucalyptus trees. Koalas need eucalyptus trees so they have the leaves to eat. It is very important that we do not set fires or cut down eucalyptus trees so we can keep koalas alive.

FIGURE 6–5 *Vanessa's and Lauren's versatility with exposition*

Assessing the Nonfiction Writing of Older Writers

The articles in Vanessa's and Lauren's (grade 4) *Koala News* illustrate Newkirk's final developmental category of ordered paragraphs (see Figure 6–5). The girls are able not only to structure basic paragraphs, but also to arrange these paragraphs in a logical order. As you read the three paragraphs, decide which paragraph engages you the most, and why.

My hunch is that you chose "Why They are Endangered." Langer's work on the development of exposition in older children's writing extends Newkirk's work and helps to illuminate the appeal of this article. Langer asked third, sixth, and ninth graders to write a report on a topic about which they knew a lot, and then analyzed their writing samples (1992). Langer concluded that young writers "have a systematic and well-developed knowledge of exposition" (1992, p. 34). Analysis of the children's work resulted in the following continuum of predictable, rule-governed structures. Each expository structure is briefly explained in Figure 6–6. (You will note some overlap with Newkirk's scheme.)

Using Langer's continuum, it is easier to understand our preference for Vanessa's and Lauren's article, "Why They are Endangered," over, for example, "Info About the Koala." Their latter piece falls into Langer's category of *simple description*. It opens with a fact rather than with a topic sentence, and then strings together one descriptive statement after another. One instance of elaboration through description is evident (differing weights of male and female). "Why They are Endangered," on the other hand, opens with a problem and ends with a solution, and it uses description to bolster the expository structure. In this piece, the girls have clustered related information and have included the following rhetorical devices: a causal relationship ("Fires are why koalas are endangered."); an explanation ("They don't really have any enemies except fire."); an adversative statement which compares alternatives ("Even though they are now protected . . ."); and an evaluative statement which reveals their opinion ("It is very important that we do not set fires . . ."). This piece is linguistically complex enough to be classified as a *topic with elaboration* on Langer's continuum.

Do Older Writers Move Through a Developmental Sequence in Exposition?

Intriguing, then, is the challenge that Vanessa's and Lauren's Koala pieces (at two different levels of expository sophistication) presents to Langer's notion of a "developmental trajectory" (1992, p. 36). Langer postulates the existence of a developmental continuum that suggests an ever-increasing refinement of expository knowledge as children move through the grades. She found, for example, that while twenty-nine percent of the third graders wrote simple descriptions, only eight percent of the sixth graders and none of the ninth graders wrote such pieces. Ninth graders (thirty percent) were the only cohort to write pieces at the most

---

HOW OLDER CHILDREN GROW AS NONFICTION WRITERS

SIMPLE DESCRIPTION:
> Writers tell you everything they know about a topic in chain fashion with little attention to an organizing principle or generalization. Their pieces can begin with an introduction to their topic or with a fact. These pieces tend to be brief.

TOPIC WITH DESCRIPTION:
> Writers open with a topic sentence that holds the piece together. They continue to sequence their information, and at times elaborate. However the elaboration is accomplished through further description. Little discussion of the topic is evident.

TOPIC WITH DESCRIPTION AND COMMENTARY:
> Description still drives these writers' experimentation with exposition, however their texts also evidence beginning elaboration and commentary. Writers in this category may begin to incorporate some of the following language features: causal relationships signaled by word markers such as *so* and *because*; evidence to support an argument; evaluative statements which gives the writers' opinions or commentary. Writers also begin to cluster their information into subtopics.

TOPIC WITH ELABORATION:
> Writers produce linguistically more complex and comprehensive exposition. Topics are introduced and elaborated upon using the above-mentioned language features: causal relationships, response relationships (question/answer; problem/solution), evidence of support, evaluation, and so forth. These writers are able to weave these features through their descriptions, rendering a more fully developed piece of prose.

POINT OF VIEW WITH DEFENSE:
> Writers at this advanced point on the continuum begin not with a topic but rather with a thesis about a topic. The writer's point of view drives the piece. Successful negotiation of the thesis demands a high level of elaboration.

FIGURE 6–6 *Langer's (1992) continuum of expository types*

advanced level (*point of view with defense*). However, Langer found that children across the grade levels experimented with the remaining expository structures. The most prominent structures at each grade level were as follows: forty-three percent of the third graders wrote *topics with description*; thirty-nine percent of the sixth graders wrote *topics with description and commentary*; thirty-nine percent of the ninth graders wrote *topics with elaboration*. While there is no implication on Langer's part that these points on the continuum represent distinct stages through which expository writers must move, she implies that younger writers are unable to negotiate the more rhetorically complex structure such as point of view.

But, then, how do we account for the fact that Vanessa and Lauren crafted two expository pieces on koalas at the same point in time but at two different levels of difficulty (*simple description* and *topic with elaboration*)? According to Vanessa, the girls wrote each article together. "We just put our ideas together and wrote each sentence together." In double-checking to see if one girl wrote the final draft of one piece, and the other girl wrote another final draft, Vanessa reiterated that they created each piece collaboratively. Trusting her perceptions, it is interesting to speculate on the range of writing here. My guess is that the range has more to do with their topic choice than with their stage of expository development. A piece on the habitat of koalas lends itself to the lower end of Langer's trajectory; most writers would tend to write a descriptive piece about any species's habitat. However, the topic of endangerment, by its very nature, pulls the writer to the more advanced end of the continuum—*topic with elaboration* or *point of view*. Vanessa and her partner intuitively understood this and responded accordingly.

One wonders what Langer's findings would have revealed if her directions to the children were: "Think about something that is happening in the world about which you are concerned. Write a letter to the President. Let him know your thoughts and what you think should be done about this issue." My guess is that many of Langer's third graders would have expressed their point of view and defended it quite adequately. A case in point is found in Shane's writing folder. In October of 1991, President Bush, in one of his radio addresses, solicited the advice of American citizens on challenges facing the nation. The local newspaper in Shane's town contacted the schools and offered to publish any letters that children might write. Shane wrote the following letter in Figure 6–7.

Shane's opening sentences attempt to juggle two theses: a) the drug problem in this country, and b) a local senator's proposal to increase the number of school days from 180 to 220 to bring American education in line with that of the Japanese. Shane's lead sentence suggests that he felt compelled to talk to the President about a "big" societal problem (drugs).

That said, he moves quickly to his real agenda—length of the school year. Shane shares his point of view about extending the school week and makes the case that students will clock more hours but will not get short-changed on summer vacation. Shane's letter of persuasion fits Langer's *point of view with defense* category at a very rudimentary level. While the degree to which third graders can propose and sustain a thesis in a piece of writing will differ from older writers, Langer's work suggests

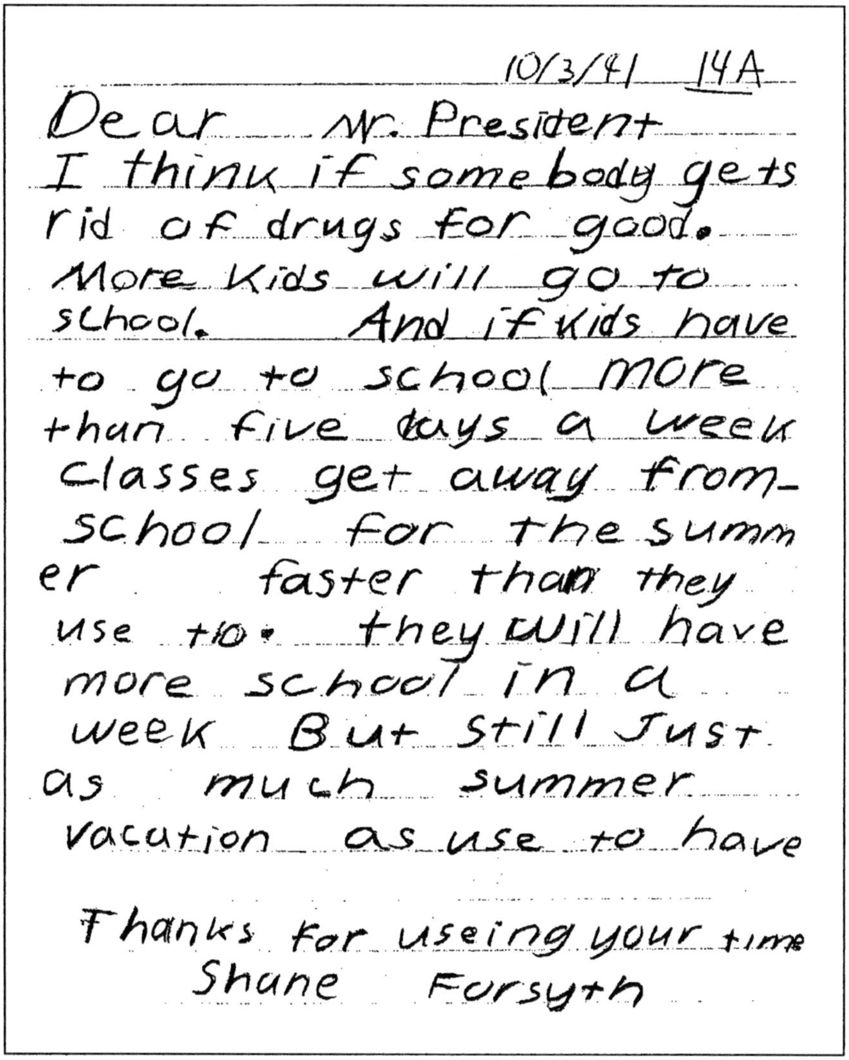

> 10/3/91 14A
>
> Dear Mr. President
> I think if somebody gets
> rid of drugs for good.
> More Kids will go to
> school. And if kids have
> to go to school more
> than five days a week
> classes get away from
> school for the summ
> er faster than they
> use to. they will have
> more school in a
> week But still Just
> as much summer
> vacation as use to have
>
> Thanks for useing your time
> Shane Forsyth

FIGURE 6–7 *Shane's letter of persuasion*

that young writers will gain more control of exposition over time. While we should be careful not to expect children's exposition to advance along Langer's continuum in a lockstep fashion, we should heed Langer's observation that each category of expository writing from *simple description* to *point of view with defense* has its own descriptive value. Like Newkirk's work, Langer's continuum provides us with a lens through which we can look at children's writing.

Shane on Shane: Self-Assessment of Report Writing

As reported in Chapter 3, with the exception of two business letters, Shane's third-grade writing folder evidences the "expository gap" about which Daniels talks (1990). In light of the earlier review of the literature which suggested that children don't write exposition because they don't read or hear non-narrative literature, it is interesting to note that Shane chose and enjoyed nonfiction literature. His third-grade reading record lists books such as *Babe Ruth, Chief Joseph,* and *The Magic School Bus: Inside the Human Body.* His ability to retell and to respond to this nonfiction literature during conversations about his reading record was impressive. In addition, nonfiction books were read on a regular basis to the class. Shane may have chosen not to write expository pieces during writing workshop because he wrote learning log entries about science and social studies topics in his Investigation Notebook a few times a week.

In asking about report writing that he did in fourth and fifth grade, Shane proudly showed me his one "big" fourth grade report on "New Zealand," and one "hard" report on "Maintaining Clean Water," written in grade 5 (in addition to numerous fictional book reports in both grades). It was clear from the smile on his face that these reports held an aura of importance for Shane. Thus, I was surprised at his responses to the survey questions in Figure 6–8.

I expected Shane's response to question 2 to be "the report." I was struck by the fact that while Shane had thrown away his fictional stories from grade 4, he had saved his reports. He had saved his fifth grade reports too. Recall, also, the importance of "the report" in his fictional story, "The Missing Report" in Chapter 5. As we talked about his responses to questions 1, 2, and 10 (Figure 6–8), it became clear why fictional writing ranked first:

CAROL: Explain the difference between a report and a story.

SHANE: A report like usually has an outline. Like usually before you have a report, the teacher will say, "This is paragraph 1, I want this;

paragraph 2, I want this." But you can make a story basically out of your own mind. You don't really have to follow any plan.

CAROL: Suppose your English teacher this year doesn't give you an outline. What will you do then?

SHANE: That would kinda make me happy because I could be able to put what I want in each paragraph so it could be like my dream report. I just wouldn't have to do whatever they wanted.

CAROL: In question 10, you said that you think teachers prefer reports because they choose the topics. Tell me more.

SHANE: They give us reports about what we are studying in class. In a story, they don't have power over what we choose.

It appears that it is not so much the genre that is at issue here as it is the principle of ownership. Shane wants to investigate nonfiction topics that matter to him, not topics exclusively assigned by a teacher. Even within the teacher-assigned country report (Figure 6–9), we see evidence of Shane's search for personal meaning, as well as audience awareness:

CAROL: Why did you pick New Zealand?

SHANE: Well, I first picked Ireland . . . My mother is Irish . . . We have all this Irish stuff. Then I came back and told my mother and father about how many people were doing Ireland, and I didn't want to do the same old thing. So, I think it was my father who gave me the idea of New Zealand. So, I went to the library and I got books on three different countries and I started studying and I thought New Zealand was pretty interesting, and my parents were right again.

CAROL: Did everyone get to pick his or her own country?

SHANE: Yeah, but say if I did Ireland and I was the last person to do my report, do you think everybody is going to be right into what I'm saying after they already heard the same thing from four people? So I kinda do something that I know nobody else will do. At first I thought about doing Laos, but I went to the library and found nothing.

CAROL: Why were you going to pick Laos?

SHANE: Because I figured it was right near Vietnam. My father was in the Vietnam War. I've seen a lot of movies about Vietnam and Laos and Cambodia. And I've read a lot of books about the war.

Here was a lost moment: Shane was on the verge of embarking on a research project that would have mattered to him. But he couldn't find the

NAME_ Shane Forsyth _   DATE_ 10/3 _

REPORT WRITING: What are your thoughts?

1. Do you think there is a difference between a story and a report? _ Yes _
Explain your answer.
A report ~~usually~~ usually has
an outline. A story is made from your
mind.

2. If you were free to choose to write a story, or to write a report on a topic that interests
you, which would you choose? _ A story _
Why?_ A story is not more interesting than
hard facts.

3. Explain the steps you follow when you write a report.
1. 1st Draft
2. Spell check.
3. Full check.
4. Final Copy.

4. What should an author do to create a good opening for a report?
They should have an interesting sentence.

5. How should an author do to close a report?
They should say something like, "I know
you are a genius" with watever the ~~story~~ was about.
                                                    Report

6. Suppose you had to write a report on sharks. How would you organize the
information you have learned about sharks in your report?
I would write an outline.

FIGURE 6–8   *Shane's responses to writing report survey*

7. When you write a report, do think about your readers? _Yes._
Explain your answer. _I think a good report that nobody can understand is a bad report._

8. How did you learn how to write a report?
I was taught in 4th Grade.

9. Pretend you have to write two reports on recycling. One report will go to the school newspaper for publication. The other report will be read by third graders. Would you give the same report to both the newspaper and the third graders? _No._
Why or why not? _They need to be more edvacated to understand the Big one._

10. What do you think teachers prefer to read - stories or reports? Why?
Reports. Teachers usually usually get to pick the topic.

FIGURE 6–8, *continued*

book, and rather than presenting his dilemma to the class or teacher for suggestions, he let it go. Helping children find their personal core of meaning significantly advances the cause of exposition (Calkins, 1994).

In the fourth century BC, Aristotle posited that the study of rhetoric was the study of three intersecting factors: the writer, the subject, and the audience. To bring readers (or listeners) into a subject, writers must establish their credibility as experts on the subject as well as attend to the disposition of their audiences. Writers need to ask: What do my readers know about the subject? What do they expect to learn? What is their attitude toward the subject (and toward me)? As the previous conversation illustrates, Shane demonstrates a burgeoning awareness of audience. His insight about the four Ireland reports is acute. While he has yet to understand that it is not the topic, per se, that holds an audience, but rather how the author breathes life into that topic, Shane does understand that the writer must keep his reader in mind as the text is created. The introductory leads of both his fourth grade report ("New Zealand"), presented in Figure 6–9, and his fifth grade "Maintaining Clean Water" report, shown in Figure 6–10 illustrate this point.

While Shane's lead in the New Zealand piece ("Hi! I chose New Zealand. As I go through each paragraph you should find New Zealand more and more interesting.") breaks the rules of exposition, it bubbles with voice and energy, and delights the reader. In time, Shane's voice will emerge in the content of his message rather than in a cheery foreword. He will, by virtue of how he shapes his actual text, engage our interest. His lead sentence in his fifth-grade piece (Figure 6–10) ("I will be explaining the hydrologic cycle.") moves closer toward that goal. This lead sentence informs the reader about the direction that the piece will take without any further extraneous prompts. Although, a comment Shane made while talking about item 4 on the survey (Figure 6–8) suggests his thinking

---

Hi! I chose New Zealand. As I go through each paragraph you should find New Zealand more and more interesting. New Zealand consists of two major islands, North Island and South Island. They are located midway between the equator and the South Pole, approximately 7,000 miles from the United States.

1)   THE GOVERNMENT

The Government of New Zealand Is based on a unicameral legislature, that is elected every three years. This is different from the United States which has a bicameral legislature, the House and the Senate. Unicameral Government means there is only one branch to legislate. Also unlike the United States, New Zealand has a Parliament instead of Congress like England.

2)   CLOTHING

The everyday clothing in New Zealand is the same as the United States. Usually you would probably think about clothes from other countries and always think they're different. It is true that the natives of New Zealand known as Maori's wear regular clothes except for ceremonies, then they wear fringed striped skirts like their ancestors wore. Men paint their faces in spiral patterns that were once permanently tattooed into their skin. The women sometimes have a "moko" (a rose tattoo that is placed on their chins).

FIGURE 6–9   *Excerpt from Shane's New Zealand report (Grade 4)*

MAINTAINING CLEAN WATER

I will be explaining the hydrologic cycle. The hydrologic cycle is the continuous movement of water between the earth and the atmosphere. Because of heating by the sun, water evaporates from oceans, lakes, streams, rivers, and land surfaces. The evaporation in the form of vapor enters the atmosphere, where it builds up until precipitated in the form of rain or snow. When the rain or snow strikes the earth, one part of the water is called run off, which flows directly into streams and rivers which in turn flow to lakes or oceans to begin the cycle all over again. The water that doesn't run off is infiltrated into the soil. Water that isn't sucked up by plant roots, continues downward to a saturation point which is called the water table. Here we get drinking water. Anything that would disrupt this cycle disrupts our way of life.

Question 1:   What are causes of polluted water?

Answer: Oil spills, over spraying of pesticides, improper landfill operations, industrial waste discharge into rivers, and untreated sewage are a few of the causes.

Question 2:   What are some ways to keep the water clean?

Answer: We must stop dumping wastes directly into the rivers and sea, we must control watercraft which dispose oily and human wastes into the oceans. It kills animals that take it into their body. On land we must recycle instead of throwing can's, bottles, and toxic wastes in the garbage to keep our drinking water clean.

Question 3:   Who is responsible for protecting water?

Answer: Although the Environmental Protection Agency is responding to this problem, it is you and my responsibility to keep our water as clean as possible. Don't litter, turn the faucet off while you are brushing your teeth and separate the recycleables in your garbage. Every little bit helps.

We must not cause pollution by over spraying plants and crops or discharge any waste at all into rivers, lakes, oceans and streams. People may think that littering can't harm the ocean but it can. Watercraft which dispose oily and human waste not only pollute the water, it kills animals which take these wastes into into their body. But remember, no matter what, maintaining clean water is everyones responsibility. It becomes a matter of survival. We must defend our precious water from ourselves. We must stop destroying the world by destroying it's water supply.

FIGURE 6–10 *Shane's clean water report (Grade 5)*

about leads is still in transition: "You have to have an interesting sentence to keep the reader into the story. Like if someone just began telling the facts in the first paragraph that would be dumb. I'd rather have it say, 'This report is about Denmark. As you read it, you will find it more and more interesting' or something like that."

Awareness of audience occurs within the text as well. In the clothing section of his New Zealand report, he talks directly to the reader ("Usually you would probably think . . ."). In the water report, his closing paragraph evidences an awareness of audience.

Langer found that only twenty-one percent of the third graders in her study expressed concern for audience when they wrote reports; forty-five percent of the sixth graders did so (1986). Furthermore, while thirty-three percent of the third graders thought about "meeting the interests" of the readers while writing reports, surprisingly only ten percent of the sixth graders considered this important. Langer makes the point, though, that while children may not be able to verbalize concern for the reader, they bring a level of tacit knowledge about audience to their report writing. When Langer asked children if they would write their reports differently for different audiences, sixty-seven percent of the third graders and eighty percent of the sixth graders responded affirmatively. Shane, not surprisingly, demonstrates this fundamental level of audience awareness. In discussing his response to question 9 on the survey (Figure 6–8), he commented, "See third graders would need to be more educated to understand a big report than a sixth or seventh grader would have to be . . . what they're learning is a snap to us . . . third graders need smaller words that have the same meaning . . . easier punctuation . . . but I wouldn't take out any of the main ideas because it has to make sense." Bravo, Shane!

Another major finding of Langer's study concerned the degree to which the children's stories and reports change with age. While the length of the third and sixth graders' stories was longer than that of their reports, the syntax and the organization of their reports were significantly more complex, particularly between ages 8 and 11. Langer concludes, "Structurally, the children's stories did not change as dramatically as did their reports, which became considerably longer, more content-laden, better elaborated, and more highly structured across the years" (1986, pp. 42–43). Langer speculates that the discrepancy between story and report writing is tied to children's exposure to the two modes of writing. Children often come to school knowing how to craft a story; this may not be the case with exposition. Langer hypothesizes that children receive more direct instruction in exposition which accounts for more pronounced change over time in expository writing.

Curious as to any instruction in exposition Shane might recall, I asked him to expand on question 8 (Figure 6–8).

SHANE: In fourth grade I started getting heavy reports and stuff. At the beginning of the year, my teacher told us what she expected in a report, what to put in paragraph 1 and 2 and the whole thing really. Same in fifth grade. And my parents gave me some hints. They helped me a lot.

CAROL: Do you remember looking at any books to see how the authors put reports together on countries?

SHANE: No.

CAROL: Do you recall learning about different ways that information can be reported in a paragraph such as cause and effect or compare/contrast?

SHANE: No.

His response to this last question is interesting since content area writing is a major focus in Shane's school. The mismatch between Shane's perception and the classroom reality probably is due to the way I phrased my question. I didn't use the terminology (e.g. "power outlining," "webbing") with which he is familiar. This mismatch alerts us once again to the critical importance of corroboration, and not relying on one data source exclusively.

I then ask Shane about the organizational scheme of each report:

CAROL: Tell me how you decide to organize your report like this: Government Clothing . . .

SHANE: Because that's what we had to do. The teacher told us.

CAROL: Were you required to use books in addition to the encyclopedia? Did she tell you how many books to use?

SHANE: Nope, on this she kinda left us on our own . . . That was better than saying "I don't want you going into the encyclopedia." Like, I like being able to do my own thing. I like being able to decide to have Economy and Industry as my first two paragraphs instead of being told one way. . . .

CAROL: Your fifth-grade piece, "Clean Water" report, has a different structure. Whose idea was it to include the question and answer section, for example?

SHANE: The teacher's. We had to do a big paragraph about the topic, three questions and the answers, and a final paragraph explaining what we can do about the problem.

Thus, while we cannot speculate about how Shane may have approached these reports if given the liberty to do so, nor about any expository spurt between grades 4 and 5, we can get a glimpse at Shane's underlying knowledge about exposition by assessing his thoughts on how he would organize a hypothetical report on sharks. In asking for specifics on question 6 (Figure 6–8), the following dialogue ensued:

CAROL: If you were going to write this shark report, what are some of the outline categories that you might include? What might you cover?

SHANE: I might cover the characteristics of sharks and how much they eat, what they depend on. I'd like do the environment that they need to live in. And I'd explain what part of the Earth they live in. And if there's been any stories. Say if a couple of days ago, I heard "Off the coast of California, a man was killed after he tipped over in his rowboat by a shark, a hungry shark." I might include this saying, "Now this might be what could happen if you ever came face-to-face with a shark."

CAROL: Why might you include this shark sighting?

SHANE: So it wouldn't be so boring—fact, fact, fact—you know.

Shane not only includes organizing concepts such as species characteristics and habitat but also incorporates the element of drama to capture his readers' attention. No doubt, some of his confidence with the organizational framework rests on the teacher-guided directions that Shane has internalized, along with his reading of nonfiction texts. There is no question that Shane has enough fundamental knowledge to take charge of his own exposition.

Assessing Shane's Expository Writing Over Time

CAROL: Now if you compare the way you set up these two reports—New Zealand and Clean Water—which do think is more interesting for the reader?

SHANE: I'd say "Clean Water" because of how I did the three questions. Like, while they're reading this first paragraph, they might say, "What are the causes of polluted water?" Then they could find out what they wondered if I have answered that question.

Shane recognizes the sophistication of one of Langer's more advanced text structures—topic with elaboration—that was required for his fifth-grade report. Even though the organizational frameworks of his reports (Figures 6–9 and 6–10) were teacher-directed, we can, to a degree, use Langer's categories to explore how Shane organizes information, within these frameworks, across the two grade levels (1986, 1992).

We can classify all of Shane's New Zealand sections as either *simple description* or *topic with description*. The section "Education," for example, falls into the *simple description* category because it presents the reader with a string of facts about this aspect of New Zealand life. Little effort is made to cluster related facts (i.e. the last sentence should follow the first with explanation). No elaboration of any of the information is offered, and no commentary is shared. Most of Shane's sections in this report would be classified as *simple description*. His section on "Clothing," however, moves up one linguistic notch to *topic with description*. In fact his opening sentence suggests an even higher rhetorical structure of comparison, but Shane doesn't develop this thesis. It seems that his interest in the Maori's ceremonial dress overtakes the piece. Evidence of commentary ("Usually you would probably think . . .") about possible stereotypical thinking, and elaboration through description (about Maori's ceremonial garb) suggest Shane's familiarity with more complex linguistic devices. Because much of this New Zealand piece hovers at the lower end of Langer's expository continuum, we need to call to mind our earlier discussions about developmental trajectories, and resist the urge to pigeonhole Shane (1992). In all likelihood, the nature of the assignment (something to the effect: "Tell what you learned about Country X. Be sure to cover these categories.") shaped Shane's response to this assignment and legitimized his descriptive thrust.

Assessing Shane's success in completing the teacher's directions to write "a big paragraph about the topic, three questions and the answers, and a final paragraph explaining what we can do about the problem," in his fifth-grade piece (Figure 6–10) is challenging. We are struck by the sophistication of his opening paragraph which adopts a fairly tight cause and effect structure, and which would be classified in Langer's scheme as a *topic with elaboration*. However, as we compare this opening with the remainder of the report, we note a discrepancy in conceptual and syntactic complexity. In talking to Shane about his opening paragraph, he confessed, "We weren't really supposed to, but I used the encyclopedia. I got it from there. I tried to make it not obvious, but I hardly used the book at all." In asking Shane to show me this section in his encyclopedia, his efforts at paraphrasing the encyclopedia immediately were evident.

His transition from the opening paragraph to the question and answer section is somewhat abrupt. There is much overlap between this section and his final plea (a potential *point of view with defense*) to protect the environment. We certainly hear a voice trying to be heard. However, given the structure of the assignment and his difficulty in weaving his bundle of information into his argument, and given his tendency to adopt popular clichés about saving the environment, he has yet to consolidate his argument.

Shane on Shane: Self-Assessment of Revision Efforts

Item 4 of the report writing survey (Figure 6–8) and the following snippet of conversation concerning Shane's ideas about revision of "Clean Water" corroborates our earlier general findings with regard to revision (Chapter 5).

SHANE: When a report is done, all you have to do is check everything and do a final copy.

CAROL: What are you checking for?

SHANE: I'd check my first draft. It doesn't have to be the most perfect thing. Then I do a spellcheck and then I give it to my parents and they do a full check of punctuation and how I use my words. See I print out my correctly spelled page, and I give it to my parents and they take a pen and they do the corrections. So that's like another first draft, and I type everything over.

CAROL: What about the actual information in the report? Do you worry about that?

SHANE: Umm, like what everybody gets from it? Sometimes, not a lot because, usually, it's covered really good.

Shane has yet to adopt the stance of critical reader when he writes nonfiction. He needs to learn to reread his text to decide whether what he has written fulfills his original intentions and goals. He then needs to resolve any dissonance noted by revising his text (Fitzgerald, 1989). Shane and other burgeoning writers need to be coached through this process of critical reading and of critical writing. They need to watch us move through the process of planning, drafting, comparing goals to actual text, reworking discrepant information, and so on. They need to watch us engage in ongoing "think alouds" in which we speculate about the import of our message or about other ways of organizing a particular text. Without direct teaching in the art of revision, writers will do what Shane did—paraphrase the encyclopedia and think they are done.

Concluding Comments and a Word About Teacher Self-Assessment

Calkins makes the case that nonfiction writing "begins with living immersed in one topic, letting everything in life remind you of it. It's about probing the topic, asking questions of it and exploring its mysteries. It's about letting exploration become a journey to new places" (1994, p. 445). Our job is to serve as the field guide.

As with the assessment of children's stories, we need to induct writers into the world of nonfiction *before* we begin the process of assessing children's expository writing. If we have not created a healthy, hearty context for the learning of exposition, we hardly are in a position to critique young writers' work with any semblance of credibility. Assessment of children's exposition (and story) begins with critical self-reflection as to the quality of the learning episodes we create for young writers.

- Have we allowed children to choose their areas of explorations within and beyond our thematic units of study?
- Have we helped writers find topics in which they have an abiding interest? Have we shared our wonderment with the world around us? Have we created a classroom environment (terrariums, butterfly cages, historical artifacts) that fosters observation and inquiry?
- Have we showed learners how to "live" like a nonfiction writer? Have we demonstrated how many nonfiction writers (ourselves included) record observations, notes, and information in their notebooks, and pore over these entries in order to find that special angle that will breathe life into their topic?
- Have we shared rich examples from nonfiction texts and asked students to examine the array of effective text structures that real authors use?
- Have we demonstrated the processes of planning, drafting, revising, and so forth with expository text?

Assessing Spelling

> Woodside July 21 1885
>
> Slept splendidly — evidently I was innoculated
> with isomnie bactilli when a baby — arose early
> went out to flirt with the flowers, & I wonder
> if there are not microscopic orchids growing on
> the motes of the air — Saw big field of squashes
> throwing out their leafy tenticles to the wind
> preparing to catch the little fleeting atom for
> assimulation into its progeny the squash gourd
> — a spider weaves its net to catch an
> organized whole, how like this is the vegitable
> living plant, the leaves and stalk catch the
> primal free atom, all are then arranged in an
> organized whole; Heard a call from the house
> that sounded like the shreick of a lost angel.
> it was a female voice three sizes too small
> for the distance and was a call for breakfast

FIGURE 7–1   *Excerpt from Thomas Edison's diary*

The above diary entries were penned by Thomas Edison, in 1885, at the
age of thirty-eight. The splendid imagery, keen insights, and playful

135

language more than delight the reader. The artistry of Edison's penmanship enhances the essence of his message and diminishes the impact of his spelling errors, his missing punctuation, and his grammatical inconsistencies.

By age ten, Edison had read tomes such as Gibbons's *Decline and Fall of the Roman Empire* and had tested every experiment in Parker's *School of Natural Philosophy* (Josephson, 1959). Although an avid reader, Edison reportedly was challenged by the conventions of written language (Josephson, 1959). An analysis of his spelling reveals the profile of a writer who prioritized meaning over mechanics during the draft stage of writing. Edison, like writers of any age, dealt with the complexity of the English language by hypothesizing about the spelling of troublesome words. Sometimes, his hypotheses resulted in conventional spellings; other times approximations resulted. Like all spellers, Edison had at his disposal three major spelling strategies upon which to draw.

Spelling Strategies

Sound (Phonemic) Strategy

Spellers employing this strategy do what comes naturally when dealing with a word that is not automatically retrieved—they sound it out. This sound strategy can be divided into two substrategies:

a) *the pure sound strategy:* A speller, using the pure sound strategy, stretches out the word, phoneme by phoneme, and writes the corresponding letters. To spell the word *laugh*, the writer records only the sounds heard—*laf*. The pure sound strategy is highly characteristic of emergent spellers (pre-K through grades 1 or 2).

b) *the sound strategy plus spelling generalizations:* More characteristic of older spellers is the sound strategy plus spelling generalizations. It is here that many of Edison's spelling approximations fall. *Shreick* is a wonderful example of Edison's attempt to rely on both the sound system and some spelling rules. His thought processes in attempting this word probably went something like this:

shr: "I'll write the sounds I hear."

ei: "Long e—to make long e, I'll need two vowels together (or silent e at the end which he rejects). Could be *ea*, *ee*, . . . *ei* looks right."

ck: "Many words that end with the sound of k are spelled with *ck* like pick, dock, check."

Unfortunately, *shriek* is not a phonemically regular word. Edison recognized this when he wrote "How is this spelled?" above his approximation. His question signaled his awareness of another critically important strategy: the visual strategy.

Visual Strategy

One of the key factors that separates good spellers from less able spellers is the ability to decide whether a word "looks right." Visualization—the ability to lock in the exact sequence of letters of a particular word and retrieve it when needed—is essential to good spelling. At some level, Edison knew that *shreick* didn't look right. Since he was writing for his own personal pleasure, he made no effort to attempt an alternate spelling or to check it in the dictionary. Throughout Edison's diary entries are a number of instances in which he spelled a word, checked its visual form, crossed the word out and either reattempted the word or settled for a synonym (see *vegitable* in Figure 7–1). Examples of his visual checking follow: *deamon* was crossed out and *demon* inserted; *horse* crossed out and *hoarse* substituted; and *disyllibic* crossed out and *dissyllabic* inserted. In addition, Edison's numerous correct spellings advance the case that he attended to the visual form of words: *patient, freight, conscience* . . .

Word Meaning (Morphemic) Strategy

Edison's final version of *dissyllabic* (Figure 7–2) is indicative of his understanding of the highly stable meaning-bearing units (morphemes) in the English language such as prefixes, suffixes, and root words. The prefix *dis* remains intact regardless of the first letter of the root word. Good

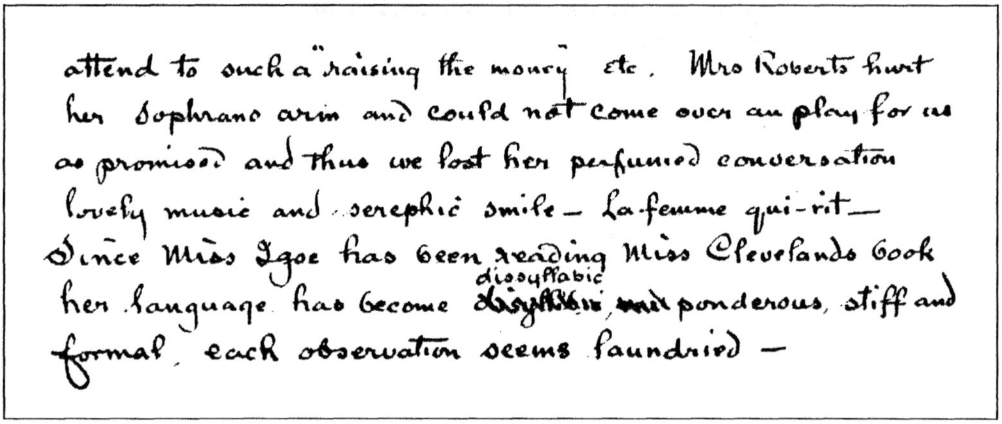
attend to such a "raising the money" etc. Mrs Roberts hurt
her Sophrano arm and could not come over an play for us
as promised and thus we lost her perfumed conversation
lovely music and serephic smile — La femme qui-rit —
Since Miss Igoe has been reading Miss Clevelands book
her language has become dissyllabic ~~disyllibic~~, ~~and~~ ponderous, stiff and
formal, each observation seems laundried —

FIGURE 7–2 *Excerpt from Thomas Edison's diary*

spellers evidence a facility with these morphemic units. They also show an awareness—tacit or otherwise—that words, related by meaning, retain a common spelling base. For example, good spellers know that if they are having trouble spelling the final syllable of the word *muscle*, they can rely on a variant form like *muscular* (Chomsky, 1970). With the exception of the variant forms of the prefix *in*, in words such as *incrusted* (p. 6), and *illimitable* (p. 14), Edison uses the morphemic strategy quite successfully (examples: *circumvent, disreputable, ponderous, navigation . . .*).

Was Edison the poor speller that many books have branded him (Gentry & Gillet, 1993)? Compare Edison's performance with that of the research findings about good spellers. Good spellers:

- often override the urge to use the phonemic strategy that characterized their emergent spelling in order to attend to the visual demands of words (Nolan & McCartin, 1984; Roskinski & Wheeler, 1972). By grade 5, good spellers rely on the visual form of words rather than on the phonemic demands (Marsh, Friedman, Welch, & Desberg, 1980).

- know when to rely on what strategy (phonemic, visual, and morphemic, or combination thereof). In interviews with good spellers (grades 3/4) about their performance on a spelling test, children reported that they broke words into parts or known words, tried alternate spellings, used spelling rules, and relied on visual imagery. Poor spellers, on the other hand, said they sounded out words letter by letter (Radebaugh, 1985).

- spell a large corpus of words automatically (Gentry & Gillet, 1993; Wilde, 1992).

- have what is termed "a spelling consciousness." Good spellers have an appreciation for the richness of language and care about spelling accuracy. They also sense when words look incorrect and act upon that hunch (Wilde, 1992; Valmont, 1972).

Edison's versatility with the major spelling strategies and his large corpus of correctly spelled words suggest that, indeed, he may fit the profile of a good speller. Since his diary entries constitute first draft writing, we are not in a position to judge his spelling competence with any degree of certainty. We would need to inspect entries which had been self-edited for the mechanics to make final judgments.

Portfolio Assessment of Spelling

Portfolio assessment of children's spelling knowledge necessitates the collection and analysis of the following spelling data:

a) *self-edits in final drafts:* With the message in final form, writers are free to concentrate on their spelling. Efforts to self-edit a word may include the retrieval of its visual form, a reattempt at encoding phonemes and/or morphemes, and/or consultation with human or text resources. Analysis of what spellers do when they rework initial spelling attempts gives us important information about strategy usage. In addition to strategy usage, analysis of self-edits offers data as to particular spelling patterns that the writer has internalized or has yet to internalize. For example, if I were to establish Edison's competence with the prefix *dis*, I would go through his drafts and list his successes with this prefix (*dissyllabic, disreputable, disappeared*). I then would log his errors and weigh his successes against his errors in order to decide his facility with this prefix.

b) *spelling across time—first drafts:* The simple fact is that no matter how full-blown our spelling program (traditional or otherwise), we cannot teach children to spell all the words they need in order to write. Wilde estimates that traditional spelling programs introduce from four to six thousand words, yet evidence exists to show that elementary children use over 6 million words in their writing (1992). Children, by virtue of the need to express themselves, problem-solve the spelling of unfamiliar or challenging words, with increasing levels of accuracy over time, and often without direct instruction. Case in point: Shane's early third-grade writing samples reveal a penchant for the phonemic strategy with regard to the suffix *tion*. In moving across his pieces over time, we find approximations of *tion* in the first term of the school year such as: *stasion, stashin, acshun*. During the second term, we find: *conventshnial, punctiashin, vacation*. By term 3, Shane has sorted out this suffix (*pretection, relations, punctuation, vacation*), prior to any formal minilessons on this particular morpheme. How does this incidental learning occur? It occurs primarily through continued experimentation and repeated exposure to print. As Smith remarks, "If you want to write with reasonably conventional spelling, then there can be no substitute for reading" (1982, p. 187). Assessment of spelling across time, particularly for primary children, yields rich data on children's ability to construct rules about how written language works.

c) *conversations:* Questionnaires, and brief conversations during editing conferences, and the like, bring us inside the writers' heads with regard to their attitudes about spelling, their awareness of spelling strategies, and their spelling knowledge.

What We Need to Know to Assess Spelling

Much has been written about invented spelling since the seminal work of Charles Read (1971, 1975). Read, in attempting to research whether young children (ages 3–6) categorize speech sounds differently than adults, became intrigued with their spelling attempts. He found remarkable phonemic consistency and logic in their invented spellings. He argued that young children hypothesize about the sound system and construct abstract, tacit rules that govern their attempts to spell. Over time, these rules are tested against the print that the writer reads (or against instruction). If the rules are confirmed, they remain viable; if rejected, they are reconstructed. While Read documented the increasingly accurate linguistic judgments that young children make about the orthographic system, he did not propose official stages through which young children progress (1971).

Read's early work on invented spelling has been corroborated by many researchers (Beers & Henderson, 1977; Buchanan, 1989; Chomsky, 1972). Schickedanz's research (1990) extended Read's work by examining the word creation strategies of very young children (ages 2–3). Bissex's (1980) and Henderson's (1990) research advanced our knowledge about developmental shifts particular to older children.

Based on these investigations, a number of authors have promulgated classification systems that describe the stages of invented spelling (Buchanan, 1989; Gentry & Gillet, 1993; Graves, 1983; Henderson, 1990; Temple, Nathan, Temple, & Burris, 1993). While the stage titles and age bands vary from author to author, considerable consistency in the descriptors of what constitutes each stage is evident.

Our inclination as educators to bring a sense of order to children's development by collapsing their ways of thinking into discrete stages has been particularly strong in the area of spelling. However, a number of experts have cautioned against reducing the intricacies of literacy development to a lockstep examination of hierarchical stages (Harste et al., 1984; Taylor, 1989; Wilde, 1992). They warn us not to lose sight of the individual child in our efforts to identify a particular stage and not to let stage characteristics limit our power of observation. In talking about children's cognitive development, Siegler writes:

. . . the typical situation is one where individual children know and use a variety of ways of thinking, rather than just one, and where cognition involves constant competition among alternative ways of thinking, rather than sole reliance on a single way of thinking at any given age. Rather than stepping up from Strategy 1 to Strategy 2 to Strategy 3, children would be expected to use several strategies at any one time, with frequency of use of each strategy ebbing and flowing with increasing age and expertise. To capture this view in a visual metaphor, think of a series of overlapping waves . . . each wave corresponding to a different rule, strategy, theory or way of thinking. (1995, p. 409–410)

The "overlapping waves" of spelling development suggest that while young writers construct, test, and refine hypotheses about written language in increasingly sophisticated ways, they can do so in a variety of ways. In order to map the range of children's hypothesis testing, then, we can experiment with the continuum of developmental spelling (Figure 7–3). Webster defines continuum as "a whole, the structure of whose parts is continuous, not atomic." While stage theory implies a hierarchical, discrete ordering of spelling development, a continuum suggests a fluid, forward-moving, at times recursive/overlapping, rhythm. It assumes that children will experiment with multiple strategies in their efforts to spell and that they may not fall neatly into any one point on the continuum. The continuum of developmental spelling rests on the findings that researchers (Bissex, 1980; Henderson, 1990; Read, 1971, 1975; Schickedanz, 1990) have shown to be characteristic of emerging spellers (generally pre-school–grade one), of developing spellers (generally grades 2–4), and of conventional spellers (generally upper elementary and beyond). Since the stage theorists used the same body of research, much commonalty in characteristics is evident. The continuum, however, allows greater latitude in describing the variability that exists among young spellers. As with all areas of writing assessment, spelling assessment goes beyond the analysis of the child's writing samples. Corroboration of our observations about writers' spelling knowledge with other critical sources of data (interviews, surveys, anecdotal records, parent input . . .) is essential.

Emergent Spellers (Points A and B)

Emergent Spellers—Point A

Upon asking Adam (age 3 years, 6 months) to tell about his piece in Figure 7–4, he explains to his Mom, ". . . It says, 'I love you' " (Schickedanz, 1990). Schickedanz in her fascinating analysis of her young son's word creation strategies notes the visual rule strategy at work in Adam's writing. Central to the visual rule strategy is the stringing together of letters

EMERGING SPELLER

A

writes strings of letters (usually capital letters) or letter-like shapes which do not correspond to sounds

does not understand the alphabetic principle

can often "read" his/her message upon request

may ask for words to be spelled; may copy words in environment

B

understands that written language is alphabetic in nature and that sounds have corresponding symbols (letters)

attends only to the most prominent sounds. Initially may only record the first consonant or first and last sound

increasingly stretches out the sounds in words (phonemic segmentation) and represents many distinct sounds

may use one letter to represent a whole word (you=U)

may substitute the letter *D* in two syllable words that contain a medial T or TT. (Both are flap consonants.) (Butter would be spelled *bodr*.)

FIGURE 7–3   *Continuum of spelling development*

DEVELOPING SPELLER		CONVENTIONAL SPELLER
C	**D**	**E**
uses long vowels but without the silent E marker or vowel digraph (two vowels together)	uses long vowels with the silent E marker; experiments with vowel digraphs and is increasingly successful	applies spelling generalizations; correctly uses vowel digraphs/ diphthongs; irregular vowel combinations
substitutes one short vowel for another	uses short vowel correctly most of the time	uses correct verb tense
approximates the sounds in the first syllable of a word but represents the second syllable with a single letter	represents the sounds in all syllables with increasing accuracy with the exception of SCHWA	spells plurals correctly
		doubles consonants
		controls homophones
spells a few high frequency words consistently	has bank of high frequency words that are spelled consistently	uses most affixes correctly
		includes most silent letters
But the developing speller (C) may not have figured out	includes nasal consonants (M, N)	spells many multi-syllabic works
nasal consonants (m and n) and omits them	uses consonant blends TR and DR with increasing success	figures out many unstressed vowels (SCHWA)
the sounds of TR and DR, and often substitutes CHR, JR, GR	shows an awareness of silent letters but often marks them incorrectly	uses multiple spelling strategies: phonemic morphemic visual
silent letters and omits them	has increasing success with verb tense and plurals	spells most words correctly
verb tense; spells past tense according to sound—T, D, or ED; plurals: spelled by sound	**But the developing speller (D) may not have figured out**	
	when to double consonants	
	how to control SCHWA	
	when to use which homophone	
	that affixes have fixed spellings	

FIGURE 7–3, *continued*

FIGURE 7–4   *Adam, an emerging speller, writes "I love you"*

in order to approximate the *look* of words. In order to create his message, Adam constructs a set of visual rules, such as "1) Don't use too many letters. 2) Don't use too few letters. 3) Use a variety of letters, with no more than two of the same letter in succession . . ." (Schickedanz, 1989, p. 103). It is clear that the phonemic strategy is not in operation because Adam does not link sounds with symbols. While emergent spellers at this point (A) on the continuum have yet to grasp the alphabetic principle, they understand the communicative nature of print. For a more detailed examination of the emergent speller's world, Schickedanz's *Adam's Righting Revolutions*, and Clay's *What Did I Write?* are must-reads.

Emergent Spellers—Point B

A literacy milestone is reached in spelling acquisition when the writer awakens to the alphabetic nature of language (Figure 7-3, Point B). Bissex captures her son's seemingly abrupt transition from writing messages in which no awareness of the alphabetic code is evident to writing the following message (1980). Unable to pull his mother away from a book she was reading, Paul decides to use rubber letter stamps to print his message: RUDF. The message, "Are you deaf?", certainly caught his mother's attention, as did Paul's leap from his earlier strategy of letter strings to phonemic spelling. Researchers acknowledge that early phonemic spelling just doesn't happen out of the blue (Bissex, 1980; Schickedanz, 1990). These early writers are in print-rich homes with literate adults who provide constant demonstrations of reading and writing, and who answer questions about print in informal but direct ways. These children watch *Sesame Street*, play with letter blocks, and are read to in extensive and intensive ways. It is from this font of print-immersion that awareness about the alphabetic principles springs forth.

Most prominent in early phonemic spelling is the child's confidence with the highly stable consonant sounds. Early phonemic spellers often initially represent a whole word with only the initial consonant. Soon both the initial and final consonant sounds are included. Other highly discernible sounds also may be represented. In addition, these early spellers often represent a whole word with the single letter that equates to that word: *R=are, U=you.*

Developing Spellers (Points C and D)

Developing Spellers—Point C

Children's ability to attend to sounds in words strengthens as they become competent at segmenting phonemes. To segment phonemes, writers stretch out the sounds in words and then represent each audible sound with a corresponding letter. For example, Jeffrey's (grade 1) journal entry (Figure 7–5) which was written the day after a story and discussion about Abraham Lincoln reveals his ability to segment the phonemes in *slavery*. (See comment about Jeffrey's piece in Chapter 3, page 51.) Prominent features of spelling development at this point on the continuum are discussed on the following pages.

FIGURE 7–5   *Jeffrey, a developing speller, writes "Read my lips. No more slavery!"*

1. Most consonants are represented accurately at this stage with two exceptions: *w* is often spelled with a *y* (the sound of letter *w* starts the same way as the name of the letter *y*); and the consonant blends *tr* and *dr* are often spelled with a *chr* and *gr*, respectively, as a result of distinct attention to articulation (Read, 1971).

2. Long vowels often are represented. Jeffrey's attention to the long vowel sounds in *slavery* is a fine example. Both the long *a* and long *e* sounds are distinguishable, and therefore represented. I suspect that the two *o*'s in the word *no* are included to signal an intonational feature; readers are to stress the word *no* when delivering Lincoln's message. However, developing spellers

at this point (C) of the continuum generally have not figured out that words containing long vowel sounds require markers like silent e or vowel digraphs (ee, ea . . .). Note Jeffrey's approximation of the word *read*.

3. Unlike long vowels, short vowels do not "say their names." Consequently, developing spellers often omit them altogether at first, as is evident in Jeffrey's approximation of *LPS*. Soon, however, Jeffrey will begin to approximate these vowel sounds. For example, Read found that since short *a* is closer in articulation to the long *e* sound than to long *a*, most young spellers will substitute for short *e* for short *a*. Characteristic, then of developing spellers, are the substitutions of short *e* for short *a*, short *e* for short *i*, short *i* for short *o*, and short *o* for short *u* (Read, 1971).

4. Efforts on the part of developing spellers to negotiate two syllable words often result in full approximations of the first syllable, and a single letter to represent the second syllable. Read noted that the vowel sounds in unaccented syllables which end in the letters *l, m, n,* or *r,* are lost in the articulation process. Hence, spellings such as *litl* and *butn* are frequent occurrences. Jeffrey did a fine job representing prominent sounds across the syllables in *slavery*.

Still beyond the grasp of developing spellers at point C on the continuum are the following features:

- silent letters—young writers who are phonemically bound obviously omit them;
- nasal consonants (*m* and *n* when they precede another consonant, i.e. *camp, dent*)—these sounds are reduced so they are omitted;
- schwa—the complexities of schwa (the short *u* sound found in unaccented syllables) escape the developing speller altogether;
- verb tenses—developing spellers stay with the phonemic information and spell *ed* inflections with the sound heard: *t, d,* or *ed;*
- plurals—as with verb tense, plurals may be spelled as they sound: *s, z,* or *ez.*

Developing Spellers—Point D

Developing spellers at point D on the continuum bring an increasing awareness about spelling conventions, learned tacitly through early reading as well as directly through any informal/formal instruction.

They often reject the pure phonemic strategy because they have begun to understand that: a) one sound may necessitate more than one letter (laugh), b) the same sound can be spelled by different letters (ate, weigh, day), and c) different sounds can be spelled with the same letters (dough, cough, through) (Buchanan, 1989, pp. 39–41). Developmental features include:

1. Long vowel–silent *e* words are marked correctly. Experimentation with vowel digraphs increases.

2. Short vowels generally are spelled correctly.

3. Most consonants are represented accurately including *w* and the nasal consonants (*m* and *n*), but the consonant blends *tr* and *dr* may continue to be spelled with a *chr* and *jr*.

4. Much closer approximations of words with two or more syllables are achieved; developing spellers now attempt the sounds heard in each syllable.

Still beyond the grasp of developing spellers (point D) are the following features:

- silent letters—inventions show a beginning awareness of silent letters but they are usually marked incorrectly (especially the doubling of consonants);

- schwa—the complexities of schwa (the short *u* sound found in unaccented syllables) continue to challenge;

- verb tenses—developing spellers show greater control over the past tense inflection but may still rely on sound and produce *t, d,* or *ed;*

- plurals—greater control of plurals is noted but occasional phonemic reliance is evident;

- homophones—still within the grasp of the phonemic strategy, these spellers' limited morphemic knowledge may not allow for attention to meaning cues while spelling. Hence, when developing spellers need to spell the word *their,* they rely on the spelling of the word that they know—*there*—or they represent it phonemically—*thair.*

Conventional Spellers

The cognitive transition from developing spelling to conventional spelling outdistances earlier intellectual leaps in remarkable ways. At this point on the continuum, writers release themselves from the grip of the sound strategy and give priority to morphemic and visual strategies.

Conventional spellers understand spelling as a problem-solving process in which they must integrate layers of knowledge about how the orthography works. Conventional spellers, from children to adults, continue to invent their spelling, especially in first drafts. Their inventions, though, are detected during proofreading and are edited with a high percentage of accuracy. While some children can move into conventional spelling as early as third grade (Bissex, 1980), most children adopt many of the features of conventional spelling by grade 5 or 6 (Buchanan, 1989). Many of these conventions take a lifetime to master (Henderson, 1990). Conventional spellers:

- use multiple strategies (phonemic, morphemic, and visual) to problem solve unknown words.
- have a spelling consciousness and care about their spelling. They also try alternative spellings for words which don't "look right."
- attend to the semantic demands of written language and show increased competence with homophones, affixes (prefixes and suffixes), and root words. They also use variant forms to figure out correct spellings. (If they're unsure about the spelling of *confidence* because of the schwa in the second syllable, they think about the variant form, *confide*, in which the vowel is clearly marked.)
- handle spelling conventions such as silent consonants and the doubling of consonants with increased proficiency;
- have an extensive bank of spelling words.

Assessing Shane's Spelling in First Drafts (Grade 3, First Term)

The selections that have already been chosen for Shane's collaborative portfolio provide the starting point for the analysis of his spelling knowledge and usage. To determine whether he is an emerging, developing, or conventional speller, portfolio pieces chosen for their content (see below) during the first marking term are used for spelling assessment. As mentioned earlier, since the research on developmental spelling patterns emerged primarily from analysis of children's first draft writing, assessment of Shane's developmental spelling trends can be anchored in his first drafts. These drafts include his personal narratives: "The Dentist" (Chapter 3, Figure 3–5), "Stickers" (Chapter 4, Figure 4–7), and "The Visitors" (Chapter 4, Figure 4–5). A quick scan of these entries shows relatively few spelling approximations. A percentage check on these journal entries yields the following accuracy rates, respectively: ninety-eight percent, ninety-four percent, and ninety-three percent. Shane is a strong speller. However, since these high rates of accuracy give us few spelling approximations to analyze, other pieces of his portfolio are examined. Since his story "Lizard and the Motorcycle" (Appendix D) is rich with spelling approximations, it can serve as one source for our analysis.

As you scan the first page or two of Shane's story, make a list of his spelling approximations. Begin to note any patterns. Note, in particular, Shane's successes and approximations with two-syllable words and with short vowels. These two features tend to be good predictors of the developing speller. Use your very tentative findings to predict Shane's place on the continuum of developmental spelling (Figure 7–3).

My review of the first few pages of the Lizard story reveals accurate spelling of multisyllabic words (problem, lizard, motorcycle, animal) as well as no difficulty with short vowels in one syllable words (crashed, smell, locked). I note the homophone confusion (their, no) and some difficulty with double consonants words (botom, imposable, hapend). My hunch is that Shane is a developing speller. To test my hypothesis, I plot Shane's spelling approximations as well as his successes on the Continuum Worksheet (Figure 7–6). It is important to weigh his spelling successes against his approximations. Under the evidence column, I list successes of each feature noted, using a check mark to note accuracy. I, then, list approximations for this same feature in a column to the right.

Upon completion of the worksheet, I confirm my initial hunch about Shane as a developing speller. He demonstrates good control over short vowels, nasal consonants, and silent letters. With one exception (hapend), past tense is marked correctly (*climbed, laughed, crashed, ransaked* . . .). Spelling challenges that remain include homophones, schwa in unaccented syllables, and double consonants. Note, though, that in each of these categories, Shane has some degree of success, signaling the range of his spelling versatility.

As emphasized earlier, one of the primary purposes of assessing children's spelling is to inform our instruction. Analysis of Shane's worksheet suggests his readiness to tackle some of the more advanced spelling features. For example, while schwa is a challenge (*luckaly, crockadile, refridgearator*), he is successful in controlling schwa in words like *police* and *problem*. Shane also indicates a readiness to tackle double consonants, and perhaps the derivational suffix *tion*. Whether instruction occurs informally in an individual spelling conference or more formally in a whole class minilesson depends on our overall assessment of where the rest of the class is with respect to schwa, and so forth.

Shane

Continuum Worksheet

"*The Children's Muesam*"

Developing Speller "*Lizard and the Motorcycle*"   Conventional Speller "*Swiss Army Knife*"
D

Evidence		Evidence of Success	Evidence of Approximation
* uses long vowels with the silent e marker; experiments with vowel digraphs and is increasingly successful	name✓ zoming near✓ swoped cheese✓ corse found✓	* applies spelling rules: vowels digraphs/diphthongs; irregular vowel combinations; nasal consonants (m/n); consonant blends: tr and dr	head really screw special scout	muesam
* uses short vowel correctly	rob✓ twenty✓ Flash✓ kid nap✓	* uses correct verb tense	liked odered using	
* represents the sounds in all syllables with increasing accuracy with the exception of schwa	building✓ rezist Lizard✓ refridge- motorcycle avatn	* spells plurals correctly	telaphones places	
*uses consonant blends tr and dr with increasing success	drove✓	* doubles consonants	button scissor's bottle	
* includes nasal consonants (m,n);	bank✓ found✓	* controls homophones	There would	
* has increasing success with verb tense and plurals	ransaked✓ shoveing crashed✓ hepend years live-	* uses affixes effectively	pretend opener	
* shows an awareness of silent letters but often marks them incorrectly	climbed✓ wrong✓ tonigt night✓	* includes silent letters	climb alright knife	
* has bank of high frequency words that are spelled consistently	some✓ where✓ friend✓	* spells most multi-syllabic words	personal different special opener	different muesam
But the developing speller may not have figured out				
* when to double consonants	supper✓ botom better✓ hapend stepd	* figures out unstressed vowels (schwa)	machine personal magazine	telaphone nostrel
* how to control schwa	police✓ luckaly crockadile imposable refridgearator	* uses multiple spelling strategies: phonemic, morphemic and visual	✓	
* when to use which homophone	know✓ no herd their cell	* spells most words correctly	✓	
* that affixes have fixed spellings	imposable✓ stashin stasion misschif			

FIGURE 7–6   *Continuum worksheet*

Assessing Shane's Spelling in First Drafts (Grade 3, Third Term)

Shane's spelling profile at the beginning of third grade evidenced some features associated with conventional spelling. While this final point on the continuum takes all spellers years to master, we are ready to look for evidence of Shane's expanding knowledge base, and of a more sophisticated level of hypothesis-testing. Writing samples, completed in January/February, show growing evidence of conventional spelling. Since his percentage of accurate spelling continues to be high on nearly every writing sample, two samples, "The Children Muesam" (Chapter 4, Figure 4–8) and "My Swiss Army Knife" (Appendix H) are used to map the Continuum Worksheet (Figure 7–6). As Figure 7–6 indicates, Shane demonstrates increased facility with verb tense (*liked, odered, using*), with double consonants (*buttons, scissors, bottle*) and with schwa (*personal, machine, magazine*). Schwa in words such as *telaphone* and *nostrel* continue to challenge him, although an effort at self-editing may be all that is needed. If not, instruction in more advanced prefixes like *tele*, as well as encouragement to try alternate spellings and to do a dictionary check for rarely used words such as *nostril*, would be appropriate.

A side note on Shane's spelling of *diffrent* and *odered*: One of the confounding factors in spelling is pronunciation. Shane's ability to spell these two words appears to be tied to his pronunciation and to his prioritizing of the phonemic strategy. A series of minilessons on variant word forms—differ, different, difference—is critical for the conventional speller. In addition, demonstrations of how good spellers develop a system of alternate pronunciations for certain words (Fe*bru*ary) should be discussed.

A word of caution concerning the continuum (Figure 7–3) is in order. Placing Shane's two writing samples in conventional spelling does not necessarily mean that all of his subsequent entries will fall neatly into this point of the continuum. Spelling does not develop in steady, gradual increments. It would not be surprising, for example, to find some of Shane's later writing samples showing problems with past tense endings. His self-editing attempts, however, should reflect his knowledge base and result in correction.

Assessing Shane's Spelling in Final Drafts (Grades 3 & 5)

Detecting developmental trends in spelling in first draft writing constitutes only one dimension in the assessment of spelling. Critical, also, is the analysis of what young writers (primarily grades 2 and up) do when they edit their work for spelling.

Shane's first draft, "The Visitors," (Chapter 4, Figure 4–5), at the end of the first term reveals the following spelling approximations: vistors, Andrae, there (for their), there (for their), and of (for after). None of these attempts were fixed by Shane during the editing step; the changes were made by Alice. The same pattern is evident in his "Vacation" piece, written later in the year (Chapter 8, Figure 8–7). When Shane edits for mechanics, he tends to target only capitalization (see Chapter 9). Perhaps, because he a fairly competent speller, he doesn't realize that writers edit for spelling. Perhaps, because editing is a complex task for all writers, let alone burgeoning writers, he can only hold so many areas of concern at once. The demands of revising ideas and of editing spelling, punctuation, and grammar are difficult for writers at all levels to choreograph. Therefore, no additional information about his spelling competence is revealed in his self-edits.

However, an interesting piece of longitudinal data on Shane's spelling is available. Recall that Shane, in fifth grade at the time, offered to rework his third-grade piece, "Lizard and the Motorcycle" (Appendix F), during one of our sessions. Figure 7–7 presents Shane's original third-grade spelling attempts, and his fifth-grade self-edits. The plus mark (+) indicates that he corrected the word; the notation *no* indicates that he did not edit his original spelling error.

Of the thirty-three spelling approximations in the third-grade piece, Shane, as a fifth grader, found twenty-four of these approximations and respelled twenty-two of them correctly, with two approximations remaining (happend, misscheif/misschef). When challenged to find the remaining ten approximations, Shane found six more. This reminds us that proofreading and editing require intense concentration. When children don't find all their approximations in their first sweep, encourage a relook.

Figure 7–7 shows a surge in his morphemic knowledge of homophones. He has sorted out homophone pairs like *herd/heard*, *sell/cell*, *no/know*, and *there/their*. Also evident is Shane's success with doubling consonants in words such as *botom* and *hapend*. In addition, he employs the visual strategy to edit words such as *tonight*, *resist*, and *caught*. Shane's editorial successes indicate his increasingly sophisticated understanding of the spelling system.

One area of phonemic understanding that continues to challenge Shane (and most expert spellers) is schwa. Schwa is the vowel sound found in the unaccented syllable of words; schwa sounds like short *u* but can be represented by any vowel. Shane's decision not to correct *crockadiles* (twice), *imposable*, and *luckaly* suggests that Shane needs instruction in this area.

Ideally, an analysis of some of Shane's self-edits of his fifth-grade pieces would corroborate some or all of the above preliminary observa-

ORIGINAL	SELF-EDIT	ORIGINAL	SELF-EDIT	ORIGINAL	SELF-EDIT
their	no	hapend	happend	imposable	no
when ever	no	ransaked	+	kid nap	+
misschif	misschef	crockadile	none	shoveing	+
rezist	+	corse	+	swoped	+
when ever	no	tonigt	+	herd	+ (heard)
no	+ (know)	caugh	+ (caught)	stashin	+
zoming	+	luckaly	no	the	+ (they)
refridearator	+	lizar	+	live	+ (life)
botom	+	there	+ (their)	for ever	+
seen	+ (seem)	sell	+ (cell)	animal	+ (animals)
shore	+ (sure)	stasion	no	live	+ (lived)

FIGURE 7–7   *Shane (Grade 5) edits the spelling in his third grade story*

tions. However, upon asking for such samples, Shane quickly informed me that he composes exclusively at the computer and uses spell-check as he goes along.

Shane on Shane: Self-Assessment of Spelling (Grade 5)

In an attempt to corroborate some of the above tentative findings, and to examine his strategy usage, I asked Shane to complete the Spelling Strategy Inventory featured in Figure 7–8. Adapted from Powell and Hornsby (1993), this activity asks children to spell three different groups of words. Each group of words taps one of the spelling strategies—phonemic, visual, morphemic—explained at the beginning of this chapter. (Note: The words in Figure 7–7 were chosen for a fifth grader; choose words appropriate to your age group.) Shane was encouraged to cross out as often as needed. After each set of words was dictated, Shane was asked to proofread and make any corrections. He, then, was instructed to describe what he did in order to spell each group of words (or individual words within a group).

Group A

The words in Group A were chosen for their phonemic irregularity with the goal of having Shane rely on his visual memory. As the following conversation reveals, Shane relies on the visual strategy when spelling phonemically irregular words.

```
                    Spelling Strategy Inventory


Group A Words            What did you do to spell this group of words?
1.  Laughter             All the words have been taught to me before..

2.  Knowledge            Knowledge is stuff you know.

3.  Shriek               It was in a book.

Group B Words            What did you do to spell this group of words?
1.  Dictate              I sounded it out — I checked it to see
                Delapabated   if the letters made the right noise.
2.  Delapidated

3.  Simmer

Group C Words            What did you do to spell this group of words?
1.  Disatisfied          I saw the word Trans Am on
                         my neighbors car.
2.  Telegraph

3.  Transportation
```

FIGURE 7–8   *Shane's responses to Spelling Strategy Inventory*

CAROL: What did you do to spell *laughter*?

SHANE: I just know how to spell it. It's a common word.

CAROL: Why didn't you spell *laughter, l-a-f-t-e-r*?

SHANE: Because I noticed how in school we learned about different words. They sound like they're supposed to be done a different way but they're not.

CAROL: What about the word *knowledge*?

SHANE: I checked to make sure it had *know* at the beginning because knowledge is stuff you <u>know</u>, and I knew *know* was spelled k-n-o-w.

CAROL: How did you figure out *shriek*?

SHANE: I'm not sure if that's right because I've seen the word *shriek* in a book about this giant, named Shriek, or something. But I'm not sure if his name was spelled the same way as the actual word or if the author changed the actual word and gave it an unusual spelling.

CAROL: So, why did you spell *shriek* the way you did?

SHANE: Because that's how it was spelled in the book.

If there is one area of agreement among all the spelling and writing experts, it is that if children are to increase spelling competence, they must read extensively. Shane, not surprisingly, is an avid reader.

Group B

Further support for Shane's increasing facility with spelling generalizations is found in his two successes in this category, *simmer* and *dictate*. As was evident in his editing of the Lizard story, Shane understands when to double consonants (*bottom, happend*). Likewise, he has figured out when to represent the hard *c* sound with a single consonant as in *dictate*, and when to spell it with a *ck* (self-edit of *ransacked* in Lizard story). Since the word *dilapidated* was unfamiliar to Shane, he relied on the sound strategy. Interestingly, his first attempt at this word resulted in correct usage of schwa in the third syllable (*delapitaded*). However, Shane rejects this spelling and reverts back to his standing hypothesis about the schwa sound. As his approximation of *delapadated* and his approximation in his self-edit of the lizard story (*imposable, luckaly, crockadile*) show, Shane represents the schwa sound with the vowel *a*. In asking Shane how he arrived at *dilapadated*, he replied:

SHANE: Well, I've never seen that word, so I sounded it out. Then I checked it to see if it made sense with the noises the letters made.

CAROL: How could you find out if your spelling is correct?

SHANE: I'd probably get a different piece of paper. I'd write maybe four or five different ways it could possibly be spelled and the one that looks neatest and correct would probably be the one.

CAROL: Would you do anything else for a final check?

SHANE: No.

Shane's procedure for checking his spelling of *dilapidated* represents one of the higher level problem-solving strategies (Wilde, 1992). In talking with elementary-age writers about what they do when they don't know how to spell a word, Wilde found the following range of strategies:

a) *placeholder spelling:* The writer uses any spelling to hold the word's place.

b) *human resources*: The writer asks someone how to spell the word.

c) *textual resources*: The writer consults a dictionary, chart, or other print source. Interestingly, at no point during my prompting about "a final check" did Shane mention the use of the dictionary. Only when asked what he'd do if he couldn't decide among his alternatives, did he say he'd go to the dictionary. However, he added quickly that he would use the dictionary only if his computer was not nearby. He said he often types a word, and then runs it through his spellcheck.

d) *generation, monitoring, and revision*: The writer tries out alternative spellings and chooses the best alternative. It is this high-level strategy about which Shane talks.

e) ownership: The writer simply knows how to spell a word.

While Wilde suggests that these strategies are hierarchical in the sense that items *c–e* represent a more sophisticated response to the challenge at hand, she reminds us that, in fact, both children and adults use all of strategies depending on the circumstances (1992).

Group C

Overall, Shane's morphemic knowledge of affixes (prefixes and suffixes) is strong. The suffix *tion* is spelled correctly in *transportation* as well as in his self-edit of *stashin* in his Lizard story. As for *telegraph*, Shane remarked, "I've seen *tele* on other words like *telephone*, and *graph* is a common word." When asked what the prefix *tele* means, he said he wasn't sure but said that *trans* means "to move from one place to another." However, prefixes which end in *s* continue to elude Shane. His approximation, *disatisfied*, along with his self-edit of *misschef* in the Lizard story, and his spelling of *mispelling* (Figure 7–9, item 3) suggest that he doesn't understand that *dis* and *mis* remain constant regardless of the first letter of the root word.

The discussion about the strategies that writers use to generate each group of words in the Spelling Strategy Inventory is as important as the spelling task itself. Such a discussion helps children understand that a) the sound strategy is only one way to spell and is often not the most reliable strategy, b) they need to pay attention to the visual form of words, and c) knowledge of meaning-bearing units such as the affixes and root words facilitates spelling.

Additional information about strategy usage, as well as information about children's attitude toward spelling, can be gleaned through use of the spelling survey (Figure 7–9). This survey, adapted from Wilde's

Spelling Advice

1. How did you learn to spell?

My Mother is a good speller and she taught me

2. What do you do differently now when you spell words that you didn't do when you were in first grade?

I think before I spell a word.

3. Should writers care about the way they spell words? Why or why not?

Yes. Who would want to read a book full of mispellings?

4. When you are writing a story, when do you check to see if your words are spelled correctly?

When the story is finished.

5. What do you do when you come to a word that is hard to spell?

I sound it out, then I spell what I think is right, then I check it later.

Do you do anything else?

No.

FIGURE 7–9   *Shane's responses to a spelling survey*

6. How do you know if you've spelled that hard word right?

_I spell the word in a few different
ways, and I use the one that looks Good._

7. If you had to give some advice to a friend about spelling, what would you tell your friend?

_Don't give up if you are having Spelling
Problems._

8. If a friend spelled the word, laugh, like this: laf, what would you tell your friend?

Try some different spellings.

9. Who do you know that is a very good speller? _My Mother._

Do you think that this person always spell words correctly? Explain your

thoughts. _No. Everyone makes mistakes._

10. How do you feel about yourself as a speller?

_I think I don't realize how
Important spelling is._

FIGURE 7–9, *continued*

Spelling Interview, can be completed by children at the beginning, mid-point, and end of the school year. Analysis of Shane's spelling survey lends further corroboration to our preliminary conclusions. It is clear that Shane by grade 5 has developed a spelling consciousness (items 2, 3, 10). He knows when in the writing process to attend to spelling (item 4). He uses phonemic and visual strategies (item 5) as well as the generation, monitoring, and revision strategy for hard words (items 6, 8). The spelling survey encourages children to bring to a conscious level whatever understandings they have about the spelling process. It also allows us inside their heads, to assess their understandings, and to provide appropriate instruction.

Concluding Comments and a Word About Teacher Self-Assessment

Spelling is not a low level skill that can be learned through isolated drills. Rather, it is a complex cognitive process in which "knowledge begins globally and develops through greater differentiation and greater abstraction or integration . . ." (Wilde, 1992, p. 20). The transition over time from invention to convention is facilitated when writers have extended opportunities to read and write. Informal and formal spelling instruction, especially on strategy usage, during editing conferences or whole class minilessons, supports the development of spelling (Atwell, 1987; Wilde, 1992).

As we have observed in earlier chapters, teacher assessment is a critical feature of portfolio assessment. We have to ask ourselves, "Are we creating the conditions in our classrooms that foster spelling growth?" Prior to assessing the children, we need to assess our beliefs and our actions and answer the following questions in the affirmative:

- Do we share our love of language by integrating word study and word play throughout the day?

- Do we view spelling as a complex, developmental, cognitive activity that is learned informally through extensive, daily reading and writing as well as formally through instruction?

- Do we provide formal spelling instruction which includes strategy building as well as direct instruction on key spelling generalizations?

- Do we explain why spelling is important? Do we help children develop a spelling consciousness—a positive attitude about spelling and a concern for accuracy?

- Do we demonstrate how our first drafts often contain spelling errors, some of which we catch right away and fix, and some of which we catch during the editing process? Do we stress the editing process as the place where I concentrate on my spelling?

- Do we show children how to proofread and edit their spelling on an ongoing basis?

- Do we ask children to keep a spelling log of words learned (particularly grade 2 and up)? If spelling lists are used, do we encourage children to select the words from their writing samples (with our support, if necessary)?

- Are our classrooms rich in print resources (dictionaries, atlases, thesauruses . . .) and do we model use of these print resources?

Assessing Handwriting

8

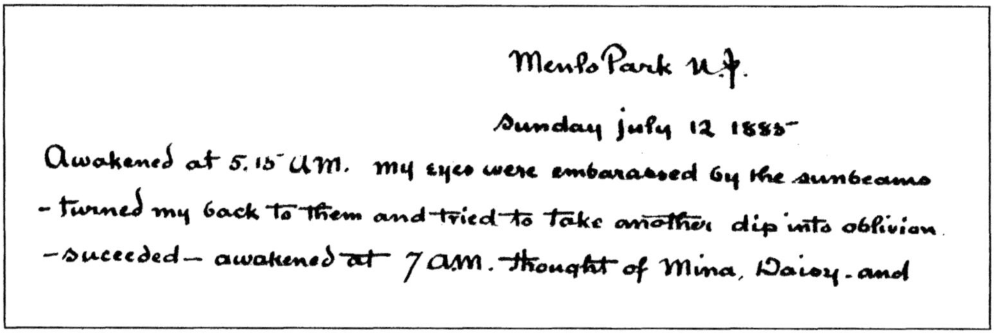
Menlo Park N.J.

Sunday July 12 1885

Awakened at 5.15 AM. my eyes were embarassed by the sunbeams
- turned my back to them and tried to take another dip into oblivion.
- suceeded - awakened at 7 AM. thought of Mina, Daisy - and

FIGURE 8–1 *Excerpt from Thomas Edison's diary*

From beginning to end, Thomas Edison's deft hand graces each page of his diary. His handwriting achieves a level of artistry that most of us would not be able to approximate in a final draft, let alone a first draft. Penmanship of this calibre, according to Smith, must have its origins in practice: "Handwriting is improved through practice that is not boring . . ." (1982, p. 204). And practice Edison did. As a sixteen-year-old telegraph operator for Western Union Telegraph Company, he transcribed Morse code night after night, cultivating his skill as a scribe in the context of purposeful writing.

Unlike Edison, though, few of us wrote with such purposeful regularity in school. Try as we may, the goal of Palmer-perfect penmanship eluded many of us. Since handwriting was viewed as an end in itself—as a product—our writing grades often reflected our skill as scribes. The neater the handwriting, the better the writing grade. In talking about his first-grade teacher, Fletcher writes:

> I revered this woman. It pained me to live with the knowledge that while I excelled in many areas, I consistently let Mrs. Damon down in

one: My handwriting was horrific. I simply could not get my fingers to make the pencil dance the way a pencil should dance. My letters leaned, wandered, wobbled, and trembled so violently even I could not read them most of the time. I drooled over the perfectly printed papers that girls in our class produced with such apparent effortlessness. No matter how hard I tried, I could not replicate anything even approaching their work. In that classroom, writing was penmanship, and no paper of mine ever received higher than a C . . . One afternoon, Mrs. Damon took me aside and looked deeply into my eyes. "Listen Ralph," she said softly. "You're going to have work harder on this. You've got sloppy penmanship, and sloppy penmanship means a sloppy personality." (1993, p. 11)

Fletcher's experience is not unique. Markham asked fifth graders to write a piece on a teacher-chosen topic (1976). Their essays were typed, and rated in terms of the quality of their content. A group of children with varying levels of handwriting then rewrote these essays. Elementary teachers rated these papers on a scale of 9 to 1. Markham found that elementary teachers gave significantly higher grades to students with good penmanship *regardless of the quality of the content.*

If Markham were to replicate her study today, my guess is that teachers would not equate good writing with good handwriting. The work of Graves (1983), Smith (1982), Calkins (1986), and others have helped us understand the place of the handwriting in the writing process. Handwriting is a functional tool that enables writers to communicate their message effectively. When we write early drafts, we focus on the quality of our message, not on the legibility of our handwriting. However, publication of our messages necessitates legible, neat (but not Palmer-perfect) handwriting.

Handwriting, then, is a functional aspect of literacy that warrants assessment. Poor handwriting interferes with the act of composition (Shaughnessey, 1977; Graves, 1978). When the physical act of putting pen to paper is laborious, writers struggle to craft their ideas. As Frank Smith aptly remarks, "You do not learn to dance wearing heavy boots" (1982, p. 194). Young writers compose at a rate of about 1.5 words per minute; third graders write eight to nineteen words per minute. It is little wonder that first graders' lack of speed impacts adversely on the quality of the message (Graves, 1978). In addition, poor handwriting is the cause of about 20 percent of spelling errors (Barbe, Lucas, & Wasylyk, 1984).

What We Need to Know to Assess Children's Handwriting

Historically, investigations into handwriting have ebbed and flowed (Hildreth, 1960). The 1960s and 1970s marked a period of intense interest in the *surface* aspects of handwriting. An overview of the questions researchers asked, along with their often inconclusive or contradictory findings, follow. Remember, most of these studies predate the writing process movement.

What Kind of Paper Should Young Writers Use?

- First graders copied ten letters more legibly on wide-lined paper than on unlined or on regular-lined paper (Leung, Treblas, Hill, & Cooper, 1979). Given a teacher-assigned topic, first graders wrote more legibly on unlined paper (Lindsay & McLennan, 1983).

- Given a teacher-assigned topic, second graders wrote more legibly on the lined paper than on unlined paper (Burnhill, Hartley, & Davies, 1978). Lindsay and McLennan found no difference between lined and unlined paper (1983).

- Given ten minutes to write on a teacher-assigned topic, third graders wrote as legibly on unlined paper as they wrote on lined paper (Krzesni, 1971; Lindsay & McLennan, 1983).

- Given a teacher-assigned topic, fourth graders demonstrated greater legibility on lined paper (Lindsay & McLennan, 1983).

What Kind of Instruments Should Children Use?

- Beginner pencils and crayons (wider in diameter) or pencils with grips do not enhance legibility (Lamme & Aris, 1983; Ziviani & Elkins, 1986).

- Young children prefer adult-size pencils (Askov & Peck, 1982).

- Ballpoint and felt pens enhanced the legibility of two groups of third graders (Askov & Peck, 1982; Krzesni ,1971).

Is Manuscript Writing Slower and Less Fluent than Cursive Writing?

- Upper elementary and intermediate children who continue to use manuscript write as fast and as legibly as those who use cursive (Hildreth, 1960; Peck, Askov, & Fairchild, 1980).

Because the majority of these studies were undertaken prior to, or during the infancy of, the writing movement, they treat handwriting as a purely mechanical skill. They fail to take into account the relationship between the act of writing and handwriting. They fail to assess handwriting within the context of children's authentic writing and at the appropriate phase of the writing process. They inappropriately judge the legibility of children's handwriting (grade 2 and up) on first draft writing. To find answers to the questions that these researchers posed, we need to observe and talk with children as they are writing in purposeful ways with different kinds of paper and writing instruments. In sum, the aforementioned empirical research offers few insights for the assessment process. For those insights, we need to turn to the pioneering efforts of Clay (1975) and Graves (1983) whose work marked a significant shift away from researching surface facets of handwriting toward exploring the developmental nature of handwriting.

Clay's Research on the Early Development of Handwriting

While Clay makes it clear that the research in her book *What Did I Write?* is not about handwriting per se, she uncovers some critical principles that very young writers adopt as they put pen to paper. These principles significantly advance our understanding of the development of handwriting. Through careful observation of young writers, Clay documents how letters/letterlike figures emerge from early drawings. For example, approximations of *O* constitute a common form of scribble for two- and three-year-olds. When the child accidentally joins a descending stroke with the *O*, the letter *P* takes form. Clay believes children discover this flexibility principle, as well as other principles, as they create letters. While asserting that this learning is highly idiosyncratic and that no particular sequence of letters can be tracked, "the child's early attempts at drawing and scribbling develop into later writing behavior" (Clay, 1975, p. 15).

Two of Clay's principles pertinent to school-age children deserve mention:

a) *Directionality Principle:* Within the first six months of school, most children figure out the principle of directionality, namely the English language is written from left to right, top to bottom. Obviously, directionality impinges directly on legibility and is an important facet of handwriting development.

b) *Principles of Page Arrangement*: What do young writers do when they run out of space on a line or a page? They suspend their knowledge about directionality, find an empty space on the paper, and stick in the leftover word(s). If space is limited, they may string the word vertically down the page or they may turn the page around and continue the text "upside down."

Philip, a first grader, encountering page arrangement problems in his piece in Figure 8–2, resolves not to violate the principle of directionality. Rather, he opts for a more advanced strategy—squishing.

Clay's work disputes the notion that handwriting is a low-level, perfunctory motor skill. Clay believes that children are indefatigable problem solvers who observe the global (and eventually the specific) aspects of print in the world around them, and who actively construct theories about the creation of this print. Using this tacit knowledge base, they puzzle out the intricacies of letter formations, directionality, page arrangement and so on.

Graves's Research on the Development of Handwriting

Take a minute to read James's innovation of the predictable book *Boss for a Week* (Handy, 1982) in Figure 8–3.

Now examine Graves's five general phases of handwriting development (Figure 8–4) (1983). Decide which phase characterizes James's development.

While we need to examine a few of James's other writing samples in

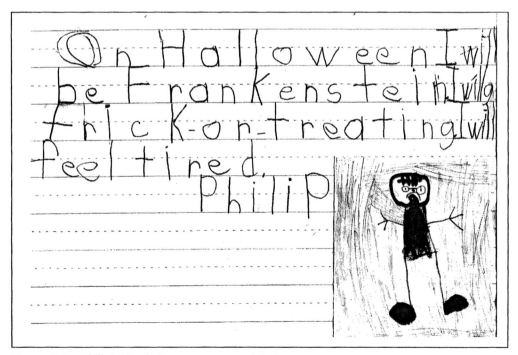

Figure 8–2 *Philip's (Grade 1) page arrangement strategy*

the same time period to make a final judgment, a preliminary conclusion places James's piece (Figure 8–3) in the first aesthetics phase. While only a kindergartner, James displays an interest in how his letters are formed. He decides that his *c* in the word *TAC* is too small, so he enlarges it without crossing out his original attempt. In the word MANDA-e-N, he comments that he used dashes so the letters "don't get too close." James is well on his way to understanding the tentativeness of first drafts. Graves makes the point that many children, with the right support from teachers during writing workshop, move through these phases during first grade. Graves, however, cautions that since more research is needed to validate these phases, they should not be viewed as fixed developmental stages (1983). Unfortunately, virtually no subsequent research has been undertaken.

Assessing Shane's Handwriting

In order to identify Shane's phase of handwriting development according to Graves's scheme (Figure 8–4), we can review any of the pieces in Shane's third grade collaborative portfolio. For example, if we inspect his September draft of the story "Lizard and the Motorcycle" (Appendix D), we note the following occurrences: a) revisions during his first draft writing which have been tucked into his existing

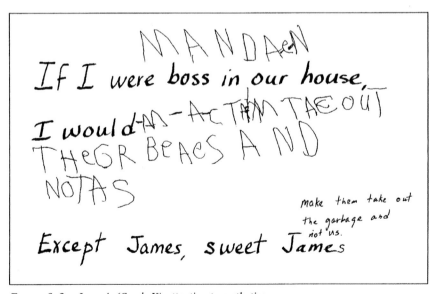

FIGURE 8–3   *James's (Grade K) attention to aesthetics*

How Children Grow as Scribes

GET-IT-DOWN-PHASE:

For emerging writers, the physical act of putting pen to paper is exciting in and of itself. They take pleasure in spraying letters and/or words across the page without concern for the finished product. Within a few weeks, most writers attend to directionality in a general sense but have little concern for spacing.

FIRST AESTHETICS:

Children soon move from no awareness of aesthetic dimensions to noticing and fixing a poorly formed letter or a crunched word. Learning to control the eraser is a challenging task. Ripped, smudged papers distress these young writers. Having the paper "look clean" (Graves, 1983, p. 174) is important to these burgeoning writers.

GROWING AGE OF CONVENTIONS:

Resolute in the knowledge that there is a right way and a wrong way to form letters, to sit words on the line, to space words and so forth, children, usually by the end of grade one, begin to attend to the conventions of print. Sensitive to comments of teacher and peers, they begin to care about how their piece looks. Graves notes that this awakening to conventions often slows writers down, making them more cautious in their approach to writing, and less productive.

BREAKING CONVENTIONS:

When young children are encouraged to revise their pieces, their devotion to aesthetics has to dissipate if revision strategies are to take hold. However, the realization that their first draft is not permanent can be disconcerting. With guidance, children in this phase of handwriting development begin to accept the proposition that handwriting in first drafts can be a messy affair.

LATER AESTHETICS:

Writers come full circle now. Attentive first to their message, they write without excessive concern for the conventions, knowing that the mechanics will come into full focus in the final draft. Cross-outs, rather than erasures, are an important marker of this phase.

FIGURE 8–4 *Graves's (1983) phases of handwriting development*

text, b) more efforts at fixing rather than at erasing misformed letters, and c) cross-outs. Informal observations of Shane as he writes reveals that he prints with good speed and doesn't seem to obsess about his handwriting. He keeps his message at the forefront. Taken together, these data suggest that Shane is operating at Graves's highest phase of handwriting development: later aesthetics (1983). As the following conversation and artifacts show, Shane prioritizes meaning over production in the drafting stage and then shifts these priorities in the publication stage.

Shane on Shane: Self-Assessment of Handwriting

In asking Shane to locate his best piece of handwriting from the beginning of the year, and his best piece from the second half of the year, he comments, "That's easy. My final drafts are the ones." Shane pulls out "The Visitors" (Figure 8–5), and "I Will Be going on vacation" (Figure 8–7).

CAROL: Why are these your best examples of handwriting?

SHANE: 'Cuz I wrote them over. We had to, so now they are neat.

CAROL: If you had to pick the best one, which would you pick?

SHANE: That's hard—they're both good but I think this one (pointing to Figure 8–5) is a little better. It's a little smaller. I'm writing smaller now.

CAROL: If you compare your first draft (Figure 8–6) and final draft (Figure 8–5) of "The Visitors," tell me what you notice.

SHANE: Well, I notice that I'm a lot messier here (Figure 8–6), but it's because I had to change stuff around like Mrs. Earle said. See it's okay to be messy first time 'cuz you can fix it later on.

CAROL: What else do you notice?

SHANE: Well, sometimes I don't have enough space (pointing to "they have" in line 8). So, sometimes I don't write good letters and I have to do them again (pointing to the *U* in United, line 10). I'm a fast writer, that's why.

In addition to understanding that his handwriting changes in accordance with the draft on which he is working, Shane pinpoints two of the important factors that affect his legibility: letter formation and spacing. With further prompting, Shane may have been able to articulate those letters which he forms well and those which need attention. He may have been able to assess other legibility factors which we will now review. The greater the degree to which children are involved in self-assessment, the stronger the ownership of learning over time.

Assessing Shane's Legibility

Traditionally, assessment of children's handwriting has been carried out within the context of the handwriting scales that accompany most of the major commercial handwriting programs. Typically, the handwriting scale consists of a rubric of five levels of handwriting performance (excellent to poor) by grade level. Teachers (and children) are instructed to compare each child's handwriting sample against the scale and to rate the writer's performance accordingly. Such practice seems of limited utility. First, instead of setting neat, legible handwriting as an attainable goal, these scales set "perfect" handwriting as the goal. Second, these scales expect children to write sentences for the artificial purpose of the rating procedure. They ignore the relationship between handwriting and the writing process.

Assessment of handwriting must occur in genuine pieces of writing and must keep legibility at the forefront. While we can analyze first draft writing across time to pinpoint growth in a writer's control over the legibility elements, the most effective analysis takes place when we place a first and final draft side by side and explore what happens when the writer has only to attend to the physical act of transcription.

As mentioned in previous chapters, the collaborative writing portfolio contains selected pieces that serve to document a writer's progress in both content and mechanics. Our first responsibility is to ask the young writers to select those pieces that matter to them, and to assess their decisions through conversation and observation. Depending on the child's selections, we may need to supplement their choices with additional pieces that capture the evolution of the writer's facility with fictional and nonfictional genres and so forth. When possible, it is these pieces, selected for their content, that should be used for the analysis of the mechanical aspects of writing, including handwriting. On occasion, it is appropriate to include a new piece, not previously analyzed, that provides important information about handwriting or spelling and so on. Therefore, in looking at pieces already chosen for the portfolio, we capitalize on Shane's choice of "The Visitors " (which was analyzed for content in Chapter 4) and compare his handwriting in first (Figure 8–6) and final draft (Figure 8–5). For easier reference, the lines in each piece have been numbered.

Most handwriting experts agree that four primary elements constitute legible handwriting: shape, spacing, slant, and size. These elements commonly are referred to as the 4 *S*'s. Two additional elements, alignment and line quality, can also be considered. As you read Figures 8–5 and 8–6, note Shane's strengths and weaknesses with regard to these legibility factors.

Shape

Letter formation—how the writer shapes his letters—often is considered the most important legibility factor. When a writer closes the loop on the letter *e* (creating a *c*), forgets to cross the letter *t* (creating the letter *l*), and doesn't complete the loop on the letter *d* (creating the letters *cl*) or the letter *a* (creating the letter *u*), legibility is compromised. While we are not looking for Palmer-perfect execution, we do expect readable letter shapes. As you scan the letter shapes in Shane's first and final drafts, it is helpful to inspect letters by the following categories: ascenders, descenders, and baseline to midline.

Ascenders Let's look first to see how Shane is doing with letters that contain ascending strokes in his final draft: *b, d, f, h, k, l, t*. In line 1, we note the crunched *t* in the word *visitor*, and *f* in the word *from*. The letter *k* in the word *took* (line 6) and *York* (line 12) is also reduced. Since we are not interested in isolated errors, we need to see if he reduces these ascending letters repeatedly. We can collect data on his *t's*

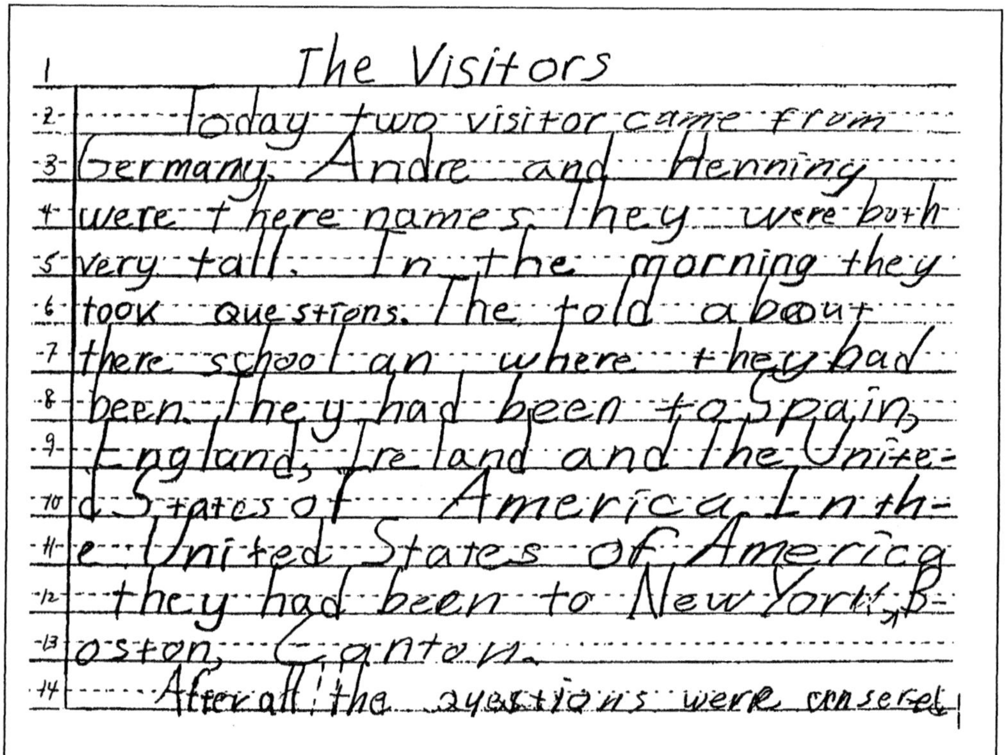

1 The Visitors
2 Today two visitor came from
3 Germany. Andre and Henning
4 were there names. They were both
5 very tall. In the morning they
6 took questions. The told about
7 there school an where they had
8 been. They had been to Spain,
9 England, Ireland and the Unite-
10 d States of America. In th-
11 e United States of America
12 they had been to New York, B-
13 oston, Canton.
14 After all the questions were answered

FIGURE 8–5 *Shane's choice for best handwriting (Term 1)*

(*there* and *both* in line 4; *tall, the, they* in line 5; *took* and *told*, line 6 and so on). His *t's* consistently are smaller than his *l's, b's, d's* and so forth. Shane tends to start the downstroke of his *t* just above the midline and to cross at or below the midline. We note the same tendency in his first draft. It would be informative to check this finding against another final draft in this same time period. If the same pattern is evident, Shane should receive one-on-one instruction on the letter *t*. Such instruction should capitalize on his strengths with other ascen-

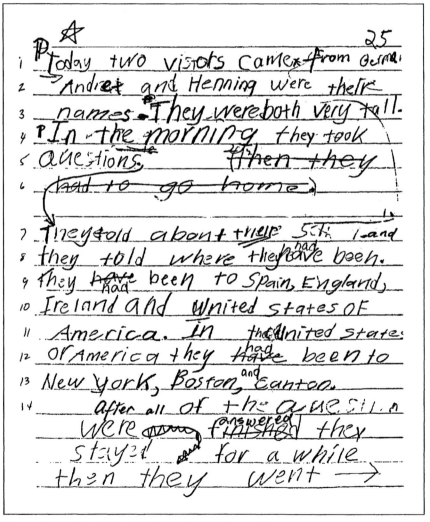

FIGURE 8–6 *Shane's handwriting in first draft*

ders. Since we don't have any other *f's* in this piece, we need to suspend judgment until we can investigate other final pieces. His *k's* also should be checked.

Descenders We move onto letters with descending strokes: *q, g, p, y, j*—the five hardest letters for children to form (Lewis & Lewis, 1964). The most obvious letter of concern is *q*. Shane substitutes the uppercase *Q* for the lowercase *q* in two instances (the word *Questions*, lines 6 and 14) in his final draft. (Note that these uppercase shapes are much improved over his *Q's* in his first draft.) It is important to try to corroborate this finding about the letter *q* by scanning surrounding drafts (preferably final). None of his journal entries prior to "The Visitors" contain *q* words; however, two subsequent entries do. In one first draft, Shane wrote, "And when we got in the classroom we sat down Quietly." Five pages later, he wrote, "They flew On Times SQuare air." Our results suggest that Shane needs direct instruction in lowercase *q*. Shane has done a fine job on his *y's* (*Germany*, line 3; *very*, line 5; *they*, line 7) overall. He does reduce the descending stroke on the *y* in the word *they*, in line 7. However, three strong *y's* and one weak *y* suggest that this letter is more of a strength than a weakness. We don't have enough information on the letter *g*. He doesn't close his *g* in the word *Henning* (line 2), and does an acceptable job on the *g* in *morning* (line 5). As illustrated above, we need to consult other pieces. We do note that his only *p*, in the word *Spain* (line 8), has been self-corrected in his final draft; the midline may have facilitated this shift.

Letters Between the Baseline and Midline While a number of small letter shapes are questionable in his first draft: *w* (*two*, line 1, line 3 and line 8), *r* (*visitors*, line 1; *from*, line 1; *where*, line 8); *n* (*been*, lines 8 and 12), these letters appear to approximate more conventional formation in Shane's final draft and do not seem to warrant attention.

Spacing

Thereisnoquestionthatlegibilityiscompromisedwhenwriterscrunchwords together, or when they crunch letters within words together. Difficulties also arise when writers   leave   too   much   space   between   words or between letters in words; it takes the reader a longer time to process such texts. As we look at Shane's first and final draft, we are reminded of the importance of carrying out our primary assessment of the legibility elements in the writer's final draft. Shane's spacing, both between words and within words, in his first draft is inconsistent. (For example, more space is needed between letters in the words *visitors* and *Germany*, in line 1.) Too little spacing exists between the words *were* and *both*, in line 3; too much spacing is evident between *Questions* and *Then* in line 5.) His final draft, however, evidences fine control of spacing in gen eral. His tendency to leave a little too much space between words (line 8) seems minor at this point.

Slant

When writers slant letters too far to the right or to the left or mix the slant of letters within words, legibility issues arise. Slant generally is assessed by drawing lines through letters to determine the degree of parallelism (Figure 8–5, line 14). It is clear that Shane's control of slant is stronger in his final draft because he only has to concentrate on his handwriting. Even though only the title is marked, a quick scan of the remainder of the piece tells us that Shane leans his letters in a consistent and appropriate fashion.

Size

The large handwriting (uppercase letters are twice as large as lowercase) in Shane's final draft is characteristic of young writers (Tompkins & Hoskisson, 1991). In time, writers learn to control the size variable. In examining the size of Shane's final draft in Figure 8–7 which was written four months after "The Visitors," we note an overall reduction in size. Even though the print size in "The Visitors" is large, we note an excellent level of consistency. Uppercase letters are evenly tall, lowercase letters are evenly small. We might mention to Shane in a brief conference that, at times, his capital letters merge with or top the baseline of the previous line (i.e. *Spain*, line 8; *England* and *Ireland*, line 9). But, in the final analysis, when we pose the question, "Does the size of Shane's print impinge on legibility?" we answer, "No."

Alignment

While not a major detractor from legibility, how a writer aligns her letters—rests letters on the baseline—impacts overall neatness. As we pursue Shane's first draft, we notice that many words and/or letters float above the baseline (*from Germany*, line 1; *Henning were*, line 2; *school*, line 7 . . .). This tendency to float letters disappears in his final draft. Alignment in this piece is not an issue for Shane.

Line Quality

As with alignment, line quality impacts more on neatness than on legibility. Line quality has to do with the amount of pressure and with the steadiness of hand that a writer brings to letter formations. Wobbly strokes and uneven thickness of strokes detract somewhat from appearance. For example, in Shane's first draft, we note the restroking effort in the letter *a* in the word *Germany* (line 1) and the letter *t* in the word *about* (line 7). With the exception of the restroked letter *f* in the word *of*

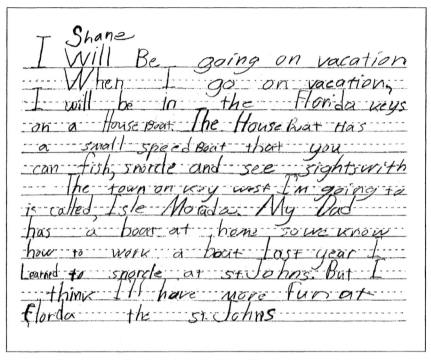

I Shane
I Will Be going on vacation
When I go on vacation,
I will be in the Florida keys
on a House Boat. The House Boat Has
a small speed Boat that you
can fish, snorcle and see sights with
The town on key west I'm going to
is called, Isle Morada. My Dad
has a boat at home so we know
how to work a boat Last year I
Learned to snorcle at st Johns. But I
think I'll have more fun at
Florda the st Johns

FIGURE 8–7   *Shane's choice for best handwriting (Term 3)*

(line 10), line quality issues do not surface in significant ways in his final draft.

In summary, we conclude that, overall, Shane's handwriting in final drafts is highly legible. Shane should be complimented on the quality of his penmanship. Over time, demonstrations of a few of the difficult letter shapes such as *q* and *j* and a reminder about not overspacing between words can occur in one-on-one writing conferences.

Since the legibility elements are concrete in nature, Shane can be asked each marking term to assess his facility with letter formations, spacing and so forth. Using a final draft, Shane can complete a self-assessment checklist such as the one in Figure 8–8. Demonstrations on how to use the checklist must be provided over a series of minilessons. Engaging children in such a self-analytical task, each term, increases their awareness of the legibility factors, and facilitates the goal-setting process. (Note: The checklist in Figure 8–8 could be modified as a record-keeping device for the teacher to use as well. The response column [*Yes, Sometimes, No*] could be substituted with Term 1, Term 2 and so on.)

Assessing Shane's Handwriting Over Time

Analysis of final drafts across the year give the truest portrait of the writer's progress in handwriting. For example, when comparing Shane's October piece, "The Visitors," (Figure 8–5) and his February final draft, "I Will Be going on vacation" (Figure 8–7), Shane noted a change in the size element of his handwriting (see transcript on page 170). The handwriting in the February piece is noticeably smaller. In addition, a number of his ascending letters start below or at the three-quarter mark rather than at the top line (in line 5: the *l*'s in *small*, the *d* in *speedboat*, the *h* in *that*; in line 11: *the l* and *d* in *learned*, the *l* in *snorcle*). Many of the cross strokes on capital letters occur just under the topline, making them more easily distinguishable. The size of the small letters are also smaller in general. While his October piece demonstrated greater consistency of size from a holistic standpoint, some variability is to be expected as Shane learns to control this smaller, more readable size.

As far as letter shapes, we see a continuation of his tendency to start the letter *t* at the midline (*to* in lines 7, 10 and 11), and the letter *k* (*Keys* in lines 3 and 7). This finding definitely warrants attention. We also note the use of the capital *B* in *HouseBoat* (line 3). Since he uses small *b*'s appropriately in other words, we can surmise that this is more a capitalization issue than a handwriting issue.

Slant in general isn't problematic. Spacing between words, however, shows more variability than did the October piece. The degree of spacing noted here, however, is considerably less than that exhibited in a first draft of "On My New Bus," (Figure 8–9) which preceded the February piece. In my interview with Shane about his writing record (see Chapter 3), recall his comment about the length of his first story:

CAROL: Are you finding that you write longer stories now?

SHANE: Yeah.

CAROL: Why is that?

SHANE: Because in the beginning of the school year, I didn't know what to write about because I didn't know much about writing. Now I do. But then I saw that everybody was having so many pages of getting writing done. So then I tried to write a lot.

CAROL: (Flipping through his writing folder and pulling out the piece in Figure 8–9): Shane, I notice that you leave big spaces here between your words compared to your Lizard story. Any reason?

SHANE: I get more pages 'cuz I spread out the words.

My Handwriting Checklist

Name _____ Date _____

	Yes	Sometimes	No

☐ LETTER SHAPES

Do my tall letters reach above the dotted
  line or midpoint?   ____   ____   ____

Do my tail letters reach down below the
  bottom line?   ____   ____   ____

Do my small letters stay between the
  bottom line and the dotted line or midpoint? ____   ____   ____

Do I close my a's, d's, e's, g's and o's?   ____   ____   ____

I need help making the letters: _____   ____   ____   ____

☐ SIZE

Do I make some of my words too big?   ____   ____   ____

Do I make some of my words too small?   ____   ____   ____

Do I make some of my letters too big?   ____   ____   ____

Do I make some of my letters too small?   ____   ____   ____

☐ SLANT

Do my letters lean in the same direction?   ____   ____   ____

☐ SPACING

Do I squish my words together because I
  forget to leave a space?   ____   ____   ____

Do I squish the letters in my words together?   ____   ____   ____

Do I leave too much space between my words?   ____   ____   ____

Do I leave too much space between the letters
  in my words?   ____   ____   ____

FIGURE 8–8 *Children assess their handwriting*

	Yes	Sometimes	No
☐ ALIGNMENT Do my letters rest on the bottom line?	____	____	____
☐ LINE QUALITY Do I make wobbly letters? Do I make my letters too thick? Do I write neatly?	____ ____ ____	____ ____ ____	____ ____ ____

- Look over this form and place two stars in the box next to your best handwriting area.
- Place one star on the line next to your next best handwriting area.
- The area that I will work harder on next term is _____

_____

FIGURE 8–8, *continued*

In accordance with his criterion of what's important when you write—lots of pages—Shane arrives at a pretty clever solution! Illustrated here, also, is the importance of talking with writers about their work. What appears to be a problem with legibility (too much spacing) is not a legibility issue at all. It is another indication of his attempt to sort out what constitutes "good" writing. Continuing discussion about the essence of writing as well as the readability of one's writing will help to move him forward.

Assessing Vanessa's Cursive Writing

The assessment of cursive writing follows the same guidelines that were spelled out previously. Since Shane used manuscript exclusively during third grade, it would have been interesting to examine Shane's handwriting in later grades. However in asking Shane—now in grade 5—about cursive, he commented, "I don't really use cursive unless my teacher asks for it." Further verification of this fact can be found in all of the surveys Shane completed for this book. All responses are printed, quite legibly and neatly, supporting the research finding that children who continue to print maintain a high, if not higher, level of legibility and speed than those who transition to cursive in grade 2 or 3 (Otto & Anderson, 1969).

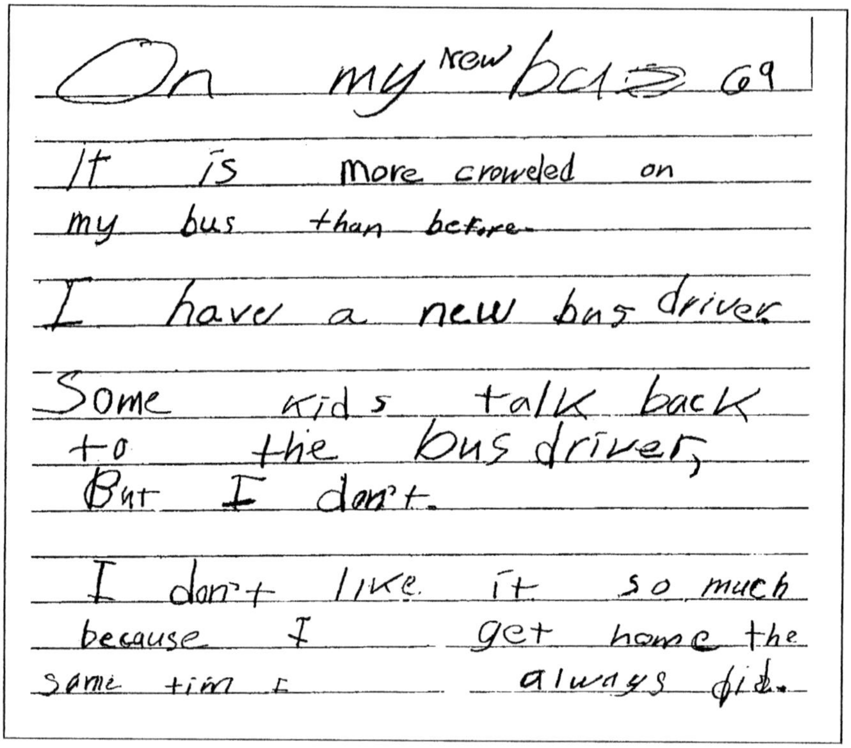
On my new bus 69
It is more crowded on my bus than before.
I have a new bus driver.
Some kids talk back to the bus driver, But I don't.
I don't like it so much because I get home the same time I always did.

FIGURE 8–9 *Shane's strategy for accumulating pages of text (spacing).*

Therefore, an excerpt from Vanessa's final draft of her autobiography (Figure 8–10), written in fourth grade, is used to make additional observations about the assessment of cursive writing.

Myers found that four letters—*a, e, r,* and *t*—cause almost fifty percent of writers' difficulty with cursive shapes (1963). Troublesome, also, are the connecting strokes that follow the letters *b, o, v,* and *w* because the connection occurs above the baseline. As we examine the letter shapes in Vanessa's piece, we are impressed to find good control over the letters *a, e,* and for the most part, *t.* We are not surprised to find some difficulty with the letter *r,* as it is the most problematic of the four letters. The *r's* in the words in the opening sentences have greater legibility than the later ones (i.e. *problem,* line 4; *children's,* line 7; *there,* line 9; *first,* line 11). Overall, Vanessa does a good job with her above-baseline connecting strokes. She correctly connects the *w* to the *a* in the word *was* (line 10), the *v* to the *e* in the word *very* (line 3), and so on. More challenging for Vanessa is the connecting stroke between the letter *o* and the following letter (i.e. *born,* line 4; *morning,* line 7; *Hospital,* line 8; *of,* line 8).

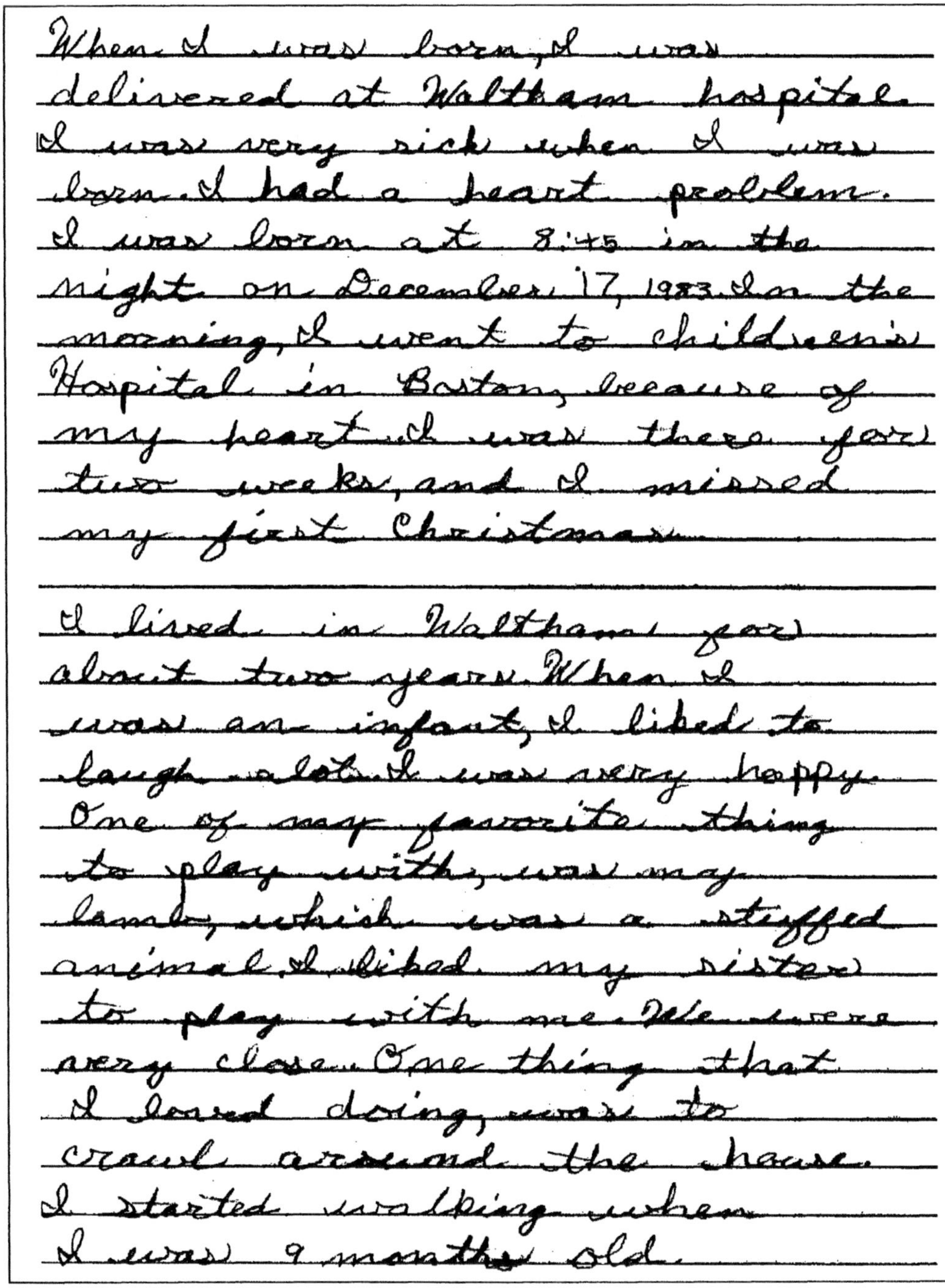

When I was born, I was
delivered at Waltham hospital.
I was very sick when I was
born. I had a heart problem.
I was born at 8:45 in the
night on December 17, 1983. In the
morning, I went to children's
Hospital in Boston, because of
my heart. I was there for
two weeks, and I missed
my first Christmas.

I lived in Waltham for
about two years. When I
was an infant, I liked to
laugh a lot. I was very happy.
One of my favorite thing
to play with, was my
lamb, which was a stuffed
animal. I liked my sister
to play with me. We were
very close. One thing that
I loved doing, was to
crawl around the house.
I started walking when
I was 9 months old.

FIGURE 8–10   *Vanessa's cursive writing*

With attention to this particular connecting stroke, to the formation of the letter *r*, and possibly the letter *b* (i.e. *problem*, line 4; *born*, line 4), Vanessa will master all of the cursive letter formations.

With the exception of not leaving enough space after each period, Vanessa demonstrates good spacing between words. Spacing within words is a little inconsistent at times (*my*, line 9; *weeks*, line 10) but does not impact significantly on legibility. When the letter shapes described above are tightened, the slant of her letters will be fairly consistent. Neither size nor alignment are major issues, although a reminder not to hug the bottom line would be beneficial.

Concluding Comments and a Word About Teacher Self-Assessment

Unlike previous chapters, where current investigations into what children do when they write have helped to guide our assessment decisions, this chapter on handwriting rests on a thin layer of research. Studies undertaken in the 1960s and 1970s were so far removed from authentic writing that their results have limited applicability. While Clay (1975) and Graves (1978, 1983, 1994) have moved us to new frontiers with regard to the investigation of what children actually do when they transcribe ideas, their research momentum has not been carried forward by other researchers. In 1978, Graves noted that ". . . research on handwriting is in its infancy when viewed within the context of the entire field of language arts" (p. 399). To my knowledge, this research has still not been undertaken.

What we have learned from Graves (1983) and Clay (1975) is that our assessment of children's handwriting must find its anchor in the current principles that underlie the writing process. Analyzing our own beliefs and practices with regard to handwriting development and instruction is an essential first step to effective assessment:

- If, as with all other aspects of learning, children create, test, and refine hypotheses about the physical act of transcription, are we observing and conferring with children about their hypotheses?
- If handwriting is not an end in itself, do we hold legibility, not perfection, as our goal?
- If four primary factors—shape, size, slant, and spacing—constitute legibility, do we collect (and ask children to collect) ongoing data on these factors, and provide developmentally appropriate instruction accordingly?

- If writers (generally grade 2 and up) concentrate on the physical aspect of writing in their final drafts, do we collect our essential assessment data from their final drafts? While analysis of first draft writing over time paints a broad picture of handwriting development, it is the analysis of handwriting in final drafts that details progress.

- If children, like adults, prefer different writing utensils and paper, do we provide a variety of materials and encourage experimentation and evaluation?

- If "handwriting is improved through practice that is not boring," do we encourage children to write every day on topics of their choice (Smith, 1982, p. 204)?

- If legible handwriting is linked to the degree of investment a writer has in a final draft of a piece, do we help children find writing projects that matter to them?

Assessing Punctuation and Capitalization

9

Thomas Edison's journal entries (see Chapters 7 and 8) show his preference for dashes over periods and, at times, for no punctuation at all. Edison probably would be pleased to know that the early Greeks wrote and understood texts that contained no punctuation, no spacing, and no capitalization, and that languages like Chinese use no punctuation. It wasn't until the 1600s that grammarians began to punctuate texts with periods and commas so that readers would know when to pause during oral chanting of a piece. This notion that writers punctuate so that readers can adopt the appropriate intonational features prevails today (Bromley, 1992; Norton, 1993), even though few modern writers expect their texts to be read aloud.

Smith, however, would counter that if we need punctuation in order to read, how is it that we have little difficulty negotiating Edison's entries (1982)? Smith makes the point that a period at the end of a sentence is of little value to the reader who is trying modulate pitch. The period in the sentence, "I will come.", gives the reader little indication of what voice to bring to the text. It is only when reader attends to the surrounding context ("I will come," she said angrily.) that appropriate intonation is harnessed. Likewise for the question mark: It comes too late in the sentence to be of any help to the reader.

If punctuation has limited utility in helping the reader navigate the text, what then is its purpose? Smith (1982) and others postulate that writers use punctuation to ensure that their intended meaning reaches the reader (Cronnell, 1980; Shaughnessy, 1977; Wilde, 1992). Punctuation marks grammatical boundaries within and between sentences, thereby signaling the author's meaning. As Smith notes, "Punctuation marks out the connected and embedded meanings in text, tracing how an argument or narrative is progressing—indicating where a particular train of thought comes to an end, where there has been a digression, and where an incomplete thread is picked up again" (1982, p. 156).

Since Edison wrote his journal entries for personal pleasure and not for publication, he adopted a system of dashes (along with occasional use of periods and commas) to mark new thoughts. Since first draft writing is the place where writers live with their ideas, formal attention to punctuation vacillates according to the writer. Hence, first drafts (grades 2 and up) are not the places where formal assessment decisions about a writer should be made. Just as with spelling, though, first drafts provide a window on the evolution of punctuation in children's writing.

What We Know About Early Punctuation Development

While the research on spelling development is rich and extensive, the research on punctuation development is paltry (Smith, 1982; Wilde, 1992). What little research exists suggests that the acquisition of punctuation parallels that of spelling development. Children attend to the punctuation they see in their print and hypothesize about its uses and functions in increasingly sophisticated ways.

Bissex (1980) notes that, at age five, Paul's earliest punctuation mark was the exclamation point which he used continually and accurately to express emotion (DOTGATNERAKOR! = Don't get near a car!). Soon thereafter, he learned with his mom's coaching that it helps the reader if the writer spaces between words. Three days later he typed a long sentence, with surprisingly accurate spaces between each word and without any prompting from his mother. Paul, however, soon rejected this notion of a blank space to mark the segmentation between words. Instead, he decided to represent segmentation with dots. From about 5 years, 6 months until 6 years, 7 months, Paul placed a dot after each word or sometimes after each syllable in order to signal spacing for the reader. Paul also showed an affinity for capital letters. Young writers show a definite preference for capital letters and make the shift to lowercase letters toward the end of first grade (Cordeiro, Giacobbe, & Cazden, 1983; Wilde, 1992).

Bissex then documents a surge in Paul's experimentation with punctuation during the second half of first grade. Within about a two month period, Paul incorporates the following punctuation marks into his writing: the apostrophe (which he uses to signal possession and contraction as well as his attempts to mark plurals with apostrophes), a question mark, parentheses, and a colon (*FROM:* and *TO:*). Bissex also notes the occasional use of the period (which she attributes to school instruction). In addition to this burst of punctuation activity, Paul abandons his dot segmentation system in favor of spaces. Learning to punctuate is not a process of steady accumulation. Young writers do not learn the form and function of the period (independently or with instruction), and then proceed to use the period faithfully in their writing. Rather, they experiment with the period by overusing it, underusing it, ignoring it—until they have finally sorted out its purpose. Meanwhile, three or four more punctuation marks may surface simultaneously and move through their own level of spurious experimentation.

The ebb and flow of the learning process is further illuminated in a fascinating study of first graders' adoption of three punctuation marks over the course of a school year (Cordeiro, Giacobbe, & Cazden, 1983). The first graders in Mary Ellen Giacobbe's classroom wrote every day on self-selected topics. They conferred frequently with her on content, chose pieces for publication, and learned one new skill (i.e. quotation marks) during an editing conference. If a child used this new skill in his next piece of writing and could explain the skill's usage, the child decided whether to record this new skill on his skills record. Such a recording indicated that the child would edit all future pieces for this skill. In examining all of the first graders' writing folders, Cordeiro et al. found three punctuation marks (possessive apostrophes, quotation marks, and periods) that received the most instruction during conferences. The researchers gathered data on the frequency of usage of each of these marks prior to any instruction, as well as after instruction. The after-instruction data was collected from the time of instruction until the end of the year. Their findings are presented in Figure 9–1.

In discussing their findings, Cordeiro et al. make the point that children's knowledge and use of punctuation evolve over time toward conventional punctuation. They note, though, that punctuation development is slower than that of spelling (the study also included a look at spelling attempts). Explicit instruction on some punctuation marks is productive, as long the writer shows a readiness to learn particular features. They advocate a process approach to writing because it affords on ample opportunities for children to learn about punctuation intuitively as well directly.

Assessing Vanessa's Punctuation Over Grade 1

To highlight the high level of experimentation that accompanies the development of punctuation, we are ready to inspect Vanessa's first-grade pieces.

In October of first grade, Vanessa's journal entry (Figure 9–2) shows accurate usage of a parenthesis, an apostrophe, a period, an exclamation point, and capitalization of the name of a holiday and the pronoun *I*. Vanessa intuitively understands that secondary information is enclosed in a parenthesis. Since the reader can infer that the author likes Halloween because she gets candy, Vanessa chooses to make this information

---

What Children Know About Punctuation: Before and After Instruction

PERIOD:
> Thirteen children were taught (and retaught and retaught) the function/form of the period. Prior to instruction, twenty-five percent of their attempts to punctuate with a period were correct. After instruction, fifty-seven percent of their attempts were correct. Interestingly, the nine children who received no formal instruction came close to matching their peers; forty-nine percent figured out the period on their own over the course of the year.

POSSESSIVE APOSTROPHE:
> Six out of twenty-two children showed a readiness to learn the function/form of the apostrophe. Before instruction, only sixteen percent of their attempts were correct. After instruction, fifty-six percent of their attempts were correct. The children's approximations included the overgeneralization of the apostrophe to plurals and to verbs. Of the sixteen children who received no instruction, only twelve percent of their attempts over the course of the year were accurate.

QUOTATION MARKS:
> Six children were taught when and how to use quotation marks. Prior to instruction, none of the children used quotation marks. After instruction, fifty-three percent of their attempts to use quotation marks were accurate. Of the children not receiving instruction, seventeen percent of their sentences containing dialogue were marked correctly.

Figure 9–1 *Findings on children's experimentation with punctuation—before and after instruction (Cordiero et al., 1983)*

optional. Characteristic of many young (and not so young) writers is Vanessa's run-on sentence (. . . I gaut candy and I,m going to be a ciowgirl.) Learning to mark sentence boundaries with periods occurs over time (Figure 9–1) and can be facilitated with feedback during writing conferences. While placement of the apostrophe in *I,m* dips below its usual placement, it is an indication that Vanessa has some awareness of the apostrophe. Her exclamation point appropriately signals her excitement about Halloween. Basic elements of capitalization seem in order with the exception of capital *B* (*Because* and *Be*) in midstream. We noted earlier that for many young writers, capital letters prevail over lowercase letters for much of first grade. Vanessa, however, already has adopted lowercase letters. It is not surprising that *B* is the last uppercase letter to

I like Halloween (Be <u>because</u> cos) I gaut ^{get} candy and I'm going to be a ciowgirl ^{Cowgirl}. Happy Halbween!

Wonderful Work Vanessa You did a great job Sounding out words I really like your picture

FIGURE 9–2   *Vanessa's personal narrative: Punctuation in October*

prevail, given the directionality issues that lowercase *b* and *d* present to most young writers.

As Figure 9–3 reveals, Vanessa's experimentation with punctuation is put on hold as she attends to the ingredients in her gingerbread recipe, written two months after the Halloween piece.

Notice that while her first sentence doesn't end with a period, she does capitalize the word *Then* to signal the start of a new sentence. Notice also that, at least in this piece, lowercase *b* is intact. This gingerbread entry was selected from a flurry of journal writing in which Vanessa engaged over the two weeks prior to Christmas to make the point about variability in writer's growth. The lack of punctuation in this entry doesn't mean her earlier (October) understandings about punctuation have disappeared. In fact, the entries which surround the gingerbread piece indicate that she uses many periods to mark sentence boundaries, although run-on sentences continue. She experiments with two commas in one entry, suggesting a beginning understanding of the role of commas in lists. Thus, Vanessa's punctuation development hasn't receded; it simply manifests itself in spurts. At times, these spurts consolidate old understandings; at other times they evidence new understandings. It is possible, also, that Vanessa adopts a no-punctuation stance in Figure 9–3 because of the genre (directions). She may have reasoned that since

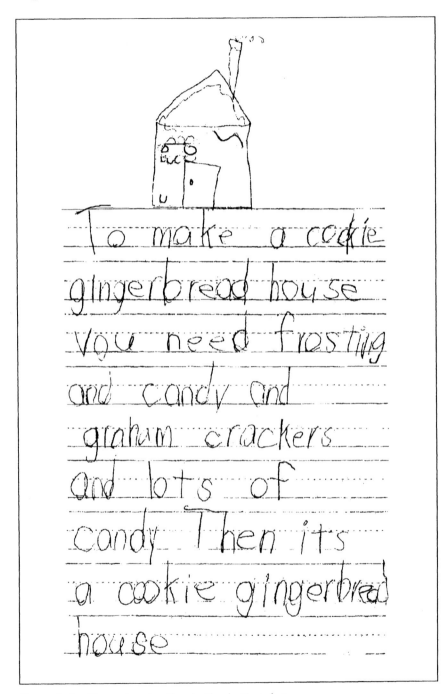

FIGURE 9–3   *Vanessa's recipe: Punctuation in December*

stories and directions have different purposes, their punctuation needs to be different: new genre, new hypotheses about punctuation.

In addition to journal entries, two stories attest to Vanessa's burgeoning knowledge about punctuation. The first story (Figure 9–4) was written early in the school year; the second story at the end of first grade (Figure 9–5).

Vanessa successfully uses dialogue to bring her teddy bear to life (Figure 9–4). While she has yet to learn how to punctuate dialogue, she intuitively understands the role of dialogue in character portrayal. Her adoption of the conjunction *and* essentially eliminates the need to mark sentences with periods. While we saw her earlier use of the apostrophe in the contraction *I,m* we note that neither *whats* nor *yours* is punctuated. Capitalization is reserved for parts of the story title, for one of the characters in the story (*Vanessa*), and for the pronoun *I*. An occasional capital is sprinkled throughout the text (Said, My, Sore [sure] . . .) which may be more a feature of handwriting than capitalization.

Approximately six months later, Vanessa authors and publishes her first story, "The Mean King and Queen." The initial part of the story has been typed and is presented on the top of Figure 9–5; Vanessa's original ending is at the bottom.

Indeed, compared with "The Day My Bear Came to Life," Figure 9–5 is bursting with punctuation. Of the sixteen sentences included, Vanessa correctly marks thirteen sentence boundaries with periods. Run-on sentences that characterize much of her earlier first grade writing are not evident in this piece. For the first time, we note Vanessa's attention to internal sentence structure with the placement of two essential commas. The first comma is used to mark off the dependent clause (one night when the king and Queen were asleep, someone Broke in.). The second comma is used to separate the dialogue carrier from the dialogue (The witch said, "You are mean and that's why I came here to night."). Delightful, also, is Vanessa's adoption of quotation marks, and accurate use of the apostrophe to signal the contraction (*that's*) and as well as to mark possession (*King's Birthday*).

As for capitalization, Vanessa successfully marks each new sentence with a capital letter, with two exceptions. She also uses capitals to signal semantically important information such as King and Queen with much consistency. Once again, we see her tendency to use uppercase *B* (*Birthday, But, Because, Broke*) throughout this piece, although some lowercase *b*'s are included (*big, beautiful*). Interestingly, Vanessa also capitalizes most words that begin with the letter *t*, especially in the first half of the story. She does not capitalize the letter *t*, however, when it occurs in the middle or at the end of a word. Since this phenomenon was not observed in any of her earlier writing, it may represent the creation of a

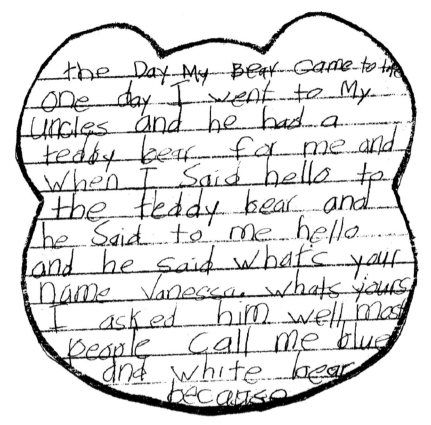

FIGURE 9–4 *Vanessa's story: Punctuation in Fall*

new hypothesis, or it may be an issue of penmanship. A quick conversation with Vanessa might shed some light on her thinking here. Researchers who have interviewed first graders about their understandings of spacing and punctuation report that children know that letters and punctuation have different functions but are not able to conceptualize these differences nor are they able to specify attributes of each punctuation mark (de Goes & Martlew, 1983).

What Do We Know About Later Punctuation Development?

By third grade, if children are immersed in daily writing workshops, they are able to use and to explain an impressive array of punctuation (Calkins, 1980b). At the end of the school year, Calkins interviewed children from two classrooms about the form and function of punctua-

FIGURE 9–4, *continued*

tion. One classroom used writing process as described by Graves (1983); the other received traditional instruction in mechanics through language workbooks. Calkins first asked children questions like "Do you like punctuation?" "What's it good for?" Then, she wrote fourteen punctuation marks, one at time, and asked, "What's it for?" Her findings, summarized in Figure 9–6, are instructive.

As Calkins's study demonstrates, children who use punctuation in order to give voice and clarity to their messages internalize significantly more advanced understandings about the function and usage of punctuation. Children who come to punctuation through language workbooks view it as something separate from writing, as a series of isolated exercises. As Calkins points out, "Forty-seven percent of the explanations writers gave for punctuation referred to the way it affects the pace and inflection of language. Only nine percent of the non-writers' definitions referred to this" (1980b, p. 570).

Once upon a time
There lived a King
and Queen. They
had a mean old
cat. They wiere
rich and They
lived in a big old
castle. One day
it was The
King's Birthday

But The King did
not get any presents
Because every one
knew That He was
mean. He was The
meanest king in The
world

The King was mad.
Even though
the Queen is mean
The Queen is still
beautiful. The King
was a warlock.
and the Queen
was a witch

one night when
the king and Queen
were asleep,
someone Broke in.
It was a witch.

FIGURE 9–5 *Vanessa's story: Punctuation in Spring*

WRITERS LEARN TO PUNCTUATE BY WRITING

Traditional Classroom

Children explained 3.8 marks on average.

50% or more of the children defined/ explained the following marks by reciting rules:

.

?

!

Writer's Workshop

Children explained 8.66 marks on average.

50% or more of the children defined/ explained the following marks by demonstrating use in their own writing:

.

?

!

,

" "

,

^

FIGURE 9–6   *Calkins's (1980b) findings about third graders's punctuation development*

Assessing Shane's Punctuation at the Beginning of Grade 3

Recall our previous discussion about Graves's (1983) findings concerning children's perceptions of "good" writing (Chapter 4, Figure 4–6). For emerging writers, spelling and handwriting equate to good writing. After children gain some facility with spelling and handwriting, the conventions of punctuation, capitalization, and grammar take precedence. Finally, concern for content prevails; young writers understand that good writing is tied to the quality of their message.

Shane, like many third graders, is preoccupied with punctuation. As Figure 9–7 demonstrates, Shane's concern about punctuation continues throughout the school year. However, Figure 9–7 also demonstrates his increasing awareness about the importance of content.

Analysis of Shane's use of punctuation begins with his one of his earliest personal narratives on the dentist (Chapter 3, Figure 3–5). (This dentist piece is included in his collaborative portfolio as baseline data for personal narratives.) Since it is important to assess across samples in the same time period, we also include another entry, "The red sox game" (Figure 9–8). Together, these pieces serve as tentative baseline data against which later work can be compared. (This baseline is considered tentative because assessment of punctuation in first draft writing permits only preliminary conclusions to be drawn. Formal assessment needs to occur in self-edited final drafts.)

Of the fifteen sentences that comprise both entries (Figure 9–8), Shane has successfully marked seven sentences with both capitals and periods (i.e., "Wade boggs hit a home run."). A number of the remaining sentences exhibited one sentence boundary marker, either the capital or the period but not both (i.e., "I had fun"). No internal punctuation (commas, semicolons, colons) is evident.

When examining the opening sentences of each entry ("When i went to the baseball game." "When I went to the dentist."), we initially might conclude that Shane has yet to sort out the difference between a dependent clause and an independent clause, and the corresponding punctuation. However, in the Red Sox piece, we note some level of clausal understanding in the sentence "When i got home I went right to

---

SHANE'S RESPONSES TO ATWELL'S *WRITING SURVEY* IN SEPTEMBER
(See original in Appendix A):

4. What do you think a good writer needs to do in order to write well?
   use captial and peeriods

5. How does your teacher decide which pieces of writing are the good ones?
   if the writing is like it showd be

SHANE'S WRITTEN REFLECTION ON MEETING HIS WRITING GOALS IN JANUARY:
   I have learned punctiation, not to always skip lines, and that the more you write the better your storys should get.

SHANE'S RESPONSES TO ATWELL'S *WRITING SURVEY* IN MARCH
(see original in Appendix B):

4. What do you think a good writer needs to do in order to write well?
   Making a story people understand

5. How does your teacher decide which pieces of writing are the good ones?
   the ones that have good punctuation

FIGURE 9–7   *The place of punctuation in Shane's thinking over time*

SHANE'S EARLY SEPTEMBER ENTRIES

The red sox game
When i went to the baseball game. Me and my dad had to borow my grandmothers car.
And on the way we saw some of my dad's friends they had seats next to us. And we
stoped at burger king i got a cheese burger then we went to fenway park. The red sox
wer vs the angels. Wade boggs hit a home run. Then some body got a run The red sox
won. When i got home i went right to bed. I had fun

When I went to the dentist. I already had one tooth out. And two were loose. The
denist took ex rays then they cleaned my teeth. Then it was my brothers turn. And
before we left he pulled one of my teeth.

FIGURE 9–8 *Baseline data on Shane's punctuation at the beginning of third grade*

bed." While Shane doesn't set off the dependent clause with a comma,
he also doesn't use a period. In looking at the lead sentences in some of
his subsequent pieces written during the first term, an interesting pattern emerges:

> When I went to the batting cages. the balls went 45 miles per hour.
> Today when I went to reading. Greg had to remind me.
> When I go to soccer practice. I bring a snack.

My hunch is that Shane has created a unique strategy for titling his
personal narratives. It appears that he uses his dependent clause to signal both the title of his piece and the opening part of his sentence.
Shane only places a period at the end of the dependent clauses in his
lead sentences. In other sentences which contain dependent and independent clauses, he uses no punctuation to separate his dependent
clauses. Over time, Shane refines his hypothesis about titling personal
narratives. In January, he uses both a title ("the Children muesam")
and the dependent clause of the lead sentence (When I went to the
children's muesam,) to signal his topic. Commas now seem to replace
the periods. He organizes this piece (original in Chapter 4, Figure 4–8)
as follows:

> the Children muesam (Title)
> When I went to the Children's muesam, (Subtitle of sorts)
> (Shane skips a line.)
> I did alot of fun things like they had these special telaphones you could
> press a button and you could talk about something personal. They had . . .

Shane's problem-solving strategy is a wonderful example of the cognitive powers of the young mind. He decides he wants to provide the reader with a context for many of his personal narratives. However, because he hasn't read any published journals, he doesn't have any models on which to rely. So he invents his own strategy for titling and refines it over time.

Returning to Figure 9–8, Shane shows no awareness of commas and apostrophes. He does not set off dependent clauses, nor does he set off phrases ("And on the way home we saw. . . . ; And before we left he pulled. . . ."). He does not show possession ("grandmothers car"; "dads friends"; "brothers turn"). Remember, we cannot conclude, with any certainty, that he does not understand these punctuation marks because we are inspecting first drafts.

Shane's understanding of sentence capitalization seems solid. Whenever Shane ends what he considers to be a sentence, he capitalizes the first word of the next "sentence." Capitalization of the personal pronoun *I* fluctuates in the pieces in Figure 9–8. In the Red Sox piece, he includes two *i*'s and one *I*; this is a step forward from his very first entry (not included) which contained only lowercase *i*'s. In the dentist piece, he shifts to appropriate usage. A look at subsequent pieces in his writing folder shows correct usage of this personal pronoun. Capitalization of proper nouns does not seem to be internalized yet (red sox, angels, boggs, burger king, fenway park). Interestingly, though, he does capitalize the proper nouns in the titles of the pieces he records on this writing record (e.g. Red Sox, Riverside Park, President). Capitalization of the days of the week and month seem intact.

To this point, we have concentrated on Shane's developing knowledge of punctuation in his first draft writing. Now we turn to a primary source of assessment data—Shane's edit of his "best" piece—written at the end of the first term. His final draft of "The Visitors" (original in Chapter 4, Figure 4–11) enables us to see what punctuation knowledge he brings when he is not attending solely to meaning. Because the photocopy of Figure 4–11 in Chapter 4 makes it difficult to distinguish Shane's edit from Alice's final edit, a typed version of this piece is presented in Figure 9–9.

Given Shane's concern about punctuation on his writing survey (Appendix A), it is somewhat surprising to find that he made only two changes in capitalization (York and Canton) and no changes in punctuation. Learning to self-edit is a complex activity that takes time to develop and that needs much demonstration on our part.

We note his continuing tendency in this piece to use part of his opening sentence as a title for his piece. Of the ten sentences included,

Today two vistors came. From Germany. Andrae and Henning were there names. They were both very tall. In the morning they took Questions. They told about there school. they told where they have been. they have been to Spain, England, Ireland and united states of America. in the united states of America they have been to New york, Boston, and canton. of the Questions were finished they stayed for a while then they went →

FIGURE 9–9   *Shane's edited version of a personal narrative*

four sentences contain appropriate capitals and periods. Not surprisingly, these are his first four sentences. Many writers tend to start pieces with attention to the mechanics but then shift focus as meaning takes over. The next five sentences are marked appropriately with periods, but first words are not capitalized. Commas are used to separate items in his list of countries and of cities. Shane does not use commas, though, to mark phrases or dependent clauses.

Capitalization of foreign countries is excellent; cities fare pretty well also. Shane's performance with capitals synchronizes well with Odom's findings on fourth graders' knowledge of capitals (1962). Seventy-nine percent of the fourth graders capitalized cites; seventy-one percent capitalized the personal pronoun *I*; sixty-seven percent, countries; sixty-four percent, days of the week and the months; fifty-seven percent, proper names. Only thirty-nine percent capitalized the first word in a sentence.

Given the above analysis, and a review of what Shane does with punctuation in surrounding pieces, we venture a reflective note that will be attached to his pieces at the end of the first term. The content of the note is shown in Figure 9–10:

Shane's ability to mark sentence boundaries continues to improve. By the end of the term, he uses periods to end his sentences, and capitalizes the first words in sentences about half of the time. His capitalization of countries and cities, days of the week, and months is strong; his capitalization of proper nouns is improving. With the exception of setting off items in a list with commas, no internal punctuation is evident. He uses an interesting strategy for titling his pieces which needs clarification. Preliminary data on contractions and possessives suggest he has yet to internalize these operations, although data is scarce. When editing his work, Shane gives some attention to capitalization, but none to punctuation.

FIGURE 9–10   *Reflective note on Shane's punctuation growth (Term 1)*

Assessing Shane's Punctuation
at the Midpoint of Grade 3

Having collected preliminary data on Shane's punctuation usage, we now examine portfolio pieces at the midpoint of the year to substantiate (or challenge) our initial conclusions, to mark further refinement, and to note the emergence of new punctuation knowledge.

We start with the piece, "On My New Bus" (Figure 9–11) (original in Chapter 8, Figure 8–9). Perhaps most noticeable about this piece, and many of the entries written around this time, is Shane's omission of the conjunctive links (e.g., *and, then, and then*) that characterized much of his writing at the beginning of the year. Omission of these links appears to have tempered Shane's proclivity for run-on sentences. Noticeable also are the physical breaks (see original, Figure 8–9) that Shane inserts between each sentence. Perhaps this phenomenon is a result of the paragraph instruction that Shane and his peers received during minilessons on editing. As with any new skill, learners often go through a phase of overgeneralization.

Shane demonstrates not only strong sentence sense in this piece but also more advanced use of punctuation and capitalization. Sentence boundaries are clearly marked with appropriate capitals and periods (with the exception of the opening sentence—the first letter in the first word, *it*, looks like a very tall, lowercase *i*). For the first time, Shane uses internal punctuation, inserting a comma before the conjunction *But* in the sentence: "Some kids talk back to the bus driver, But I don't." Shane probably capitalized the conjunction *But* out of habit. In a number of previous pieces, he begins many of his sentences with *But* and capitalizes it appropriately. Thus, his capitalization of *but* in this sentence suggests a tenuous understanding of role of internal punctuation. This observation is supported by the fact that he does not use internal punctuation to separate clauses in the other sentences in this piece. We continue to note proper capitalization of the personal pronoun *I*. As for capitalization of

---

it is more crowded on my new bus than before.
I have a new bus driver.
Some kids talk back to the bus driver, But I don't.
I don't like it so much because I get home the same tim I always did.
When I am on the bus I usually sit with michael.
My dad said if I be good I'll be none as a good kid to the bus driver.
And so far I have been good.

FIGURE 9–11   *Shane's punctuation development (Midyear): "On My New Bus"*

proper names, Shane doesn't capitalize his friend's name. A quick skim of November and December entries reveals increased facility with name capitalization (Mrs. Butler, Ms. Doherty, John F. Kennedy, Ken) but this concept has yet to stabilize in first draft writing (brian, griffey). We also see his use of the apostrophe to mark the contractions *don't* and *I'll.*

Additional data is available in his "best" piece of the third term, "I am going on vacation." Figure 9–12 presents his first and final draft of this piece (original of his final draft is in Chapter 8, Figure 8–7).

Shane's first draft shows continued adherence to his titling hypothesis (see page 197). Here, as in previous pieces, Shane creates a title and then uses his opening dependent clause as a subtitle. He sets off his subtitle by skipping a line between his opening dependent clause ("When I go on vacation,") and the remainder of his sentence. In his final draft, however, he abandons his subtitling strategy and correctly punctuates his opening sentence. It would be premature, though, to attribute his

---

FIRST DRAFT

                     I am going on vaction
When I go on vacation,
(Shane skipped a line.)
I will be going to the Florida Keys.
(Shane skipped a line.)
I will be at Key West on a houseboat.
(Shane skipped a line.)
The houseboat has a small speed boat that you can fish, snorkle, and see sights with. The town on Key West I'm going on is called isle marada. My Dad has a boat at home so we know how to work a boat. Last year I learned how to snorkle at St. John's.

    It was nice at St. John's but I think I'll have more fun at florida. My mom said were not going to Disney. I have never been on a houseboat but I'll have fun.

FINAL DRAFT

                     I Will Be going on vacation
    When I go on vacation, I will be in the Florida keys on a HouseBoat. The HouseBoat Has a small speedBoat that you can fish, snorkle, anzd see sights with.

    The town on key west I'm going to is called, Isle Morada. My Dad had a boat at home so we know how to work a boat. Last year I Learned to snorkle at st. Johns. But I think I'll have more fun at Florida the st. John's.

FIGURE 9–12   *Shane's punctuation development (Term 3)*

correct punctuation in this lead sentence to a true understanding of dependent clauses. Other examples with which to corroborate this finding aren't available in this piece. In surrounding pieces, dependent clauses aren't marked (i.e., "When they got their the motel seemed old.") My guess is that his placement of the comma after *vacation* is a carry-over from his subtitling strategy. His writing folder shows continued use of his titling/subtitling strategy. Two weeks after the vacation piece (Figure 9–12), Shane writes the draft:

> *Febuary Vaction at roll-land*
> (Shane skips a line)
> During Febuary vacation,
> (Shane skips a line)
> I went roller-skating with my family (my dad did good for his first time skating.) . . .

Shane's insertion of a comma before *Isle Morada* in his final draft (Figure 9–12), however, is an indication that he is beginning to notice internal punctuation in print. We can expect to see increased experimentation over the next few months.

His control of sentence boundaries in both his first and final draft is strong. All of the sentences in his first draft begin with a capital and end with a period. With the exception of a missing period in his final sentence, his final draft also contains appropriate sentence boundary punctuation. His use of commas to separate verbs in the second sentence corroborates earlier observations concerning his understanding of the importance of separating words in a series. Continued success with contractions (I'm, I'll) is noted. Shane has punctuated the abbreviation in St. John's correctly in both first and final drafts.

With the exception of *isle marada,* and *florida,* capitalization of place is excellent in his first draft. Interestingly, while Shane correctly edits both *Isle Morada,* and *Florida* in his final draft, he doesn't capitalize *st. John's* or *key west* in his final draft. There is a chance that, in fact, Shane thought he capitalized *st. John's* and *key west.* Notice his capitalization of the words *HouseBoat* in sentence two as well as *Has* and *speedBoat* in sentence three in Shane's original piece (Chapter 8, Figure 8–7). He squeezes these capital letters between the bottom and dotted lines. It is possible that since Shane usually writes on regular paper, he may have had a little difficulty negotiating this dotted-line paper. It is interesting that Shane edited *houseboat* in his first draft to *HouseBoat* in his final draft. He must have decided that since it was a particular kind of boat, it deserved proper noun status.

In an investigation of punctuation usage, Calkins found that third graders at the beginning of the year

> . . . only needed an average of 2.2 different kinds of punctuation to correctly punctuate a piece of writing, and they used an average of 1.25 kinds. They wrote mostly simple sentences, without dialogue, sound effects, supportive information, or exclamations . . . By February, . . . they used an average of five different kinds in one piece. (1980b, p. 571)

Shane's early September pieces included only periods. His January "muesam" piece (Chapter 4, Figure 4–8) included: periods, a semicolon, parentheses, exclamation points, an apostrophe, and a comma. Shane's progress in the areas of punctuation and capitalization is tied to the daily opportunities that he has had to read and write. It is tied to his ability to create, test, and refine hypotheses about how written language works, including the conventions of punctuation and capitalization. His progress also is tied to the instruction he received in these areas—instruction that addressed his and his classmates' demonstrated needs and interests.

Shane's Punctuation Development (Grade 5)

Recall that in one of my meetings with Shane, I asked Shane, now a fifth grader, to reread and react to his third-grade story, "The Lizard and the Motorcycle." Shane graciously did so and then offered to rewrite his third-grade story. The revision of this story is presented in Appendix F.

It is impossible to compare and contrast the punctuation in Shane's third-grade and fifth-grade versions of "The Lizard and the Motorcycle" without first marveling at Shane's increasingly sophisticated ability to construct meaning. Shane's revision shows marked sensitivity to the syntactic and semantic aspects of written language. The more complex his grammatical structures, the greater his need for punctuation. Consider the following example.

Original third grade version	*Revision two years later (fifth grade)*
And he climbed out and when he got there he found his motorcycle and then he went back to his room but it did not seen the same but he said hmm i'm shore this is my room but what hapend to it.	They climbed out, found Lizard's motorcycle and went back to Lizards room. But it did not seem the same. He said, "Hmmm. I'm sure this is my room but it does not seem the same. What happened to it? . . ."

Shane, the fifth grader, has transformed the chain of kernel sentences that were linked by the string of *ands* into more syntactically complex and appropriate sentences (Appendix F). We note that he not only reduces the redundancy in the first part of his text but also uses a comma to separate the predicates. In addition, he uses commas to:

- separate a series (monkeys, tiger, lions, bears, and crocodiles.)
- mark dialogue carriers (He said, "Hmmm . . .")
- set off parenthetical expressions (Meanwhile, . . .)

In addition, Shane uses commas to punctuate some of his dependent clauses ("Before they ran out of food, . . ."), but not all ("But whenever Lizard went near any other animal they would laugh at him."). As we would suspect, Shane's comma knowledge and usage has grown dramatically over two years.

Shane punctuates dialogue in the above example, and elsewhere in the revised piece, with great accuracy. Quotation marks were rarely used by Shane in third grade. Two years of extensive reading, along with classroom instruction, have contributed to his understanding of dialogue markers.

On a side note, you may be wondering about Shane's shift from *he* to *they* in the previous example. In the original story, both Lizard and Owl start out on the motorcycle, but Owl somehow drops out of the picture. Shane, the fifth grader, recognizes this inconsistency, and decides to rebuild the cohesion by substituting *they* for *he*. Children as early as second grade use primary cohesive devices such as personal pronouns (he, she, him, her, them . . .) to signal referents in their texts or relative pronouns (who, whom, whose) to clarify relationships (King & Rentel, 1981).

Concluding Comments and a Word About Teacher Self-Assessment

We conclude this chapter with a comparison of Shane's rate of punctuation accuracy on his self-edited Lizard story (Appendix F) with the findings of NAEP's *The Writing Report Card* (Applebee, Langer, Mullis, & Jenkins, 1990). Using fourth graders' first drafts of a persuasive piece, written "on demand in a relatively short time" (p. 7), these researchers found that children made an average of 3.1 punctuation errors in 100 words. Most of these errors were errors of omission (an average of 2.9 words per 100), rather than errors of commission (average of .2 per 100 words). In calculating Shane's total number of punctuation errors per

100 words in his self-edited piece, an average of 3.5 errors were noted: 3 punctuation omissions and .5 actual errors per 100 words. Shane, like most of the NAEP writers, makes relatively few errors in punctuation. The NAEP researchers, Applebee, Langer, Mullis, and Jenkins, remind us that:

> In 1984 and 1988, it is clear that most students were able to control the conventions of written English. If many fourth graders still have difficulties with spelling and with some aspects of grammar and usage, most of these problems disappear by grade 11. Even the best papers written for the assessment contained some errors, and these are to be expected in first-draft writing. . . . Thus while focused instruction in the conventions of written language may be necessary for certain individuals or subpopulations of students, additional whole-class drill and practice is not likely to be useful for the majority for students. (1990, p. 58)

In previous chapters, we emphasized that before assessing children's work, we must first assess ourselves and the kind of learning environment we have created for and with children. This principle holds true in this chapter on punctuation. Since most of teacher self-assessment questions at the end of Chapter 7 parallel the questions that would end this chapter (with the substitution of the word *punctuation* for *spelling*), they will not be repeated here. If we view writing as both process and product, and have adopted the philosophy and practice of the writing workshop (Atwell, 1987; Calkins, 1986, 1994; Graves, 1983, 1994), rich in mediated instruction, we can expect learning to be as active in the area of punctuation as it is in the area of spelling.

But How Do I Do All of This? *10*

When I turned forty years old, I enrolled in an Irish Ceili dancing class. I explained to family and friends that I wanted to reclaim a small part of my heritage. Of course, my thirty-nine-year-old sister countered that I was in the grip of a midlife crisis. Whatever my motivation, I vividly recall my first class. I arrived (with my mother because I was too cowardly to go alone) and expected to sit along the sidelines for most of the evening. Instead, my Ceili teacher, Maureen Keohane, tossed me into the first dance of the evening. While the other seven members of the group used a basic step, called the sevens, to move around and through the circle, I skipped. My patient partner dragged me in one direction or another. Maureen, at times, took my hand and moved me through a step. And so the night went, dance after dance. I desperately wanted to be taken to a corner and to be introduced to the basic step. I wanted to be introduced to one dance, not six. I also wanted to dance only with the newcomers, and not with the experienced dancers. But I had no choice. By the end of the evening, I felt so overwhelmed, and so awkward that thoughts of quitting ran rampant. If it wasn't for the kindness and encouragement of my fellow dancers, and for the laughter and camaraderie, I probably would have quit.

At about the same time I began Ceili dancing, I began experimenting with portfolio assessment. Moving into portfolio assessment was as exciting, frustrating, and overwhelming as Ceili dancing. Doubts about my ability to implement portfolio assessment surfaced regularly. Unsure what to collect, and when to collect it, I waited until the end of the marking term to gather data. After taking home my first crateful of portfolios to analyze and being overwhelmed by the enormity of the task, I vowed never to set myself up for failure again. The more I read about portfolios, the more I realized that I instinctively had taken charge of the assessment process and had not factored the children into the assessment equation. With that realization, I became checklist-happy, swamping children with one form after another. Their robotic approach to the checklists subsequently caused me to question the validity of the whole process. Indeed, I had a great deal to learn.

Five years have passed since that first Ceili lesson and first batch of portfolios. Thanks to the brief but intensive one-on-one tutoring of my teacher and codancers, and to a fair amount of practice, I have learned my sevens. I have committed a few dances to memory but still rely on the whispers of my more experienced partners. I also have come to appreciate Maureen's wisdom. It was through her modeling that I came to realize that Cambourne's (1988) conditions for optimal literacy learning apply to all learning situations, including the implementation of portfolio assessment.

This realization occurred one evening as I watched Maureen observe a newcomer stumble through a dance. The new dancer used a sliding step, didn't have her arms in position, and wasn't in time with the music. Maureen ignored all of this emerging behavior and concentrated on helping her with the overall choreography of the dance. As I watched, it dawned on me that this was yet another example of Cambourne's condition of "approximation." Maureen understood that this learner needed to feel the rhythm of the music, and to dance the dance with whatever approximations she could muster. Driving home that evening, as I was chastising myself about my overuse of checklists, I realized that I needed to give myself permission to "approximate." I needed to accept the fact that I would make mistakes during portfolio implementation and that my penchant for perfection would have to be kept in check. Learning a new way of thinking and of performing—whether it be Ceili dancing, literacy, or portfolio assessment—necessitates a tolerance for ambiguity and error. It also necessitates the presence of the other essential conditions (Cambourne, 1988).

Conditions for Portfolio Assessment Learning

Immersion and Responsibility

For me, the desire to attain intellectual mastery of a subject precedes the desire to act. However, if I waited to master all of the available research, I would never start. I had to immerse myself in the process of portfolio assessment even though my knowledge was rudimentary. As noted in Chapter 1, the acquisition of knowledge emerges from two sources: focused observations of children and self-study. I needed to observe what children did with their portfolios. I needed to create hypotheses about their understandings and to test those hypotheses against further observation and the accumulated research. New knowledge requires the continual interplay of both of these dynamics. But the responsibility of deciding how the process of portfolio implementation would unfold remained mine. As

Cambourne notes, ". . . the learner . . . is left to decide just what part of the task will be internalized at any one time" (1988, p. 36). I had to figure out what I could handle at any one point in time and pursue that goal.

Demonstration

In order to consolidate my understanding of portfolio assessment, I needed to read about it, talk about it with colleagues, observe it in action, and read more about it. Immersion in the portfolio literature, participation in professional workshops, direct observation of colleagues' implementation, feedback on my implementation, and ongoing discussions with colleagues and experts constituted essential demonstrations. It is through these layers of self-study and collegial exchange that I found the energy to continue, and the strength to sustain.

Expectation and Engagement

Demonstration after demonstration, however, would not pull me into portfolio assessment unless I deemed such activity as purposeful and as within my capabilities. I had to accept that my confidence and skill levels would ebb and flow and to believe that I could succeed over time. Once I vowed to march ahead, I set high standards for myself and problem-solved as I went. I learned to trust my own judgment and to lean on what I had learned from the literature and from my colleagues.

Response

How did I know I was on the right track? All learners need feedback on their performance. Historically, though, the school culture has been one in which teachers operate in isolation with occasional administrative visits for the purpose of formal evaluation (Lortie, 1975). Fortunately, with the recent resurgence of Dewey's notions about the social nature of learning, professional collaboration in the form of teacher study groups, inclusion, and peer coaching has taken hold in many schools (1959). Joining (or starting) a study group to examine the complexities of portfolio assessment or inviting a respected colleague into our classroom signals our readiness for genuine self-assessment. I accept the viability of Vygotsky's "zone of proximal development" for the children with whom I work; I need to accept that same zone of proximal learning for myself (1978, p. 86).

Use

Children need continual practice reading and writing—practice which occurs in the context of genuine literate activity (Cambourne, 1988). Practice, also, is essential to the art of assessment. I need to use my assessment knowledge on a daily basis as I observe and confer with writers and as I examine their writing samples. I need to keep the goal of marking children's writing development over time at the forefront, and to try not to get tangled in the technical aspects of the portfolio process. This is not to suggest that a preoccupation with the details of portfolio assessment did not consume my attention periodically. As the following overview of the teacher change research shows, meaningful change is a process of persistent, ongoing inquiry.

Teacher Change

The research on initiating and sustaining change in the classroom shows that teachers tend to move through identifiable phases (Berman & McLaughlin, 1978; Emrich & Peterson, 1978). One of the most popular developmental schemes suggests that we advance from the initiation phase of change, to the implementation phase, and finally to the adoption phase. Each phase is accompanied by a shift in our focus of concern (Hall & Loucks, 1979):

1) Self

At the onset of change, our primary response is personal in nature: "I am interested in portfolio assessment and would like to find out more about it." An introduction to portfolio assessment leads to questions like, "Do I want to do this? Can I do this? What do I need to know to do this? How much time do I need to invest?. . ."

2) Task

With a tentative commitment to portfolio assessment, our concern shifts to management of the task. Questions related to time and resource management prevail: "How do I fit this into an already bulging curriculum? When do I introduce the portfolio to the children? What is included in the portfolio? Who fills in what form? Where do I store the portfolios?"

3) Impact

Having worked out the technical aspects of the change, our concerns shift to the questions of consequence and collaboration: "How can I best document progress through analysis of writing samples? What happens when children self-assess? How does portfolio assessment impact on my classroom instruction?" According to Hall and Loucks it is not until we have reached this stage of expertise that we are ready to collaborate with peers in order to refine our thinking (1979).

As with all stage theory, the temptation to view these phases as discrete and hierarchical should be resisted. In all likelihood, these phases overlap and intertwine. Hall and Loucks's study was undertaken at a time when curricular innovation was a top-down enterprise—teachers were lectured at about a new idea and instructed to implement it. Today, with the advent of the teacher-researcher and of teacher study groups, informed teachers do collaborate from the onset. They also assess the impact of a curricular change on student learning at each phase of implementation. Nevertheless, Hall and Loucks's work lends some credence to the fact that our brains cannot process everything at once. As we implement portfolio assessment, our preoccupations will shift over time. As one concern recedes, another takes its place. If reflective practice is to be sustained, though, it must stay the course and be nourished by persistent inquiry, ongoing intellectual study, collegial support and feedback, and time (Figure 10–1).

Getting Started with Portfolios

Change is a trial and error process. As Miles and Louis found, "Good problem coping (dealing with problems promptly, actively, and with some depth) is the *single biggest determinant* of program success" (1990, p. 60; italics in original text). One way to cope with the complexity of portfolio implementation is to start small:

Start with the Showcase Portfolio

Children are delighted to select and to reflect upon pieces for their showcase portfolios. They are able do this without much prompting from you. Enjoy their burst of engaged activity; pull up a chair beside various learners and hear what they have to say. Over time, as your understanding about the critical role that demonstrations play in the selection/reflection process increases, their decision making will strengthen. Your ability to assess their selections and reflections also will increase over time.

Select a Few Students and Begin Collaborative Portfolios

While all children can create their showcase portfolios, it makes sense to ease into the collaborative portfolio. At the beginning of a school term, choose three to five children whose work you will evaluate more closely. Review their writing notebooks/folders on a regular basis, and keep notes on information learned in conferences. Select and reflect on the pieces that mark growth. Meet with each child to share findings. Starting the analysis process with a small number of children reduces anxiety and gives you time to hone your assessment skills and to work through management issues.

Assess as You Go

Observing what learners do and say on a daily/weekly basis is central to portfolio assessment. Waiting until the end of the school term to assess

What We Need to Know About the Change Process

Research findings on the change process include:

- Change in beliefs frequently *follows* change in practice (Huberman and Miles, 1984).

- Every successful innovation is accompanied by early implementation problems (Huberman and Miles, 1984); a repertoire of effective problem-solving strategies is essential (Miles and Louis, 1990).

- Teacher knowledge, in conjunction with sustained practice, drives the change process (Joyce, Wolf, and Calhoun, 1993).

- The greater the level of in-class and out-of-class support and reflection during implementation, the greater the chance of sustained adoption (Berman and McLaughlin, 1978; Huberman and Miles, 1984; Joyce, Wolf, and Calhoun, 1993; Lieberman and Miller, 1984).

- Varied kinds of support before and during implementation is critical: simulations, workshops, videotapes that are critiqued, peer/mentor visitations, group problem solving sessions (Berman and McLaughlin, 1978; Cox, 1983; Huberman and Miles, 1984; Sussman, 1977).

- Change is a developmental process that occurs over time (Berman and McLaughlin, 1978; Lieberman and Miller, 1984).

- Full adoption of a new curricular paradigm takes two or more years (Huberman and Miles; Johnson and Johnson, 1984; Shepard, 1995).

- The stronger the bonds of collegiality in the school culture, the more successful the change process (Little, 1982; Fullan and Pomfret, 1977).

- Public support of administrators facilitates change and fosters collegial support (Berman and McLaughlin, 1978; Cox, 1983; Lieberman and Miller, 1984).

Figure 10–1   *Research findings concerning teacher change*

each child's writing across genres and conventions violates a fundamental principle of assessment—namely that we assess continually so we know what to teach. When you pull up a chair beside a child in writing workshop and confer about a report she is writing, you are collecting assessment data. Record the child's comments, inquiries, and responses to your questions; they provide a window into her literacy understandings.

Solidify Your Assessment Knowledge of One Genre Each Term

As the previous chapters illustrate, there is a significant body of knowledge about children's writing development with respect to specific genres. Reading the chapter, for example, on story writing probably affirmed much of what you know intuitively. However, in order to assess children's story writing effectively, a *working* knowlege of this research is essential. This knowledge guides the questions you ask children and the comments you offer. To illustrate, Ernie has just written a story about a little mouse named Pat who gets lost in a store. During a conference, Ernie reads his story. As you listen for the story grammar elements, you note that his story jumps from story problem to resolution without including the character's attempts to solve the problem. You compliment Ernie on creating a good story problem and tell him that you are curiuous about what the little mouse did when she realized she was lost. Aware of the pervasiveness of intertextuality, you might ask him where he got the idea for his story. Knowledgeable about Graves's (1989b) research on how children create characters, you might ask where he got the name for his mouse, and so forth. You use his responses to assess his level of story understanding and to inform your instructional decisions. It takes time and practice, however, to attain this working knowledge. It makes sense, then, to concentrate on only one genre over the course of a school term. Choose a genre which appeals to you or to which your young writers are drawn. What do you do about the other genres that children are writing? You rely on the body of knowledge that you have been using over the years, and set a goal to expand your knowledge base.

Demonstrate Every Aspect of Portfolio Assessment

If there is one lesson I have learned about portfolio assessment, it is the significance of demonstrations. The more you "show" children what you expect in terms of the procedural and the conceptual aspects of portfolio assessment, the easier it will be for them to grasp the essentials. Keep in mind that one demonstration will not suffice most of the time. Children need repeated but varied demonstrations. Think-alouds—moments in which you literally "think aloud" and share your thoughts, questions, uncertainties about a particular part of the process—are invaluable.

Read, Talk, Observe, Find a Coach, Read . . .

In 1928, John Dewey wrote that learning is rooted in ". . . respect for self-initiated and self-conducted learning; respect for activity as the stimulus and centre of learning; and perhaps above all belief in social contact, communication, and cooperation . . ." (1959, pp. 115–116). Collegial exchange, mentoring, and self-study must accompany portfolio endeavors.

Set Realistic Goals

There are no hard and fast rules for portfolio implementation. It begins with a personal vision that is juxtaposed with the perennial demands and tensions of teaching, and with an honest appraisal of what can be accomplished within the first term or so. Short-term goals are designed and revised as you go along. However, the long-term commitment to professional growth stays front and center.

Go Public with Your Goals

Portfolio assessment is like dieting—if you don't tell someone, you're probably not going to do it. Once you set your goals, share them with the children in your class, another teacher, members of your teacher study group, your principal, or whomever. The mere act of telling others about your goals signals your willingness to take action, whether you feel ready or not.

Thus far, the broad strokes that underpin the successful implementation of portfolio assessment have been sketched. We turn now to the finer strokes that detail the interplay of theory and practice.

Portfolio Assessment in Action

Portfolio assessment does not exist in a vacuum. It is not an add-on to the writing workshop. Rather, it is at the center of the writing workshop. Preparing for portfolio assessment means preparing for writing workshop, and vice versa. In this section, I highlight a hypothetical portfolio implementation plan. In order to illustrate the inextricable link between assessment and instruction, I weave threads of Shane's third grade work into a suggested time frame. The implementation draft, which begins in August and culminates in Shane's portfolio conference at the end of first term, is not meant to be prescriptive or inclusive. Rather, it is one way to think about portfolio possibilities.

August

A letter is sent to Shane and his peers welcoming them to third grade (Calkins, 1991; Harwayne, 1992). The letter explains the essence of the reading and writing workshop. It also suggests that they bring a) a book(s) they would like to read the first week of school, b) a notebook for writing workshop, and c) a story/poem/report they may have written over the summer. Children are invited to write a return letter.

A letter is also sent to parents which shares my excitement about the upcoming year, and my beliefs about literacy (Atwell, 1987) and portfolio assessment (Tierney, Carter, & Desai, 1991). It asks parents to write a return letter in which they share their thoughts about their child: "What is your youngster like? What are the things you, as a parent, know that would be important for me to know? What are your child's interests? I want to know how your child thinks and plays and how you see your child as a learner and a person" (Calkins, 1991, p. 15). It also asks parents to save writing samples the child does at home, and to bring them to student-parent-teacher conferences. Such requests give credence the maxim that "parents are our children's first teachers" and forge the link between home and school.

Summer also is the time to create or update my personal writing portfolio. I have learned that the best way to introduce the concept of the showcase portfolio is to share my writing portfolio. I wish I could boast that I have been keeping a portfolio of my writing over my lifetime. I have not. I confess that, at the prodding of Donald Graves (1992) to practice what we preach, I decided to create one. My plan was to pull together a few scraps of writing from my school days, along with some current pieces. But, as I rummaged through the "box of stuff" that my mother had kept of our schoolwork, I found small treasures of my past. I found the comic strips that I wrote and illustrated in sixth grade—inspired, in no small part, by Archie and Veronica. I found the journal that my Dad made me keep on our trip to Ireland, complete with the best examples of bed-to-bed narratives. As I sorted the pieces that mattered to me, I realized that nearly all were written outside of school. The copied Mother's Day poems and the Halloween story dripping with "descriptive" adjectives held little appeal. I left this box with a mission to find other pieces I had written that held personal significance—the slide show presentation for my parents fortieth anniversary, the article I had written about an adult learner for whom I had great admiration, and so on. I now understand why Donald Graves is adamant about teachers creating their own portfolios.

August also is the time to make decisions about the logistics of collaborative portfolios: how to house them and where to store them. Pocket folders with the three-ring insert, recommended by Mary Ellen Giacobbe, work well for the collaborative portfolio. A summary of the portfolio contents is typed; as the year progresses dates of portfolio pieces are recorded on the content page. This summary page is placed in the 3-ring insert for easy reference. A plastic crate with hanging files is prepared for storage of the collaborative portfolios. Since the showcase portfolios will belong to Shane and his peers, decisions about how to house the contents of their portfolios will be made by the students in September. Their portfolios will be organized on a table that is easily accessible to them.

September: Week 1
Joyful Learning

Creating a climate for "joyful learning" (Fisher, 1991) and a mindset about the importance of literacy is probably my most important undertaking of the year. From day one, literature and language swirl around Shane and the others. I read and talk about my favorite children's books (Trealease, 1989), and we share personal responses (Rosenblatt, 1978). I read some pieces from my writing portfolio (without a formal discussion about what a portfolio is at this point), and talk about why and how I wrote them.

Writers Self-Assess

Sometime during the week, I read my literacy autobiography—my memories of learning to read and write (Calkins, 1991; Harwayne, 1992). I ask the children to talk about their memories with a partner and invite them to write their histories as readers and writers. I encourage them to take their histories home, share them with parents, and add any memories that may emerge in their discussions. We share their stories during the week. Later in the week or the following week, I ask children to complete Atwell's (1987) reading and writing surveys (see Appendix A). Results are tallied and shared with the class. We talk about why writers must read and readers must write. The importance of self-assessment is introduced.

Writers Write (and Read)

Time is set aside each day for independent writing (without formal introduction to the writing workshop). Basic guidelines such as where to keep their writing notebooks are discussed. Informal conversations about topic choice occur as well as conferences.

September: Weeks 2 and 3

Shane and his peers are ready for a more formal introduction to the rhythm of writing workshop. Much has been written about the philosophy and the organizational scheme of the writing workshop: mini-lessons; sustained, independent writing; writing record; status of the class; individual conferences; and group sharing (Atwell, 1987; Calkins, 1986, 1991, 1994; Graves, 1983, 1994). While ongoing assessment of children's writing has been a central feature of the writing workshop, the integration of portfolio assessment into the writing workshop necessitates additional action. Children need to understand the purpose, principles, and procedures of the showcase and collaborative portfolios. They need to learn how to select and to reflect on pieces for their portfolios. In order for these understandings to take place, the writing workshop needs to integrate assessment events from the beginning of the school year. A brief overview of this integrated writing workshop cycle is presented below. This overview is followed by numerous examples and scenarios which illustrate the assessment components of the cycle over the course of first term.

Writers Learn: The minilesson—a concentrated period of interactive instruction—is an essential feature of the writing workshop. What to teach in minilessons is tied to my assessment of the children's needs and interests. For example, if many of the children begin their stories with "Once there was . . . ," a series of minilessons on the literary element of story leads may be appropriate. Rather than one half-hour lesson on leads, three or four minilessons are presented. Each minilesson, five-to-fifteen minutes in duration, builds on and extends the previous one. Minilessons typically are designed to teach children about the process of writing, the literary elements, the procedures of the writing workshop, and language skills. Minilessons are also the essential vehicle for bringing children into the assessment process.

Writers Write and Confer: Children engage in daily, sustained, independent writing. They choose their own topics, and write at their own pace. They talk about their ideas, drafts, and so forth with peers and others.

Assess-as-you-go Conference: Central to the success of the writing workshop is the student-teacher conference. During this conference, I listen to and receive their pieces. I help them problem-solve, offer feedback, and so forth. As writers share their thoughts, they provide me with important assessment data. Their insights, confusions, and so on are recorded in my assessment notebook. (The assessment notebook or three-ring binder is divided into sections, one section per child. It travels with me to writing conferences.) Hence, the assess-as-you-go conference is synonymous with the traditional writing conference with an accent on note taking.

Writers Share: Social interaction undergirds the writing workshop. Writers need readers for feedback, response, and recognition for a job well done. Author's Chair, partner share, and small group share serve the goal of response.

Writers Self-Assess: Long before the official portfolio conference at the end of the term, children need to be inducted into the self-assessment process. Self-assessment begins with literacy autobiographies and surveys at the start of the school year, moves to periodic selection and reflection of important pieces, and culminates in completion of the portfolio and in the portfolio conference.

Assess-as-you-go Weekly Review: While writing conferences keep us abreast of children's writing endeavors, they do not give us a sense of the whole. Therefore, I plan to read each child's writing notebook on a weekly (or so) basis (Giacobbe, 1995). A commitment to review five writing folders a night, and to record assessment observations in my notebook keeps this essential task manageable (see Figure 10–4). I then use this information to plan my minilessons, and to confer with individual writers.

Needless to say, while the assessment components of the integrated writing workshop are presented above in a linear fashion, the assessment process is anything but linear. In addition to formal assessment events, assessment data will appear during minilessons I conduct, during periods of sustained silent writing, and during sharing periods. Let's turn now to a more detailed look at some of the specifics of the integrated writing workshop cycle during the second and third weeks of September.

Minilessons with the Accent on Assessment

Since the writing record (Chapter 3, Figure 3–1) provides important assessment data, I decide to explain its purpose and procedures through a series of minilessons. I begin by placing my writing record on the overhead and explain what it is and why I keep it. I demonstrate how I record information on a recent piece. I then ask the children to take out their notebooks and to record the first piece they wrote during writing workshop on their blank writing record. Together, we move from column to column and fill in the data. We end this minilesson with a promise to complete a few more entries tomorrow. I expect that Shane and many others will need repeated minilessons in order to master this record keeping. At some point, I show a writing record of a previous student and talk about what he does well as a record keeper and what he needs to remember.

I also use minilessons to introduce the class to the concept of portfolio. As already noted, I brought my portfolio to school the first or second day of school and shared some of my special pieces. I am now ready to demonstrate the process of selection. I hold up my portfolio and ask if anyone recalls some of the selections I shared. Memories jogged, I explain that I chose each piece after careful thought. I bring out my mother's "box of stuff" which contains other pieces of my writing. I hold up the Halloween story and explain why I chose not to put it in my portfolio. We review the idea that portfolios are places where we keep the writing that matters to us.

Sessions of genuine sharing result in genuine activity. I am not surprised when one child arrives the next day with a bag of "stuff" that his mother kept of his writing and artwork. Six more arrive the following day. Discussions about the fact that not everyone has a bag of "stuff" at home are important; assurances that all of their writing will be saved so they can choose their special pieces for their portfolio are given. The portfolio is launched.

Writers Self-Assess

Discussions about what writers use to package their portfolios (folders, three-ring binders, cereal boxes, etc.) continue over the week. Children design their portfolio covers and begin the process of selecting special pieces for their portfolios. Children understand that this selection process is tentative and that they will have opportunities to review their choices and make changes.

Writers Write

After each daily minilesson, writers take out their writing folder/notebooks and write. While they write, I confer with individual children. Much of the conferring that I do during these first weeks focuses on procedural aspects of the workshop and on topic choice.

Assess-as-you-go Conference

I check in with Shane and ask how he is doing with his writing record (Chapter 3, Figure 3–1). He explains that he has listed his four titles and dates. I notice that with the exception of one piece, the actual pieces in his writing folder are not titled. I compliment Shane on creating titles for these pieces for his writing record. We talk about how titles help readers understand our pieces, and how it would be helpful if he titled each of his actual pieces and then transferred these titles to his record. I also mention that he has recorded "Sept 7" next to "Rivesidie note," but note that September 7th was last Saturday. He explains that he records one date after another. We rethink his strategy of chronologically listing the dates. We also talk about the importance of recording the actual date on each of his pieces to facilitate the transfer of the date to his writing record. Since Shane has left the column "Fiction or Non-fiction" blank, we review the discussion (which occurred the week before) about the difference. Shane identifies his pieces accurately. I then ask Shane how his current piece is going. He shares his topic and says he doing fine.

Before I leave Shane's desk, I dash off notes on what I have learned about Shane in this quick conference in my notebook. Notice in the following anecdotal record that my notes go beyond the content of our actual conversation. (Note: These notes are on his writing record only. I haven't read his pieces yet.)

> 9/11—Excellent sense of titling in writing record—doesn't title individual pieces in writing folder. Starts a new piece each day. Understands the distinction between F and NF but doesn't record. Dates pieces chronologically without regard to actual day; showed him how to date pieces. Spelling is strong overall. Alignment of handwriting varies—some titles above the line; may be more an issue of space constraints. Good job on capitals of proper names (Riverside Park, Red Sox)—not sure if he knows the convention for capitalizing titles (The dentist).

September: Weeks 3 and 4
Assess-as-you-go Weekly Review
One of the five folders I take home on Thursday night belongs to Shane. As I read his entries, I record the following in my assessment notebook:

> 9/18—Shane hasn't recorded his last five pieces on writing record—need to address.
> *Content:* With the exception of one list ("The pet"), all entries are personal narratives of one day duration. Seems to have little trouble finding topics. Started a topic list but doesn't use it; doesn't seem to need it. His narratives record yesterday's events and are straight chronologies of the "and then . . . and then . . ." nature. Good sequencing sense. No effect other than "I had fun." No reflection about events. Narratives about future events are very short (i.e. "soccer practice" piece is three lines in length).
> *Mechanics:* Impressed with his spelling; few errors per piece. Seems to rely on phonemic strategy for unfamiliar words (*strate, thar*) but uses visual strategy to check (edited *saterday* and *wright*). Morphemic strategy seems strong for *ed* suffixes (*tried, used*). Successful with many two syllable words (*bucket, dragon*) and high frequency words (*friend, because, would*). May need the doubling consonant rule (*stoping, bobing, hiting*); schwa (*luckaly, mechines*); and homophones (*there/their*). Handwriting is legible overall; some ascending letters are too short in first drafts—check final draft eventually. Some punctuation of sentence boundaries evident—uses period or capitalizes first word. He uses commas in list ("*spin, twist, go up, and down*"), and capitalizes some but not all proper names (*Wade boggs, burger king*)—check final drafts. Successful shift on personal pronoun from small *i* to *I*.

Minilesson Possibilities
What to teach in minilessons comes primarily from my observations of the children's writing in conjunction with my notes of our conversa-

tions. I have to weigh what they know against what they need to know and when they are ready for this new knowledge. By the end of September, minilessons shift from a focus on workshop procedures to the art of writing. Minilessons on topic choice, genres, literary elements, writing process and so on are emphasized from this point on. The conventions are also addressed in minilessons. (Occasional procedural minilessons will be scheduled as the need arises.) My review of the children's work results in the following decisions:

a) Personal Narratives as Genre   While I could conduct a one-on-one conference with Shane about the essence of personal narratives, I note that many of Shane's peers also are writing bed-to-bed narratives (see pages 61–62) (Graves, 1983). I decide to do a series of minilessons over the next week or so on journal writing. I begin by showing the children an entry from the journal I kept at the age of twelve during a vacation in Ireland (Chapter 4, Figure 4–4). The entry is a bed-to-bed narrative which includes brief mention of a tumble I took while trying to ride my grandmother's horse. I ask the students to ask me questions about this incident which I record on the board. (I expect questions such as: Did you get hurt? How did you feel?) I then tell the children that I can't answer their questions because I don't remember. We start the conversation of what makes a good journal entry. The next day I show two more of my Ireland entries. Each entry reads like the previous one: I got up, had bacon and eggs for breakfast, went somewhere, had lunch . . . went to bed. After reading two entries, I ask children to predict the next one. They do so without difficulty; we talk about the sameness of these entries. I encourage the children to tell me what I should have included in these entries to make better pieces. We talk about why good journal entries do more than tell the facts. I ask the children to look over the entries in their writing notebooks to find one in which they shared their thoughts and/or feelings. I ask them to put a post-it on that entry so they can share it tomorrow, if they choose to do so. At some point later in the week, we read and respond to the journal entries of Zlata Filupovic, a Bosnian child caught in the ravages of the war (1994). Or, I could use Henry David Thoreau's (Lowe, 1990) or Laura Ingalls Wilder's (1962) journal. Or, I could read the journal entries of characters in literature: *Dear Mr. Henshaw* (Cleary, 1983); *The Diary of a Church Mouse* (Oakley, 1987); *Three Days on a River in a Red Canoe* (Williams, 1981); *A Gathering of Days: A New England Girl's Journal* (Blos, 1979). Over the next week or so, I note who is absorbing the essence of the personal narrative and is transferring this essence to their journals. I ask permission to share these entries on the overhead. I know that, in time, many children will respond to the call of journals as places to think and feel deeply. I make a note to revisit and extend their understanding of this genre later in the term and school year.

I choose to start with personal narratives not only because many of the children are writing them but because I am comfortable with this genre. I believe I have a good understanding of what constitutes a good journal entry as well as the developmental aspects of this genre (see Chapter 4). While a few children wrote poems during writing workshop, I recognize that I do not have the same level of confidence with poetry. I'm not ready to create a series of minilessons on poetry at this point in the year. I know I have much to learn but I remind myself of a Mary Ellen Giacobbeism—"Remember, you have 180 days to turn children into readers and writers. This is day 12. You have 168 days left." I decide to do my best to support their current efforts at poetry writing and to expand my knowledge base over the coming months.

b) Spelling   A glance at my weekly review notes reminds me that Shane's experimentation with the homophones *there* and *their* matches that of many of his peers. These words are among the twenty-five most frequently misspelled words across grades 1–6 (Buchanan, 1989). This homophone pair will be introduced during the spelling workshop and placed on the weekly spelling list. Children will be asked to devise and share strategies or mnemonic devices for distinguishing between these words. When they begin to edit their pieces, reminders to check these homophones will given.

In another minilesson during spelling workshop, I capitalize on Shane's attention to the visual demands of words. With Shane's permission, transparencies of the two pieces which contain his self-edits of *saterday* and *wright* are displayed. Shane is asked to explain to the class how he made these corrections. I emphasize that good spellers check to see if their spellings of words "look right." We talk about visual strategy in relation to the phonemic strategy. We talk about steps spellers can take to verify their spellings, and the notion that good spellers care about the way they spell words.

c) Minilesson with an Accent on Assessment   At the end of September or the beginning of October, I am planning to ask Shane and his peers to make preliminary selections for their showcase portfolios and to write reflections about these pieces. Therefore, I need to explain and illustrate the concept of reflection. (I know they will need repeated demonstrations on the art of writing reflections over the course of the year.) In order to introduce this concept of reflection, I read a piece from my portfolio which I previously have not shared. I then place my reflection about this piece on the overhead and read it to the children:

Just looking at this piece makes my heart pound, even now. It was fourth period, English class; the teacher said, "Write a book report on *The House of Seven Gables.*" Everyone started writing, but I just sat there. I couldn't think of anything to write. I had read the book and even enjoyed it. But, for some reason, my mind wouldn't focus. I tried one sentence but it sounded stupid, so I crossed it out and tried another. It didn't sound any better. The period was racing by and I had nothing on paper. Everyone around me seemed to be writing nonstop. My palms started to sweat; I wanted to scream. About ten minutes before the bell, the teacher asked how many of us would like to finish our reports at home. I was saved.

This was my first experience with writer's block. I often have wondered why it happened. My guess is that this was the first time I realized the importance of a lead sentence. Lead sentences set the tone for a piece and serve to hook the reader. I wanted my opening sentence to be engaging but I couldn't shape it. Maybe I should have moved ahead with the rest of the report and then returned to the lead sentence.

We talk about my reflection, and about why writing reflections is important. We talk about the notion that portfolios not only include our favorite and best pieces but also pieces which help us discover something about ourselves ("lightbulb pieces," as one child called them). I explain that I can't wait to read the reflections they will write on the pieces they choose for their portfolios.

Writers Write
The momentum of sustained writing is in full swing.

Assess-as-you-go Conference
The weekly review of writing notebooks gives me ample data not only for minilessons possibilities but also for one-on-one conferences. As already noted, my weekly review of Shane's writing folder reveals his difficulty with the writing record. During a follow-up conference, Shane remarks, "Sometimes, I forget to do the form. There is so much stuff to remember for writing workshop. And the dates don't fit." I ask him why he thinks he has been asked to keep a record of his writing. He replies, "Umm, well, I . . . I don't really know." I give a brief rationale and make a note to discover if others are unclear on this point. We talk about ways of managing the writing record. As the conference comes to a close, I tell Shane how much I have enjoyed reading his journal entries. I refer to our recent minilessons on good journal writing and explain that I look forward to reading his thoughts and feelings about his experiences in his upcoming journals.

September/October: Weeks 4 or 5

Minilessons—Showcase Portfolio-in-the-making

About a month into the first term, I present a minilesson or two in which I revisit the process of selecting pieces for my showcase portfolio. Recall that at the beginning of the term, after I demonstrated the selection process, the children created their portfolios with pieces from home and so on. Now that children have a month's worth of writing, the selection process is revisited and extended. I show children how I reread each piece I have written over the last few weeks and how I sort them into piles: one pile for my favorite pieces, one pile for best pieces, one pile for lightbulb pieces (what I learned about myself as a writer), and one pile for other pieces. I share how I pick my best piece. I show children a piece which contains my best handwriting and has no spelling mistakes but whose content is mediocre. We talk about the importance of good hand-writing and spelling in final drafts. But I emphasize that good writing is about the discovery of significant ideas and feelings.

In a subsequent minilesson, I review the importance of writing re-flection pieces for our portfolio selections. I further their understanding by placing another of my bed-to-bed narratives from my Ireland trip on the overhead and by asking the children to help me write my reflection piece for this entry. As they offer assessment comments, I record those that connect to the content of my narrative at the top of the overhead. I record comments about the mechanical aspects at the bottom of the overhead. I concentrate initially on their critique of my ideas. I am look-ing to see if they can assess my work against the criteria of a good per-sonal narrative (which we discussed in earlier minilessons). I tell the children that I will use their ideas to write my reflection piece and that I will share it with them tomorrow. The next day, I put the draft of my re-flection piece on the overhead. Using the checklist in Figure 4–9, I "think-aloud" and show the children how I evaluate this piece. I also come back to the comments they made about the mechanical aspects of my piece and write a separate paragraph on my strengths and weak-nesses.

Writers Self-Assess

Children are ready to make decisions about their September pieces for their portfolios. Since children need time to reread and sort their pieces, writer's workshop is suspended for a day or two. Logistically, it makes sense to engage five or six students a day in this process while the others continue with writing workshop. Be prepared for children's requests to take over corners of the room so they can spread out their work and take stock. With young children, Bobbi Fisher recommends that we meet individually with each child to demonstrate the selection/reflection process at the end of September (1995). While the other children are in writing workshop, one child is asked to find two best pieces and share reasons. The child's observations are recorded on a form. At the end of October, the children select their best work independently and then meet with Bobbi to share observations. By March, children select pieces and complete a yes/no form as a class activity. Throughout the year, children are asked to compare current pieces with September pieces and reflect on progress over time.

Collaborative Portfolio-in-the-making

When children have made their selections, and have written their reflections, I introduce the collaborative portfolio. I explain that the showcase portfolios belong to them. I explain that because their showcase portfolio goes home at the end of the year, a copy of the pieces in their portfolio will be made for the school portfolio—the portfolio that stays in school and that is given to next year's teacher. I share my excitement about reading the pieces they have selected and explain that while they are selecting their pieces, I will be selecting my favorite, best, and lightbulb pieces of their work. I explain that I will write a paragraph explaining why I chose my selections. At our portfolio conference, we will share our selections and our thoughts so we can learn from each other.

Minilessons

While the portfolio minilessons, presented above, take two or three days, time is still available for other minilessons. Depending on my ongoing observations, I may need to do minilessons on the range of genres, a specific genre, a particular literary element, a specific language skill, and so on.

Writers Write

Since I have chosen to rotate small groups through the portfolio creation process, only five or six children are selecting and reflecting on pieces for their portfolio each day. (Some children may need two days to complete their preliminary portfolios, especially in September.) The rest of the class is engaged in writing workshop.

Assess-as you-go Weekly Review

Five folders are reviewed each day or evening and observations noted.

Assess-as-you-go Conference

Individual conferences with Shane and others continue.

October: Weeks 6 or 7
Minilessons—Showcase Portfolio-in-the-making

A week or two before the end of the term, Shane and his peers are asked to assess their October writing and to reassess the contents of their show-case portfolio. Has one of their most recent pieces become their best piece? Do they have a new favorite piece? Do they want to keep their initial favorite pieces in their portfolios? What other pieces—written at home or at school—are important to include? New reflection pieces are written. As always, I demonstrate the reassessment process, using examples from my writing notebook/portfolio.

Writers Self-Assess

The children are introduced to the self-assessment rating form (Appendix C). With my portfolio in hand, I place a transparency of Appendix C on the overhead. As I read through the first four or five items, I ask children to help me decide which items I can rate without looking at the pieces in my portfolio. We decide that there is little in the portfolio that will help me rate an item such as "I begin work without delay." I show them how I assess myself on this item. My think-aloud contains insights about how I am task oriented once engaged but how I have a tendency to procrastinate sometimes. After sharing my thoughts, I ask children to think about this item and share their thoughts with a neighbor. I pass out the form and ask them to rate themselves. We then turn to item one of the rating scale, "My writing is neat and easy to read." We decide that this item requires a look at the pieces in the portfolio. I put my first and final draft of my best piece on the overhead and again demonstrate my rating decision. The children are then asked to the same. After two or three items, we put the scale away. Since the task of self-assessment is mentally demanding, it needs to be spread out over time. We need to show children that it is the process of self-reflection that matters, not the mechanical act of filling out the form. We can return to the rating scale the next day or two and do a few more items. (Note: Any items that are unclear to the children should be revised or deleted. Asking them to offer new items or to reorganize existing items increases involvement.)

A word about rating scales. Blind adoption of other educators' rating scales, checklists, and so on does not serve children well (Cambourne, 1988). Rating scales and the like must reflect our belief systems. Before using rating scales, we need to ask ourselves: What is it that we value? How can we best collect this information? If we decide that a rating scale facilitates the assessment process, we can consult other published scales (i.e., Rhodes, 1993) but we need to customize the final product. Do we want a rating scale that taps the content of children's pieces or one that focuses primarily on the mechanics such as the one in Appendix C? What about attitudes and work habits? In addition, we should think about how many items children can manage successfully at the beginning of the year and create the scale accordingly. Additions can be made over the year. If we use checklists, we need to draft our items, pilot them, revise, and retest.

Writers Write
On days when children are not self-assessing, independent writing continues.

Assess-as-you go Conference
Confer with Shane and others as they make their selections and write reflections.

Assess-as-you go Weekly Reviews
Continue to gather insights about children's written work; create minilessons.

End of October: The Portfolio Conference
Preparation for this end-of-the-term conference has been underway since the first week of school. This culminating conference is called to bring closure to a term of hard work, to exchange viewpoints and information about writing growth, to revel in accomplishments, and to decide what remains to be accomplished. The success of the portfolio conferences hinges on the degree to which I have prepared the children. Enter the minilessons again. What follows is a description of the minilessons (or maxilessons—lessons which can run up to a half hour) I might use to inform Shane and his peers about the portfolio conference as well as a run-through of Shane's portfolio conference. Snippets of conversations with Shane, most of which appear elsewhere in this book, are woven together to demonstrate one way of conducting a portfolio conference.

Preparing for the Portfolio Conference
Setting the tone for the portfolio conference is critical. I ask Shane (or any volunteer) to bring his portfolio to the front of the class and to explain briefly what he has included in his portfolio. I share that I am eager to learn Shane's thoughts about how he is becoming a better writer. I explain that Shane and I will meet to discuss his progress. I explain that in our portfolio conference, I also will share my thoughts about Shane's progress, and that the purpose of the conference is to learn from each other. I express my

eagerness to have a portfolio conference with each member of the class. I suggest that since they will be running the conference, it would be helpful to do a dry run. I explain that tomorrow I will pretend that I am a third grader who is sharing my portfolio with the "teacher" (any volunteer: a parent, a secretary, another teacher, the principal).

It is advisable to do some preplanning for this role play. The "teacher's" feedback should be worked out ahead of time. Built into the role-play is the importance of being prepared for the conference. For example, when it is time to share my self-assessment rating scale, it becomes obvious to the audience that I only completed the first four items. I have the uncomfortable task of explaining to the "teacher" what happened and what I plan to do about it. After the role play, we discuss what we learned—about me as a writer and about the portfolio conference. We then discuss the logistics of doing conferences—how they should be scheduled, what others will be doing while each writer is in a conference, what kinds of interruptions are appropriate, what to bring, and what we can do to be sure the conferences run smoothly. On the following day, I nudge them toward a class-designed conference agenda (which was used in the role play) which lists possible topics to be covered: the writing record, selected pieces and reflections, the self-assessment scale, goals. Having set the stage for the portfolio conference, individual conferences begin. We turn now to Shane's portfolio conference.

Shane Leads the Conference

Shane brings his showcase portfolio and writing folder to the conference table, and I bring the collaborative portfolio. I also bring my assessment notebook so that I can record any new insights that might unfold at the conference. To start the conference, I tell Shane that I can't wait to hear about his portfolio and ask him what he'd like to do first. Using his agenda, Shane moves through the conference in the following fashion.

Favorite Piece   When the class generated the conference agenda, it was decided that writers would share the contents of their portfolios in the order they wished. Shane opens with his favorite piece, "Lizard and the Motorcycle." He explains he chose it because "It's awesome 'cuz exciting things happen to Lizard and Owl, and it's a really long story—five pages." I ask him to share the event in the story that he thinks is the most important and why. We talk briefly about his choice and I make the point that this event could be a story in and of itself. I mention that Beverly Cleary, the inspiration for his story, needed eighty-five pages to develop all of her story episodes. I open the collaborative portfolio and take out a copy of my favorite piece, "Lizard and the Motorcycle." Shane smiles. I explain that I, too, chose this piece because I found one part of his story very touching. I read the excerpt ". . . And he had only had one friend his name was owl. But whenever lizard went near any other animals they laughed at him and he did not no who they were talking about so he was laughing too and once they knew that they laughed some more but the only animal that did not laugh was owl . . ." I tell Shane that this episode reminds me of the time when some kids made fun of the ankle socks I wore in seventh grade. (I learned that day that white ankle socks were not cool in seventh grade.) I tell Shane that I had not thought about this humiliating event in a long time. I point out that he has the same wonderful talent that published authors have—the ability to make their readers relive their experiences in new ways. I also explain that as I read his story I wanted to find out whether Lizard learns that he is being ridiculed and how he deals with this problem. However, because Lizard and Owl find themselves in all kinds of exciting events, I don't find out how Lizard deals with his humiliation. I ask Shane to think about coming back to this story theme in a new story. He agrees to think about it. I list this as a potential goal for next term. At the end of the conference, we will compare the goals that Shane has chosen for next term with the goals that emerge from our portfolio conversation.

Our conversation on his favorite piece comes to a close. Shane shares his choice and his reflections; I acknowledge his thoughts, and I share my thoughts in an effort to extend one aspect of his understanding of the story genre. It is important to emphasize that I do not share everything I have surmised about him as a story writer (Chapter 5). For example, I do not broach the issue of story grammar. I do not point out that he has the three unresolved story problems on the first page. Since many of the third graders are writing focused chains (Chapter 5), I plan to do a series of minilessons on story grammar elements. I'll watch to see if Shane's stories begin to reflect an understanding of the story grammar elements and will address the issue in later conferences. The portfolio conference is not the place to overwhelm Shane with all of my assessments. I prioritize one or two pieces of information that he appears ready to absorb. To make that decision, I tap a burgeoning strength and attempt to refine that strength. "Here's what you're already doing well Shane; now think about this."

Best Piece Shane checks off the space next to Favorite Piece on his agenda and moves to Best Piece. He explains why he chose "The Visitors" as his best piece: "I had to keep going over it to make it better, the periods and stuff. I had to put in all the capitals in the right place." I compliment Shane on his attention to the conventions during the editing process. Recognizing that Shane appears to be equating "good writing" with convention accuracy (Graves, 1983—see Figure 4–6 in Chapter 4), I ask why he chose this piece over his journal entry about the Red Sox game. He replies, "Well, that story is . . . you see, this is just about me (pointing to the Red Sox narrative) but this one (pointing to "The Visitors") is about real people and real places. They traveled all over the place." I tell Shane that he has drawn an interesting conclusion, and that I am going to record his idea in my notebook so that we can refer to it at a later time. I tell Shane that he has done a fine job on reporting what he learned about the visitors from Germany, and that I am curious about his thoughts about these visitors. I ask him to recall our minilessons about journals, and our conclusion that good journal entries, in addition to the facts, include our thoughts and feelings. To illustrate my point, I take out my choice for best piece, "Stickers" (see Figure 4–7) from the collaborative portfolio, and highlight its strengths. We return to "The Visitors" and I explain that readers would be interested in his thoughts about the visitors from Germany. Shane shares that he, too, loves to travel, and that someday he would like to go to Germany, but he wonders if he would miss his family too much. The connection is made. Since our best pieces differ, I tell Shane that I would like to put his choice and his reflection next to my choice in our collaborative portfolio. I also note another potential goal on our list: including his thoughts and feelings in his journal entries.

As with his favorite piece, I focus on one aspect of his journal writing. I refrain from telling him everything he needs to know about personal narratives. I realize that this information has to be demonstrated repeatedly in new and intriguing ways.

Before leaving his best piece, I return to Shane's comment about "capitals and periods." I compliment him on his excellent sense of punctuation. I tell him I am impressed that he capitalized many of the names of countries and towns in his first draft, and that he used a comma to separate a series of items. I tell him I am curious to see how he rated himself on his self-assessment scale. I use this opportunity to segue to the scale.

Self-Assessment Rating Scale   This is the place where the portfolio conference can bog down. Asking children to explain their ratings for each item will exasperate even the most fastidious learner and will lengthen dramatically the time of the conference. I pull his scale out of the collaborative portfolio. (At the time the rating scales were completed, Shane chose not include his form in his showcase portfolio.) We go to the punctuation item to which he has already referred. After discussing his rating, I ask what else he would like to learn about punctuation; we record this information. I then suggest that, instead of walking through each item on the rating scale, we use his draft and final copy of "The Visitors" to talk about the other big areas on the rating scale: spelling and handwriting. We follow the same process: talk about how he has changed as a speller/scribe; talk about what he would like to do better as a speller/scribe. I assess his observations, concur or offer clarification, and together we arrive at a course of action. I am ever mindful, though, that it is more important for him to leave the conference with a sense of his accomplishments, and with two or three new learnings (across content and mechanics) which have been prioritized than with head full of "What I didn't do right."

Other Pieces Shane shares other pieces that he has included.

Goals—Old and New Shane shares his assessment of the goals set at the beginning of the year (Chapter 3, Figure 3–2). For example, we talk about his efforts to "try to remember a lot," and some of the strategies he tried during the term but which didn't work. He proposes a checklist, like the conference agenda, to follow during writing workshop. Because we are running out of time, I tell him that we can discuss his second goal assessment, "Do as much stuff you can so you will have a lot to write about," during a regular conference.

I ask Shane about his goals for next term. He says that he wants to write another Lizard story that will be even more exciting and that will "give the characters feelings." He also wants to learn about quotation marks. I tell him that I think he has chosen two fine goals. I reread the list of potential goals that I scribbled during our conference to see if he wants to add, delete, or alter his stated goals. He adds the goal of adding his thoughts and feelings to his journal entries. I concur with his goals, and the conference ends on a congratulatory note.

This portfolio conference with Shane takes 10–15 minutes. Since I have already read and made notes on his pieces in my weekly reviews, as well as conducted regular conferences, I don't spend any time actually reading pieces in this final conference. This conference is reserved for exchange of assessment observations.

The Portfolio Retrospective

For two months, Shane and I have been gathering insights about his writing development. At this point, the collaborative portfolio contains a record of these insights in the form of Shane's individual reflections about chosen pieces and my reflections about his pieces. However, if one of our goals is to compare his progress from term to term, we will need a synopsis of our observations at the end of each term. Since it will be too time consuming to return to all of our individual reflections in order to track his progress over time, I craft a summary statement—a portfolio retrospective—of the assessment decisions made at the end of the first term. The portfolio retrospective can take the form of: a) a literacy profile (Taylor, 1989), b) an adaptation of

When asked on the Writing Survey how he felt about writing at the beginning of the school year, Shane wrote, "happy." Anecdotal notes support Shane's perception. While he delays sometimes at the beginning of writing workshop, once engaged, he stays on task. He enjoys sharing his work with others. Shane views himself as a writer.

Shane latches onto the genre of personal narrative on the first day of school, and continues writing personal narratives for most of the term. He finds topics easily, leaning primarily on his life experiences—his soccer games, activities with Dad, and afternoons with friends fill his journal entries. His earliest narratives chronicle the details of events with great precision. He records everything that happened to him without commentary or response. Toward the end of the term, Shane writes a piece which centers on one event rather than on several, and includes a glimpse of his thoughts and feelings. Attention to the affective nature of journals is just beginning. Shane starts and finishes a new personal narrative each day. He makes no attempt to carry entries over from one day to the next. Attempts at revision occur only on request.

Twice over the term, Shane leaves journal writing to try his hand at story writing. His fascination with Beverly Cleary's *The Mouse and the Motorcycle* scaffolds both of his story writing efforts. While his first mouse story loses momentum as soon as the story problem is established, his second story about a lizard rocks with activity. In this focused chain, Shane tumbles characters in and out of dilemmas with lightning speed but with little attention, as expected, to character or theme development. (Awareness of theme is evident in his second story.) It is this second story that marks Shane's first success in carrying his writing over from one day to the next. This story takes three days to complete.

With the exception of one persuasive letter, Shane does not experiment with other genres (nonfiction, poetry). His letter, written in conjunction with a school-wide event, shows his intuitive understanding about the art of persuasion. He chooses not to revise and send this letter.

FIGURE 10–2 *Literacy profile on Shane (Term 1)*

the Weekly Writing Record (Giabobbe, 1995), or c) a writing portfolio checklist. As Figure 10–2 illustrates, a literacy profile is an extended narrative which illuminates the child's engagement with and progress in writing. While literacy profiles require a strong knowledge base and take time to construct, parents are particularly appreciative of the effort and expertise that characterizes these personalized, comprehensive portraits. Because time tugs relentlessly, an excellent alternative to the literacy profile is the Weekly Writing Record (see Figure 10–3). The Weekly Writing Record was designed by Mary Ellen Giacobbe to help teachers and children keep track of weekly assessment insights and of corresponding instructional plans (1995). Mary Ellen recommends that the teacher take home five writing folders each night, review each

Use of conventions: Many of Shane's writing samples reveal high rates of spelling accuracy (93% and above). Analysis of his spelling successes and approximations suggests that he is a developing speller who is moving toward conventional spelling. Shane tends to rely on the phonemic strategy when puzzling out unfamiliar words, but increasingly uses the visual strategy to check his spellings. Shane consistently spells many high frequency words, and demonstrates good control of short vowels, vowel combinations, and silent letters. He successfully spells many multisyllabic words. Homophones, schwa, and double consonants need attention. His ability to mark sentence boundaries has improved over the term, especially his use of the period. Capitalization of the personal pronoun *I*, of cities, and of dates is fairly consistent. Capitalization of first words in sentences occurs about fifty percent of the time. While he did not use internal punctuation at the beginning of the semester, he uses commas to separate a series of items by the end of the term. Handwriting in first drafts is fairly legible, and is excellent in final drafts. Letter formation in final drafts, with the exception of the letters *t* and *q*, is fine. While variability is noted in first drafts with regard to the spacing, sizing, slanting and alignment of words and letters, final drafts evidence very good control of these legibility factors. When Shane edits for mechanics, he tends to edit for capitalization but not for punctuation or spelling.

Shane's goals for term 2 include:
- incorporating thoughts and feelings into his personal narratives;
- writing another lizard story which includes character's feelings;
- using quotation marks.

FIGURE 10–2, *continued*

child's work, and complete the Record. Implementation of this recommendation certainly facilitates the end-of-the-term portfolio retrospective. When the Weekly Writing Record is used as a summative record at the end of the term, it can be titled Writing Record: Term 1. This record accomplishes the same goal as the literacy profile and demands the same knowledge base but allows us to summarize concise assessment conclusions in list form. One notable advantage of the Writing Record is its invitation to link assessment with instruction. The third alternative for the portfolio retrospective is a portfolio checklist (Figures 10–4 and 10–5). As noted earlier in this chapter, checklists have serious limitations. Checklists do, however, provide a supportive scaffold if our knowledge base isn't extensive. They also address the time issue. Regardless of the format we choose, we need to commit to the portfolio retrospective to ensure that each writer's progress is tracked.

WEEKLY WRITING RECORD

TITLE _____   DATE _____

_____ knows how to:	...needs to know how to:	a plan of action:

FIGURE 10–3   *Weekly Writing Record (Giacobbe, 1995)*

PORTFOLIO CHECKLIST: GENRE WRITING

WRITER _____ GRADE _____

	First Term	Second Term	Third Term
I. PERSONAL NARRATIVE			
• writes a summary statement of a personal event	___	___	___
• reports events of a personal experience in chronological order	___	___	___
• reports events of an entire day in chronological order	___	___	___
• focuses on one event in a personal experience	___	___	___
• writes about topics of personal significance	___	___	___
• includes thoughts/feelings/opinions about a significant event	___	___	___
• includes self-reflections about significant event	___	___	___
II. STORY			
A. *Story Chains*			
• writes an unfocused chain in which characters and settings keep changing; no coherent storyline	___	___	___
• writes a focused chain in which characters jump from one action to the next; no central problem	___	___	___
B. *True Narrative (Story Grammar Evident)*			
• places characters in time and place	___	___	___
• creates a problem for main character	___	___	___

FIGURE 10–4 *Portfolio Checklist: Genre Writing*

	First Term	Second Term	Third Term
• tells how character feels about problem	____	____	____
• has main character make various attempts to solve problem	____	____	____
• brings story to resolution	____	____	____
• tells how character feels about solution	____	____	____
• understands that story is more than story grammar elements	____	____	____

C. *Character Portrayal*

	First Term	Second Term	Third Term
• incorporates TV/book characters	____	____	____
• incorporates friends or self	____	____	____
• invents a new character	____	____	____
• brings character(s) to life through:			
• dialogue	____	____	____
• physical description	____	____	____
• character's actions	____	____	____
• character's reaction to events/other characters	____	____	____
• other characters' reactions	____	____	____

D. *Character Development*

	First Term	Second Term	Third Term
• creates believable character(s) by			
• giving character a range of human qualities	____	____	____
• keeping actions true to character	____	____	____
• changing character's way of thinking over time	____	____	____
• linking character change to specific credible events in story	____	____	____

E. *Theme Development*

	First Term	Second Term	Third Term
• shows an intuitive awareness of theme	____	____	____
• states the moral or message of story directly but doesn't weave it into story	____	____	____

Figure 10–4, *continued*

	First Term	Second Term	Third Term
• states theme explicitly through dialogue of characters	____	____	____
• states theme explicitly through dialogue and action of characters	____	____	____
• implies theme through the dialogue of characters	____	____	____
• implies theme through dialogue, action and/or reaction of characters	____	____	____
• experiments with multiple themes but doesn't weave themes together	____	____	____
• weaves secondary theme(s) into a primary theme	____	____	____
• uses theme to hold the story together	____	____	____

III. NONFICTION WRITING

	First Term	Second Term	Third Term
• is curious about world around him/her	____	____	____
• reads/listens to nonfiction	____	____	____
• labels pictures	____	____	____
• lists words about a topic	____	____	____
• writes random statements about topic; sometimes includes personal feelings	____	____	____
• writes reasons for interest in a topic	____	____	____
• writes a paragraph with three or more sentences on topic that connect to each other	____	____	____
• opens paragraph with a topic sentence and links subsequent sentences to topic sentence.	____	____	____
• uses a text structure (problem/solution; cause and effect...) to present topic	____	____	____
• defends a point of view in topic	____	____	____

FIGURE 10–4, *continued*

PORTFOLIO CHECKLIST:
ENGAGEMENT WITH WRITING

WRITER _____   GRADE _____

	First Term	Second Term	Third Term
I. RESPONSIVENESS TO WRITING			
• writes willingly and with enthusiasm	____	____	____
• cares about quality of work	____	____	____
• writes during free time	____	____	____
• is still writing when workshop has ended	____	____	____
• writes at home (unassigned)	____	____	____
• asks for help from peers/teachers	____	____	____
• experiments with a variety of genres	____	____	____
• self-assesses in developmentally appropriate ways	____	____	____
• sets appropriate writing goals	____	____	____
• enjoys new writing challenges	____	____	____
• perceives self as a writer	____	____	____
II. AUDIENCE AWARENESS			
• targets a particular audience before writing	____	____	____
• thinks about readers' knowledge	____	____	____
• sets a purpose for audience: to inform, to persuade, to entertain, to move...	____	____	____
• adjusts language appropriate to readers	____	____	____
• uses cohesive devices—reader knows who "he" is	____	____	____
• uses text structure appropriate to genre	____	____	____
• writes for varied audiences	____	____	____

FIGURE 10–5   *Portfolio Checklist: Engagement with Writing*

	First Term	Second Term	Third Term
III. WRITING PROCESS			
• *Chooses Topic:*			
• uses personal experiences for idea generation	___	___	___
• reads published authors for writing ideas	___	___	___
• reads/listens to peer authors for writing ideas	___	___	___
• finds topics easily	___	___	___
• rereads entries to find topic of significance	___	___	___
• *Plans:*			
• rehearses ideas for pieces by drawing	___	___	___
• rehearses ideas for pieces by talking, listing, webbing, outlining.	___	___	___
• uses first draft to rehearse ideas	___	___	___
• *Drafts*:			
• focuses primarily on ideas in first draft	___	___	___
• starts and finishes pieces on same day	___	___	___
• carries same piece over from day to day (duration)	___	___	___
• revises during first draft	___	___	___
• makes first draft readable (rewrites illegible words, fixes some spelling) if others are to read draft	___	___	___
• *Revises:*			
• seeks feedback from peers/others on draft	___	___	___
• evaluates and when appropriate acts on readers' suggestions	___	___	___
• rereads first draft and revises ideas by			
• adding new information	___	___	___

Figure 10–5, *continued*

	First Term	Second Term	Third Term
• substituting new words/phrases	____	____	____
• reorganizing information	____	____	____
• deleting information	____	____	____
• *Edits:*			
• spelling	____	____	____
• punctuation	____	____	____
• grammar	____	____	____
• *Publishes:*			
• brings pieces to publication	____	____	____
• takes pride in work	____	____	____
• writes legibly on final draft	____	____	____
• participates in author's chair	____	____	____

FIGURE 10–5, *continued*

Portfolios: Are They Worth the Time and Energy?

Shane's writing portfolio conference has ended. Maureen's conference starts, then Ted's . . . Report cards, and student-led parent conferences follow. (An excellent reference on student-led parent conferences is *Evaluating Literacy* [Anthony, Johnson, Mickelson, & Preece, 1991].) Indeed, the demands of portfolio assessment are many. When these demands begin to overwhelm us, we need to step back, appreciate what we have accomplished thus far, and set our sights on our next goal. We need to remind ourselves that portfolio assessment as a field of study is still in its infancy. As Graves notes, "We need to explore the many uses of portfolios for at least five years, and perhaps indefinitely" (1992, p. 1). Valencia, Hiebert, and Afflerbach, in their discussion on authentic assessment, elaborate on Graves's observation:

> We need time to examine the intended and unintended effects, study implementation issues, and determine the feasibility of new assessments in terms of time and money. Some of these issues cannot be studied until assessments are in place of a significant period of time. This is particularly true of portfolio assessment, which must be well established in a classroom before its effectiveness as an assessment tool can determined. All the anecdotal evidence thus far suggests that this process may well take several years. (1994, p. 292)

These experts understand that the potential of portfolios to change the way we view ourselves, our children, and our curriculum will be realized only if we pursue a course of patient, persistent inquiry and continual reflection. Portfolio assessment is an evolutionary process of self-renewal that requires resolve, knowledge, and the belief that it makes a difference in children's lives. As a recent conversation with Shane reveals, it has made a difference in his life:

CAROL: Do think it is a good idea to keep a writing portfolio?

SHANE: Yes, it's fun thing to do. You can set goals for yourself.

CAROL: Tell me more about setting goals.

SHANE: I like setting goals for myself in every part of my life, not just writing. You have a better chance of achieving what you want to achieve if keep going after your goals. If you have no goals, then it's pretty hard to achieve something that you'd like to achieve.

CAROL: Give me an example of a writing goal you set.

SHANE: Like I remember in third grade, every kid set a goal. The object was to get as much writing done as possible. Except that some kids when they tried to do that, they lost the focus of good writing. They had stories of five words on a page so they had 900 pages and they needed three folders to hold all the paper. That was dumb. I got a fair amount of pages and I filled them as best as I could.

CAROL: You just finished your report on the blue whale. If you had to set a goal for your next report, what might it be?

SHANE: I would like to have an equal amount for every topic. See, my introduction (which was half a page in length) is way shorter than my physical characteristics section (three quarters of a page in length). So I have to work harder to get it even.

CAROL: Do you think that the length of each section is as important as the actual content?

SHANE: No. The reader cares about my ideas but it looks better to the reader if everything is even.

CAROL: Do you think portfolios are a good way to evaluate a writer's work?

SHANE: Yeah. If you have a portfolio, you can keep track of writing. You can open up the portfolio, flip through the pages, and say, "Ah, here's a story that I could add on to or correct." I mean like it never ends. Writing is never-ending.

CAROL: Do you think teachers should ask students to evaluate their own work?

SHANE: Our teacher really believed in us evaluating most of our work. All teachers have their different ways of teaching. She expected us to make drafts and to be the editor of our own work. We had to know all these different signs for editing—the paragraph sign, the caret. . . .

CAROL: How did you explain your evaluation to your teacher?

SHANE: We had to write her a letter talking about what grade we thought we deserved and why. I was always honest. Kids that did A+++ in their letters got bad grades so I figured I'd be honest and get a fair grade. Lots of times she gave me a little higher grade.

CAROL: Did you think it was a good idea to evaluate your own writing?

SHANE: Definitely. You get to see problems with your writing. You can't address your own problems if you don't know what the teacher is talking about. The teacher might give you something back and say you did this wrong, and you go "What? I don't see that." You might not understand the teacher's words but if you correct it yourself, you might say, "Oh there's a problem. I'll have to change that." That happened to me before.

CAROL: Any final word of advice for teachers about portfolios?

SHANE: Keep the kids doing them. You can do tests too. Most kids hate tests. Me, I enjoy tests sometimes. I like to try to impress the teacher. When you think about a test, it's kinda like having a goal—a goal to get a good mark. But only the portfolio tells you how good of a writer you are.

Appendices A–H

WRITING SURVEY

YOUR NAME _Shane_   DATE _Fall, 1991_

1. Are you a writer? _Yes_

   (If your answer is YES, answer question 2a. If your answer is NO, answer 2b.)

2a. How did you learn to write? _my Parents help me_

2b. How do people learn to write? _they go to school_

3. Why do people write? _to ask people Questions_

4. What do you think a good writer needs to do in order to write well? _use caprial and peerceids_

5. How does your teacher decide which pieces of writing are the good ones? _if thewriting is like iT showdbe_

6. In general, how do you feel about what you write? _happy_

WRITING SURVEY

YOUR NAME _Shane_   DATE _3/92_

1. Are you a writer? _Yes_
   (If your answer is YES, answer question 2a. If your answer is NO, answer 2b.)

2a. How did you learn to write? _I learned in 1st grade_

2b. How do people learn to write? _____

3. Why do people write? _to get people to read._

4. What do you think a good writer needs to do in order to write well? _Making a story people understand_

5. How does your teacher decide which pieces of writing are the good ones? _the ones that have good punctuation_

6. In general, how do you feel about what you write? _Nice._

Shane's writing survey (Spring)

_Shane___'s Writing Self-Assessment Date 4/82

(Key 1-Not Yet 2-Rarely 3-Sometimes 4-Often 5-Almost Always)

My writing is neat and easy to read.   1 2 3 4 ⑤

My words tell what I want to say clearly.   1 2 3 4 ⑤

I choose topics I am proud to share.   1 2 3 4 ⑤

I begin work without delay.   1 2 3 ④ 5

I stay on task.   1 2 3 4 ⑤

I add details that give information.   1 2 3 ④ 5

I use invented spelling when necessary.   1 2 3 4 ⑤

My sentences make sense.   1 2 3 4 ⑤

I know where to use capitals and periods.   2 3 4 ⑤

_____'s Writing Self-Assessment (cont.) Date_____

I know when to use connecting words, such as <u>and</u>. 1 2 3 4 (5)

I use paragraphs. 1 2 (3) 4 5

I organize the paragraphs in my writing. 1 2 3 (4) 5

I use dialogue form (" ") when necessary 1 2 3 4 (5)

I can find my own errors when I edit. 1 2 3 4 (5)

I can use a dictionary to correct spelling. 1 2 3 4 (5)

I use verb forms correctly. 1 2 3 4 (5)

I use pronouns correctly. 1 2 3 4 (5)

I can follow my teachers suggestions for rewriting

1 2 3 4 (5)

15

Once their was a lizard
who wanted a motorcycle.
When ever a motorcycle went
by it couldn't catch one!
And then he found one.
But He got into a lot of
misschif. And the problem
was he could not rezist
the smell of cheese
And he only had one
friend his name was owl
But when ever lizard went
near any other animal
they laughed at him
and he did not no who
they were talking about
so he was laughing too
and onee they knew that

Shane's story, "Lizard and the Motorcycle" (Grade 3)

<u>16</u>

they laughed some more but
the only animal that did not
laugh was owl. Then they
stopped laughing and he got on
his motorcycle and the owl said
Step on it. he lived in an
apartment. Then he went 20 min
down the halls. coming back he
went in the wrong room
and crashed into the open
refridgearator and it shut
and locked he could not get
out. And he stayed in for
lots of nights. Before he ran
out of food he found a hole
in the botom. And he
climbed out and when he
got there he found his motorcycle

"Lizard and the Motorcycle," continued

17

and then he went back to his room but it did not seem the same but he said hmm I'm shore this is my room but what hapend to it. It looks like it's been live in by crockadiles! and then he said wow! Thats imposable it's really been ransaked by animals. By monkeys, tigers, lions, bears crockadiles. And he even said oh my! I better get out of here before I'm the main corse for supper. And then he heard a man comii and Just before he got steped on he hid and he heard the man said where are we goin

"Lizard and the Motorcycle," continued

18

to rob tonigt a bank.
the man who asked said lets
kid nap somebody. they weren't
lucky because the got caugt
And they went to
Jail. For twenty years.
But luckily lizar called the police the lizard go
into the police car but
the door was open
And they drove of in a
flash and when they
got there sell at the
police staion. They were
pushing and shoveing.
Then owl flew over
the police stashin and
swoped on to the
roof. And herd lizard
calling for help

"Lizard and the Motorcycle," continued

19.

then owl got in
to the building and
saved lizard from
a Jeep that almost
ran over lizard. And
when the got
out owl said to lizard
i'll be a friend of you
for the rest of ~ y
live. And lizard said me
to. And they were friend
for ever. ~~The lizard got in~~
~~the police~~ car ~~because the door~~
~~was open. And lizard ca.~~
~~the Police.~~ ~~This~~ Police couldn't
~~understand but the car wen~~
by.

"Lizard and the Motorcycle," continued

Shane

Jackpot Catcher   11/12/91
Once their was a boy named Eric.

He had moved from cape cod.

He played baseball their and he
was a shortstop.

When he unpacked he saw
a bunch of kids playing
baseball, because they lived next
to a baseball feild.

Shane
Eric said "can I play," they said are
you a catcher? Eric said
yes! I am.

They said then be on are team
the Battle cats.

They practiced and practiced.

His first game was againist the
Hommer's. It was tied 0,to,0 and
some one hit a home run.

Shane's story, "Jackpot Catcher" (Grade 3)

the Hammers won. then
they Had the last
game of the
year, If they won
they would Be the
Champions. It was
the Ninth inning.
and eric was
up at Bat it was

5-5 And Eric
hit a grand slam, and
latter eric said did we
win, and they did.

The End

"Jackpot Catcher," continued

Once their was a Lizard who wanted a motorcycle. Whenever a motorcycle went buy Lizard wished he could ride on one, and then he found one abandoned in the woods. He got into a lot of mischief and the problem was he could not resist the smell of cheese, and he only had one friend, his name was Owl. But whenever Lizard went near any other animal they would laugh at him. He never knew what they were laughing about so he would laugh at himself to fit. The only animal that never laughed was Owl. Owl came and then they stopped. They both got on the motorcycle and Owl said, "Step on it."

Lizard lived in a apartment. He went zooming down the halls. On their way back, they went in the wrong room and they crashed into an open refrigerator and it shut and locked. They could not get out. They stayed in it for a long time. Before they ran out of food, Lizard found a hole in the bottom. They climbed out, found Lizard's motorcycle and went back to Lizards room. But it did not seem the same. He said, "Hmmm. I'm sure this is my room but it does not seem the same. What happened to it? It looks like crocodiles have lived in it. Wow! It's been ransacked by monkeys, tigers, lions, bears, and crocodiles. I better get out of her before I'm the main course for supper." then Lizard heard a man coming and he hid just before he got stepped on. Then he heard the man say, "Where are we going to rob tonight, a bank?" The man who asked said lets kidnap somebody!" Lizard called the police. They weren't lucky because they got caught and they were sent to jail for twenty years. Luckily Lizard got into the police car because the door was open and he took off in a flash (because the car was still running).

Owl was flying over the road leading to the police station and heard Lizard calling for help. Owl swooped down and saved Lizard right before a car accident with a jeep. Meanwhile, the kidnappers got their cell at the police station. Owl brought Lizard to the top of the police station and said to Lizard, "I'll be your friend forever." Lizard said, "Me too!" And they were both friends forever.

THE END

Shane's (Grade 5) revision of "Lizard and the Motorcycle"

THE MISSING REPORT MYSTERY
By Shane Forsyth

CHARACTERS

John Borneo	Main Character
Pat Borneo	John's Father
Kathy Borneo	John's Mother
Ralph	John's Dog
Susan Smith	John's Girlfriend
Pele	John's Best Friend
Mr. Cockroach	John's Teacher
Eunice Monique	Police Sergeant
Bill Griffey	Detective

Chapter 1
The Report

John Borneo was a young boy who didn't do well in school. He was 11 years old and he went to the Washington Junior High School. He was a medium-sized boy who loved soccer, baseball, and many other sports. So he was a typical, average, american boy.

But he had one problem...Reading. He had an average of a D. His Reading teacher was named Mr. Cockroach, the meanest teacher in the school regardless of what grade.

One day Mr. Cockroach said that everyone had to do a report on any subject. John thought to himself "Who am I going to do a report on!" After school, John went to the library to find something or someone to do a report on.

Just then he bumped into Susan Smith who dropped a book about Andrew Carnegie. John said, "Oh, I see you found someone to do a report on." Susan said, "Yes, Andrew Carnegie is a great person." John said, "Good luck!" Susan replied, "See you tomorrow!" Then Susan left the library. All of a sudden a book fell on John's head and it was called, "George Washington's Life." John screamed, "I found it!"

Chapter 2
The Book

John brought home the book and read it all night. He thought it was amazing that one man could be so important to our country. George Washington was a war hero and the 1st president of the United States.

Pat Borneo (John's Father) and Kathy Borneo (John's Mother) both walked into the room and his mother said, "It's getting late." John replied, "O.k., I will go to bed soon." His father said "Nice to see you working so hard on you report. By the way, who are you doing a report on?" "George Washington, said John."

The next morning, John up early or and read his book on George Washington. This pattern continued for about a week or until he finished this book. When he was done reading, he had so much information he didn't know if he could fit it all into one small report. The night that John finished the book he made a five page outline all about what he was going to write in his report for Mr. Cockroach. When John was all alone and he was very tired, Ralph (The Dog) came speeding into John's hot but tranquil room. He made a giant leap and he landed on John's bed. Ralph kept John company throughout the night.

Chapter 3
Pele

John's best friend was Pele. He was a 11 year boy just like John. The only difference was that Pele just immigrated from Brazil. But nobody cared, not even John. John and Pele didn't even look at there differences because they were to busy playing and hanging around that they

"The Missing Report Mystery," continued

never even noticed. They were both great soccer players. But the soccer season was over so nobody thought about soccer that much. They were both concentrating on their reports.

Chapter 4
"Where's My Report?"

When John was writing his report, he worked all day and all night just like he did when he was reading his book. After two long, strenuous, Weeks, John had his report finished. Hid mother and father said that this report was a wonderful piece of work. John said to himself, "Wow! I never knew that I could write a report so carefully and neatly."

John went parading around town showing every kid in his class how well he did (Kind of cocky...Don't you think?). His friends took his report of a bench and hid it. They all said "Let's see how cocky he is when he doesn't have a report to turn into Mr. Cockroach. He will flunk John."

When John figured out that his report was lost, he panicked. He was searching all day for at least a week. Finally, John called the police.

Chapter 5
Police

The call to the Police was very complicated. Sergeant Eunice Monique bursted out laughing on the telephone. She said, "Do you mean to tell me that you want us to send our police officers to come over to everyone's house that has lost a report? Are you Crazy! You want us to tell our officers to stop helping the community so they can help people find reports? Goodbye. Have a nice day!" John said, Oh my god! I thought that the police are here to serve and protect!" John quickly flipped through the telephone book then he screamed, "Ah-ha! I Found it!"

Bill Griffey's Detectives Office
Phone: 999-9999

"The Missing Report Mystery," continued

Chapter 6
The Detective

The Detective said on the phone he would be at Johns house in five minutes. Instead, He came two hours later. He said, "Yes sir, I am Bill Griffey." John said, "Have you ever had any cases like this before?" Bill said, "Ah...no...But it shouldn't be to hard." That made John feel happy it would be easy to find his wonderful report.

The next day Bill Griffey began his search. First he searched at a beach, then a pub, next the pound, and then the grocery store. To put in a small term, Bill searched everywhere.

Every day after school, John would meet Bill and they would both start searching for his report. Even Pele helped out. By the day that the book report was due, the report didn't turn up for Bill nor John. John just said to himself, "I am gonna have to take this like a man!" After that John wasn't scared of what would happen to him.

Chapter 7
The Report is Due

John came to school the next day. Reading was John's last class of the day so that gave John a little extra time to think about what he was going to do. John went to Social Studies, then Science, next English, fourth Computers, then last John steped into reading. Everybody who was a part of the group that took John's paper would say, "I can't wait until you show Mr. Cockroach your report! He will love it!" They pretended to not know that his report was gone.

Just then somebody stuck John's report in his back pocket. When John was called up, he felt the report in his pocket. He passed it in and he got an A. After class the children told John what they did. After that day John promised to never brag or show off. The children had taught John an important lesson.

THE END

"The Missing Report Mystery," continued

My Swiss army knit   108

I oderd a cub Scout

Knife out of a.

Boy's life magazine.

It has a: blade, Cork

screw, Can opener, bottle

opener, nail File, scissor's,

109

Screw driver I
lik it very much and
I is redewith this on
the top ok it. The good thing
is that It is
Perfeet

Shane's personal narrative (Grade 3)

Bibliography

ALVERMAN, D., & BOOTHBY, P. (1982). Text differences: Children's perceptions at the transition stage in reading. *The Reading Teacher, 36,* 298–302.

APPLEBEE, A. (1978). *The child's concept of story.* Chicago: University of Chicago Press.

APPLEBEE, A. (1980). Children's narratives: New Directions. *The Reading Teacher, 34,* 137–142.

APPLEBEE, A., LANGER, J., MULLIS, I., & JENKINS, L. (1990). *The writing report card, 1984–1988: Findings from the nation's report card.* Princeton, NJ: Educational Testing Service.

ANTHONY, R., JOHNSON, T. MICKELSON, N., & PREECE, A. (1991). *Evaluating literacy: A perspective for change.* Portsmouth, NH: Heinemann.

ASKOV, E., & GREFF, M. (1975). Handwriting: Copying versus tracing as the most effective type of practice. *Journal of Educational Research, 69,* 96–98.

ASKOV, E., & PECK, M. (1982). Handwriting. In H. Mitzel, B. Hardin, & W. Rabinowitz (Eds.), *Encyclopedia of educational research* (pp. 141–145). New York: The Free Press.

ATWELL, N. (1987). *In the middle: Writing, reading, and learning with adolescents.* Portsmouth, NH: Heinemann.

AU, K., SCHEU, J., KAWAKAMI, A., & HERMAN, P. (1990a). Assessment and accountability in a whole literacy curriculum. *The Reading Teacher, 43,* 547–578.

AU, K., SCHEU, J., & KAWAKAMI A. (1990b). Assessment of students' ownership of literacy. *The Reading Teacher, 44,* 154–156.

AU, K. (1992). Constructing the theme of a story. *Language Arts, 69,* 106–111.

AU, K. (1994). Portfolio assessment: Experiences at the Kamehameha elementary education program. In S. Valencia, E. Hiebert, & P. Afflerbach (Eds.), *Authentic reading assessment: Practices and possibilities* (pp. 103–112). Newark, DE: International Reading Association.

Avi. (1984). *The fighting ground.* New York: HarperTrophy.

Avi. (1989). *The man who was Poe.* New York: Orchard Books.

Avi. (1990). *The true confessions of Charlotte Doyle.* New York: Orchard Books.

Avi. (1991). *Nothing but the truth.* New York: Orchard Books.

Avi. (1994). *The barn.* New York: Orchard Books.

Barbe, W., Lucas, V., & Wasylyk, T. (1984). *Handwriting: Basic skills for effective communication.* Columbus, OH: Zaner-Bloser.

Bearse, C. I. (1992). The fairy tale connection in children's stories: Cinderella meets Sleeping Beauty. *The Reading Teacher, 45,* 688–695.

Beers, J., & Henderson, E. (1977). A study of developing orthographic concepts among first grader children. *Research in the Teaching of English, 2,* 13–148.

Berman, P. & McLaughlin, M. (1978). *Federal programs supporting educational change.* Santa Monica, CA: The Rand Corporation.

Bissex, G. (1980). *GNYS AT WRK: A child learns to write and read.* Cambridge, MA: Harvard University Press.

Blackburn, E. (1985). Stories never end. In J. Hansen, T. Newkirk, & D. Graves (Eds.), *Breaking ground: Teachers relate reading and writing in the elementary school* (pp. 73–82). Portsmouth, NH: Heinemann.

Bloome, D., & Egan-Robertson, A. (1993). The social construction of intertextuality in classroom reading and writing lessons. *Reading Research Quarterly, 28,* 304–333.

Blos, J. (1979). *A gathering of days: A New England girl's journal, 1830–1832.* New York: Scribner.

Blyton, E. (1939). *The enchanted wood.* London: Darrel Waters Ltd.

Blyton, E. (1943). *The magic faraway tree.* London: Darrel Waters Ltd.

Bridwell, L. (1980). Revising strategies in twelfth grade students' transactional writing. *Research in the Teaching of English, 14,* 197–222.

Britton, J., (1970). *Language and learning.* Harmondsworth, England: The Penguin Press.

Britton, J., (1993). *Language and learning* (2nd ed.). Portsmouth NH: Heinemann.

Britton, J., Burgess, T., Martin, T., McLeod, A., & Rosen, H. (1975). *The development of writing abilities (11–18).* London: Macmillan.

BROMLEY, K. (1992). *Language arts: Exploring connections.* Boston: Allyn and Bacon.

BROWN, A. (1980). Metacognitive development and reading. In R. Spiro & W. Brewer (Eds.), *Theoretical issues in reading comprehension* (pp. 453–481). Hillsdale, NJ: Lawrence Erlbaum.

BUCHANAN, E. (1989). *Spelling for whole language classrooms.* Winnipeg: Whole Language Consultants Ltd.

BURNHILL, P., HARTLEY, J., & DAVIES, L. (1978). Lined paper, legibility, and creativity. *Educational Research, 21,* 62.

BURROUGHS, M. (1972). *The stimulation of verbal behavior in culturally disadvantaged three-year olds.* Unpublished dissertation, Michigan State University.

CAIRNEY, T. (1990). Intertextuality: Infectious echoes from the past. *The Reading Teacher, 43,* 478–485.

CAIRNEY, T. (1992). Fostering and building students' intertextual histories. *Language Arts, 69,* 502–507.

CALKINS, L. (1980a). Children's rewriting strategies. *Research in the Teaching of English, 14,* 331–341.

CALKINS, L. (1980b). When children want to punctuate: Basic skills belong in context. *Language Arts, 57,* 567–573.

CALKINS, L. (1983). *Lessons from a child.* Portsmouth, NH: Heinemann.

CALKINS, L. (1986). *The art of teaching writing.* Portsmouth, NH: Heinemann.

CALKINS, L. (1991). *Living between the lines.* Portsmouth, NH: Heinemann.

CALKINS, L. (1994). *The art of teaching writing* (new edition). Portsmouth, NH: Heinemann.

CAMBOURNE, B. (1988). *The whole story: Natural learning and acquisition of literacy in the classroom.* New York: Ashton Scholastic.

CAMBOURNE, B., & TURBILL, J. (1994). What we found out from the research project. In B. Cambourne & J. Turbill, *Responsive evaluation: Making valid judgments about student literacy* (pp. 16–27). Portsmouth, NH: Heinemann.

CHALL, J., & JACOBS, V. (1983). Writing and reading in the elementary grades: Developmental trends among low SES children. *Language Arts, 60,* 617–626.

CHARNEY, R. (1991). *Teaching children to care: Management in the responsive classroom.* Greenfield, MA: Northeast Foundation for Children.

CHOMSKY, C. (1970). Reading, writing and phonology. *Harvard Education Review, 40,* 287–309.

CHOMSKY, C. (1972). Write now, read later. In C. Cazden (Ed.), *Language in early childhood education.* Washington, DC: Association for Education of Young Children.

CLAY, M. (1975). *What did I write?* Portsmouth, NH: Heinemann.

CLAY, M. (1979). *The early detection of reading difficulties.* Portsmouth, NH: Heinemann.

CLAY, M. (1991). *Becoming literate: The construction of inner control.* Portsmouth, NH: Heinemann.

CLEARY, B. (1965). *The mouse and the motorcycle.* New York: Avon Books.

CLEARY, B. (1983). *Dear Mr. Henshaw.* New York: Morrow.

CORDEIRO, P., GIACOBBE, M., & CAZDEN, C. (1983). Apostrophes, quotation marks, and periods: Learning punctuation in the first grade. *Language Arts, 60,* 323–332.

COX, P. (1983). Complimentary roles in successful change. *Educational Leadership, 41,* 10–13.

CRONNELL, B. (1980). *Punctuation and capitalization: A review of the literature.* Los Alamitos, CA: Southwest Regional Laboratory for Educational Research and Development. (ERIC Document Reproduction Service No. ED 208 404).

CROWHURST, M. (1987). Cohesion in argument and narration at three grade levels. *Research in the Teaching of English, 21,* 185–201.

DANIELS, H. (1990). Young writers and readers reach out: Developing sense of audience. In T. Shanahan (Ed.), *Reading and writing together: New perspectives for the classroom* (pp. 99–125). Norwood, MA: Christopher Gordon Publishers, Inc.

DE FINA, A. (1992). *Portfolio assessment: Getting started.* New York: Scholastic.

DE GOES, C., & MARTLEW, M. (1983). Young children's approach to literacy. In M. Martlew (Ed.), *The psychology of written language* (pp. 217–236). Chichester, England: John Wiley.

DELATTRE, E. (1988). *Education and the public trust.* Washington, DC: Ethics and Public Policy Center.

DEWEY, J. (1959). *Dewey on education.* New York: Teachers College Press.

DONNELLY, J. (1991). *A wall of names: The story of the Vietnam Veterans Memorial.* New York: Random House.

DORIS, E. (1991). *Doing what scientists do: Children learn to investigate their world.* Portsmouth, NH: Heinemann.

DURKIN, D. (1966). *Children who read early.* New York: Teachers College Press.

DURKIN, D. (1974–75). A six-year study of children who learned to read in school at age four. *Reading Research Quarterly, 10,* 9–61.

DURKIN, D. (1981). Reading comprehension instruction in five basal reading series. *Reading Research Quarterly, 16,* 515–544.

ELBOW, P. (1973). *Writing without teachers.* London: Oxford University Press.

ELBOW, P., & CLARKE, J. (1987). Desert island discourse: The benefits of ignoring audience. In T. Fulwiler, *The journal book* (pp. 19–32). Portsmouth, NH: Heinemann.

EMRICH, J., & PETERSON, S. (1978). *A synthesis of findings across five recent studies in educational dissemination and change.* San Francisco, CA: Far West Laboratory.

EMIG, J. (1971). *The composing process of twelfth graders.* Urbana, IL: National Council of Teachers of English.

FISHER, B. (1991). *Joyful learning: A whole language kindergarten.* Portsmouth, NH: Heinemann.

FISHER, B. (1995). *Thinking and learning together: Curriculum and community in a primary classroom.* Portsmouth, NH: Heinemann.

FISHER, B., & CORDEIRO, P. (1994). Generating a curriculum: Building a shared curriculum. *Primary Voices, 2,* 2–7.

FILUPOVIC, Z. (1994). *Zlata's Diary: A child's life in Sarajevo.* New York: Viking.

FITZGERALD, J. (1987). Research on revision in writing. *Review of Educational Research, 57,* 481–506.

FITZGERALD, J. (1988). Helping young writers to revise: A brief review for teachers. *The Reading Teacher, 42,* 124–129.

FITZGERALD, J. (1989). Enhancing two related thought processes: Revision in writing and critical reading. *The Reading Teacher, 43,* 42–50.

FITZGERALD, J. (1993). Teachers' knowing about knowledge: Its significance for classroom writing instruction. *Language Arts, 70,* 282–289.

FLETCHER, R. (1993). *What a writer needs.* Portsmouth, NH: Heinemann.

FLOOD, J., & LAPP, D. (1984). Types of writing included in basal reading second-grade readers. In J. Niles & L. Harris (Eds.), *Changing perspectives on research in reading/language processing and instruction* (pp. 5–10). Rochester, NY: The National Reading Conference.

FOX, M. (1988). *Koala Lou*. New York: Harcourt Brace Jovanovich Publishers.

FOX, M. (1990). *Dear Mem Fox, I have read all your books, even the pathetic ones*. New York: Harcourt Brace Jovanovich Publishers.

FREIRE, P. (1985). Reading the world and reading the word: An interview with Paulo Freire. *Language Arts, 62,* 15–21.

FULLAN, M., & POMFRET, A. (1977). Research on curriculum and instruction implementation. *Review of Educational Researcher, 47,* 335–397.

FULLAN, M. (1993). Why teachers must become change agents. *Educational Leadership, 50,* 12–17.

FULWILER, T. (1987). Guidelines for using journals in school settings. *The journal book*. Portsmouth, NH: Heinemann.

GENTRY, R., & GILLET, J. (1993). *Teaching kids to spell*. Portsmouth, NH: Heinemann.

GEARHART, M., WOLF, S., BURKEY, B., & WHITTAKER, A. (1994). *Engaging teachers in assessment of their students' narrative writing: Impact on teachers' knowledge and practice*. (CSE Tech. Rep. 377). Los Angeles: University of California, Center for the Study of Evaluation.

GIACOBBE, M. (1988). A writer reads, a reader writes. In T. Newkirk & N. Atwell (Eds.), *Ways of observing, learning and teaching* (pp. 168–177). Portsmouth, NH: Heinemann.

GIACOBBE, M. (1995). *Using writing folders as a means of informing daily instruction*. Paper presented at The 12th Annual Literacy Institute, Lesley College, Cambridge, MA.

GOLDEN, J. (1984). Children's concept of story in reading and writing. *The Reading Teacher, 37,* 578–585.

GOODMAN, K. (1986). *What's whole about whole language?* Portsmouth, NH: Heinemann.

GOODMAN, Y. (1989). Evaluation of students. In K. Goodman, Y. Goodman, & W. Hood (Eds.), *Whole language evaluation book* (pp. 3–14). Portsmouth, NH: Heinemann.

GRAHAM, B. (1986). *It's much too hot*. New York: Gallery Books.

GRAVES, D. (1978). Research update—handwriting is for writing. *Language Arts, 55,* 393–99.

GRAVES, D. (1983). *Writing: Teachers and children at work*. Portsmouth, NH: Heinemann.

GRAVES, D. (1989a). *Experiment with fiction*. Portsmouth, NH: Heinemann.

GRAVES, D. (1989b). Research currents: When children respond to fiction. *Language Arts, 66,* 776–783.

GRAVES, D. (1991). Trust the shadows. *The Reading Teacher, 45*, 18–25.

GRAVES, D. (1992). Portfolios: Keep a good idea growing. In D. Graves & B. Sunstein (Eds.), *Portfolio Portraits* (pp. 1–12). Portsmouth, NH: Heinemann.

GRAVES, D. (1994). *A fresh look at writing.* Portsmouth, NH: Heinemann.

HALL, G., & LOUCKS, S. (1979). Teacher concerns as a basis for facilitating and personalizing staff development. In A. Lieberman & L. Miller (Eds.), *Staff development: New demands, new realities, new perspectives.* New York: Teachers College Press.

HANDY, L. (1982). *Boss for a week.* New York: Scholastic.

HANSEN, J. (1987). *When writers read.* Portsmouth, NH: Heinemann.

HANSEN, J. (1992). The language of challenge: Readers and writers speak their minds. *Language Arts, 69*, 100–105.

HANSEN, J. (1994). Literacy portfolios: Windows on potential. In S. Valencia, E. Hiebert, & P. Afflerbach (Eds.), *Authentic reading assessment: Practices and possibilities* (pp. 26–40). Newark, DE: International Reading Association.

HARDY, B. (1977). Narrative as a primary act of mind. In M. Meek, A. Warlow, & G. Barton (Eds.), *The cool web: The pattern of children's reading* (pp. 6–12). New York: Lothrop, Lee & Shepard.

HARP, B. (1991). Principles of assessment and evaluation in whole language classrooms. In B. Harp (Ed.), *Assessment & evaluation in whole language programs.* Norwood, MA: Christopher-Gordon Publishers, Inc.

HARSTE, J., Woodward, V., & Burke, C. (1984). *Language stories & literacy lessons.* Portsmouth, NH: Heinemann.

HARWAYNE, S. (1992). *Lasting impressions: Weaving literature into the writing workshop.* Portsmouth, NH: Heinemann.

HAYES, D. (1982). Handwriting practice: The effects of perceptual prompts. *Journal of Educational Research, 75*, 169–172.

HEATH, S. (1983). *Ways with words: Language, life and work in communities and classrooms.* Cambridge, MA: Cambridge University Press.

HENDERSON, E. (1990). *Teaching spelling.* Boston: Houghton Mifflin Co.

HILDRETH, G. (1960). Manuscript writing after sixty years. *Elementary English, 37*, 3–13.

HILLOCKS, G. (1986). *Research on written composition: New directions for teaching.* Urbana, IL: National Conference on Research in English.

HIPPLE, M. (1985). Journal writing in kindergarten. *Language Arts, 62*, 255–261.

HOLDAWAY, D. (1979). *The foundations of literacy.* Portsmouth, NH: Heinemann.

HOLDAWAY, D. (1986). The structure of natural learning as a basis for literacy instruction. In M. Sampson (Ed.), *The pursuit of literacy* (pp. 56–72). Dubuque, IA: Kendall/Hunt Publishing Company.

HUBERMAN, M., & MILES, M. (1984). *Innovation up close.* New York: Praeger.

HUCK, C., HELPER, S., & HICKMAN, J. (1987). *Children's literature in the elementary school.* New York: Holt, Rinehart and Winston.

International Reading Association and National Council of Teachers of English. (1994). *Standards for the assessment of reading and writing.* International Reading Association and National Council of Teachers of English.

JOHNSON, D., JOHNSON, R., HOLUBEC, E., & ROY, P. (1984). *Circles of learning.* Alexandria, VA: Association for Supervision and Curriculum Development.

JOHNSTON, P. (1987). Teachers as evaluation experts. *The Reading Teacher, 40,* 744–748.

JOHNSTON, P. (1992). *Constructive evaluation of literate activity.* New York: Longman.

JOSEPHSON, M. (1959). *Edison.* New York: McGraw–Hill Book Company.

JOYCE, B., WOLF, J., & CALHOUN, E. (1993). *The self-renewing school.* Alexandria, VA: Association for Supervision and Curriculum Development.

KAMEENUI, E., CARINE, D., & FRESCHI, R. (1982). Effects of text construction and instructional procedures for teaching word meanings on comprehension and recall. *Reading Research Quarterly, 17,* 367–388.

KARELITZ, E. (1988). The rhythm of writing development. In T. Newkirk and N. Atwell (Eds.), *Ways of observing, learning and teaching* (pp. 168–177). Portsmouth, NH: Heinemann.

KING, M., & RENTEL, V. (1981). *How children learn to write: A longitudinal study.* Columbus, OH: Ohio State University Research Foundation.

KORETZ, D., McCAFFREY, D., KLEIN, S., BELL, R., & STECHER, B. (1992). *The reliability of scores from the 1992 Vermont portfolio assessment program.* Washington, DC: Office of Educational Research and Improvement.

KRZESNI, J. (1971). Effect of different writing tools and paper on performance of the third grade. *Elementary English, 48,* 821–24.

LAMME, L., & ARIS, B. (1983). Is the handwriting of beginning writers influenced by writing tools? *Journal of Research and Development in Education, 17,* 32–38.

LANGER, J. (1986). *Children reading and writing: Structures and strategies.* Norwood, NJ: Ablex Publishing Co.

LANGER, J. (1992). Reading, writing, and genre development. In J. Irwin & M. Doyle (Eds.), *Reading/writing connection* (pp. 32–54). Newark, DE: International Reading Association.

LEHR, S. (1988). The child's developing sense of theme as a response to literature. *Reading Research Quarterly, 23,* 337–357.

LEUNG, E., TREBLAS, P., HILL, D., & COOPER, J. (1979). Space, size and accuracy of first grade students' manuscript writing. *Journal of Educational Research, 73,* 79–81.

LEWIS, E., & LEWIS, H. (1964). Which manuscript letters are hard for first graders? *Elementary English, 41,* 855–858.

LIEBERMAN, A., & MILLER, L. (1984). *Teachers, their world, and their work.* Alexandria, VA: Association for Supervision and Curriculum Development.

LINDSAY, G., & McLENNAN, D. (1983). Lined paper: Its effects on the legibility and creativity of young children's writing. *Journal of Educational Psychology, 53,* 364–368.

LITTLE, J. (1982). Norms of collegiality and experimentation: Workplace conditions of school success. *American Educational Researcher Journal, 5,* 325–340.

LORTIE, D. (1975). *School Teacher.* Chicago: University Press of Chicago.

LOWE, S. (1990). *Henry David Thoreau: Walden.* New York: Philomel Books.

MANDLER, J. (1983). The function of structure. Paper presented at the Annual Convention of the American Psychological Association, 1–30.

MARKHAM, L. (1976). Influences of handwriting quality on teacher evaluation in written work. *American Educational Research Journal, 13,* 277–283.

MARSH, G., FRIEDMAN, M., WELCH, V., & DESBERG, P. (1980). The development of strategies in spelling. In U. Frith (Ed.), *Cognitive processes in spelling* (pp. 339–353). London: Academic Press.

McCONAGHY, J. (1985). Once upon a time and me. *Language Arts, 62,* 349–354.

McGEE, L. (1982). The influence of metacognitive knowledge on expository text structure on discourse recall. In J. Niles & A. Harris (Eds.), *New inquiries in reading research and instruction.* Rochester, NY: National Reading Conference.

McKeough, A. (1984). Developmental stages in children's narrative composition. Paper presented at the Annual Meeting of the American Educational Research Association. (ERIC Document Reproduction Service No. ED 249 461).

Mercier, C. (1991). Review of *The true confessions of Charlotte Doyle*. *The Five Owls, 5*, 56–57.

Miles, M., & Louis, K. (1990). Mustering the will and skill for change. *Educational Leadership, 47*, 57–61.

Moffett, J. (1968). *Teaching the universe of discourse*. Boston: Houghton Mifflin.

Murray, D. (1989). *Expecting the unexpected*. Portsmouth, NH: Heinemann.

Murray, D. (1990). *Shoptalk*. Portsmouth, NH: Heinemann.

Myers, E. (1963). *The ways and hows of teaching handwriting*. Columbus, Ohio: Zaner-Bloser.

Newkirk, T. (1987). The non-narrative writing of young children. *Research in the Teaching of English, 21*, 121–145.

Nolan, P., & McCartin, R. (1984). Spelling strategies on the Wide Range Achievement Test. *The Reading Teacher, 38*, 148–157.

Norton, D. (1993). *The effective teaching of language arts*. New York: Macmillan Publishing Co.

Oakley, G. (1987). *The diary of a church mouse*. New York: Atheneum.

Odom, R. (1962). Growth of a language skill: Capitalization. *California Journal of Educational Research, 13*, 3–8.

O'Neil, J. (1993). Portfolio assessment bears the burden of popularity. *ASCD Update, 35*, 3 & 8.

Otto, W., & Anderson, D. (1969). Handwriting. In R. Ebel (Ed.), *Encyclopedia of Educational Research* (4th ed.) New York: Macmillan.

Pappas, C. (1991). Fostering full access to literacy by including information books. *Language Arts, 68*, 449–462.

Paratore, J. (1993). Portfolio Assessment: Hearing the voices of children, parents, and teachers. *Greater Boston Council Newsletter, 30*, 4.

Paratore, J., & Indrisano, R. (1987). Intervention assessment of reading comprehension. *The Reading Teacher, 40*, 778–783.

Peck, M., Askov, E., & Fairchild, S. (1980). Another decade of research in handwriting: Progress and prospect in the 1970s. *Journal of Educational Research, 73*, 283–298.

Perl, S. (1979). The composing processes of unskilled college writers. *Research in the Teaching of English, 13*, 317–336.

PIAGET, J. (1969). *The psychology of the child.* New York: Basic Books.

POWELL, D., & HORNSBY, D. (1993). *Learning phonics and spelling in a whole language classroom.* New York: Scholastic.

PUTNAM, L. (1991). Dramatizing nonfiction with emerging readers. *Language Arts, 68,* 463–469.

RADEBAUGH, M. (1985). Children's perceptions of their spelling strategies. *Reading Teacher, 38,* 532–536.

READ, C. (1971). Pre-school children's knowledge of English phonology. *Harvard Educational Review, 41,* 1–34.

READ, C. (1975). *Children's categorization of speech sounds.* Urbana, IL: National Council of Teachers of English.

RHODES, L. (1993). *Literacy Assessment: A handbook of instruments.* Portsmouth, NH: Heinemann.

RIEF, L. (1990). Finding the value in evaluation: Self-assessment in a middle school classroom. *Educational Leadership, 47,* 24–29.

ROSENBLATT, L. (1978). *The reader, the text, the poem: The transactional theory of the literary work.* Carbondale, IL: Southern Illinois University Press.

ROSKINSKI, R., & WHEELER, K. (1972). Children's use of orthographic structure in word discrimination. *Psychonomic Sciences, 26,* 97–98.

SCARDAMALIA, M., & BEREITER, C. (1983). *The development of evaluative, diagnostic, and remedial capabilities in children's composing.* In M. Martlew (Ed.), *The psychology of written language: A developmental approach.* London: John Wiley & Sons.

SCHICKEDANZ, J. (1989). The place of specific skills in preschool and kindergarten. In D. Strickland and L. Morrow (Eds.), *Emerging literacy: Young children learn to read and write* (pp. 96–106). Newark, DE: International Reading Association.

SCHICKEDANZ, J. (1990). *Adam's righting revolutions: One child's literacy development from infancy through grade one.* Portsmouth, NH: Heinemann.

SCHICKEDANZ, J. (1995). (Personal communication, September 13)

SENICK, G., & GUNTON, S. (1991). Avi. *Children's Literature Review, 24,* 1–15.

SHAUGHNESSY, M. (1977). *Errors and expectations: A guide for the teacher of basic writing.* New York: Oxford University Press.

SHEPARD, L. (1995). Using assessment to improve learning. *Educational Leadership, 52,* 38–43.

SIEGLER, R. (1995). Children's thinking: How does change occur? In W. Schneider & F. Weinert (Eds.), *Memory performance and competencies: Issues in growth and development* (pp. 405–430). Hillsdale, NJ: Erlbaum.

SIMMONS, J. (1990). Portfolios as large-scale assessment. *Language Arts, 67,* 262–267.

SIMMONS, J. (1992). Portfolios for large-scale assessment. In D. Graves & B. Sunstein (Eds.), *Portfolio Portraits* (pp. 96–113). Portsmouth, NH: Heinemann.

SMITH, F. (1982). *Writing and the writer.* New York: Holt, Rinehart, and Winston.

SNIDER, M., LIMA, S., & DeVITO, P. (1994). Rhode Island's literacy portfolio assessment project. In S. Valencia, E. Hiebert, & P. Afflerbach (Eds.), *Authentic reading assessment: Practices and possibilities* (pp. 71–88). Newark, DE: International Reading Association.

SNOW, C. (1983). Language and literacy: Relationships during the preschool years. *Harvard Educational Review, 4,* 165–189.

SOWERS, S. (1985). The story and the all-about book. In J. Hansen, T. Newkirk, & D. Graves (Eds.), *Breaking ground: Teachers relate reading and writing in the elementary school* (pp. 73–82). Portsmouth NH: Heinemann.

STEIN, N., AND GLENN, C. (1979). An analysis of story comprehension in elementary school children. In R. Freedle (Ed.), *New Directions in discourse processing* (pp. 53–129). Norwood, NJ: Ablex.

STOWELL, L., & TIERNEY, R. (1995). Portfolios in the classroom: What happens when teachers and students negotiate assessment? In R. Allington & S. Walmsley (Eds.), *No quick fix* (pp. 78–94). Newark, DE: International Reading Association and New York: Teachers College Press.

SULZBY, E. (1985). Children's emergent reading of favorite storybooks: A developmental study. *Reading Research Quarterly, 20,* 458–481.

SULZBY, E., & TEALE, W. (1987). Young children's storybook reading: Longitudinal study of parent–child interaction and children's independent functioning. Final report to the Spencer Foundation. Ann Arbor: The University of Michigan.

SUSSMAN, L. (1977). *Tales out of school.* Philadelphia, PA: Temple University Press.

SUTTON, R. (1989). Review of *The man who was Poe. Bulletin of the Center for Children's Books, 43,* 27.

TAXEL, J. (1985). Review of *The fighting ground. The ALAN Review, 12,* 23.

TAYLOR, B., & BEACH, R. (1984). The effects of text structure instruction on middle–grade students' comprehension and production of expository text. *Reading Research Quarterly, 19,* 147–161.

TAYLOR, B., & SAMUELS, S. (1983). Children's use of text structure in the recall of expository material. *American Educational Research Journal, 20*, 517–528.

TAYLOR, D. (1989). Toward a unified theory of literacy learning and instructional practices. *Phi Delta Kappan, 71*, 184–193.

TEALE, W., & SULZBY, E. (1986). *Emergent literacy: Writing and reading.* Norwood, NJ: Ablex Publishing Corporation.

TEMPLE, C., & GILLET, J. (1984). *Language Arts: Learning processes and teaching practices.* Boston: Little, Brown and Company.

TEMPLE, C., NATHAN, R., TEMPLE, F., AND BURRIS, N. (1993). *The beginnings of writing.* Boston: Allyn and Bacon.

THOREAU, H. (1855–1856). *The journey of Henry D. Thoreau.* Boston: Houghton Mifflin Company.

TIERNEY, R., CARTER, M., & DESAI, L. (1991). *Portfolio assessment in the reading-writing classroom.* Norwood, MA: Christopher-Gordon Publishers, Inc.

TIGNER, S. (1993). Lecture presented at Boston University.

TOMPKINS, G., & HOSKISSON, K. (1991). *Language arts: Content and teaching strategies.* New York: Macmillan Publishing Company.

TRAP-PORTER, J., COOPER, J., HILL, D., SWISHER, K., & LaNUNZIATA, L. (1983). Space, size and accuracy of second and third grade students' cursive writing. *Journal of Educational Research, 76*, 231–223.

TREALEASE, J. (1989). *The new read-aloud handbook.* New York: Penguin Books.

VALENCIA, S., (1990). A portfolio approach to classroom reading assessment: The whys, whats, and hows. *The Reading Teacher, 43*, 338–340.

VALENCIA, S., & PEARSON, P. (1987). Reading assessment: Time for a change. *The Reading Teacher, 40*, 726–733.

VALENCIA, S., & PLACE, N. (1994). Literacy portfolios for teaching, learning, and accountability: The Bellevue Literacy Assessment Project. In S. Valencia, E. Hiebert, & P. Afflerbach (Eds.), *Authentic reading assessment: Practices and possibilities* (pp. 134–156). Newark, DE: International Reading Association.

VALENCIA, S., HIEBERT, E., & AFFLERBACH, P. (1994). *Authentic reading assessment: Practices and possibilities.* Newark, DE: International Reading Association.

VALMONT, W. (1972). Spelling consciousness: A long neglected area. *Elementary English, 49,* 1219–1221.

VYGOTSKY, L. (1978). *Mind in society.* Cambridge, MA: Harvard University Press.

WELLS, G. (1986). *The meaning makers: Children learning language and using language to learn.* Portsmouth, NH: Heinemann.

WHALEY, J. (1981). Story grammars and reading instruction. *The Reading Teacher, 37,* 346–353.

WILDE, J. (1985). Play, power, and plausibility: The growth of fiction writers. In J. Hansen, T. Newkirk, & D. Graves (Eds.), *Breaking ground: Teachers relate reading and writing in the elementary school* (pp. 73–82). Portsmouth, NH: Heinemann.

WILDE, S. (1992). *You kan red this: Spelling and punctuation for whole language classrooms.* Portsmouth, NH: Heinemann.

WILDER, L. (1962). *On the way home.* New York: Harper.

WILLIAMS, V. (1981). *Three days on a river in a red canoe.* New York: Greenwillow.

YOLEN, J. (1991). The route to story. *The New Advocate, 4,* 143–149.

ZIVIANI, J., & ELKINS, J. (1986). Effect of pencil grip on handwriting speed and legibility. *Educational Review, 38,* 247–257.

Index

action (instruction) demonstrations, 87
adding on, 46–47, 94
affixes, as spelling strategy, 157
Afflerbach, P., 240
all-about books, 51
alphabetic code, awareness of, 145
anecdotal notes, 26
apostrophe, possessive, children's knowledge of, 188
Applebee, Arthur, 20, 77–81, 82, 83, 84, 205
approximation, 208
Aristotle, 125
artifact (text) demonstrations, 87
ascenders, in handwriting, 172–74
assess-as-you-go conferences, 217, 219–20, 223
assess-as-you-go weekly reviews, 218, 220
assessment, *See also* portfolio assessment; self-assessment; self- assessment by children; teacher self-assessment
   cursive writing, 179–82
   handwriting, 168–83
   holistic, 22–23, 56–61
   involving children in, 66–68
   minilessons and, 218–19, 222–23
   nonfiction writing, 115–33
   nonfiction writing of older writers, 118
   over time, 66–71
   personal narratives, 56–61, 66–71
   punctuation, 187–92, 195–203, 204–5
   reports, 122–30
   spelling, 139–41
   story writing, 93–105
   by students, 14–15
   by teachers, 10, 13
assessment notebooks, 217
attribute series (hierarchical), as nonfiction writing, 116

Atwell, Nancie, 68, 216
Au, Kathryn, 12, 13, 23
audience awareness
   engagement with writing checklist, 238
   in nonfiction writing, 125–26, 128
autobiographies
   literary, 216
   sketches, 38
Avi, 1–7

Bearse, C. I., 86
bed-to-bed narratives, 61, 221
benchmark portfolios, 10–14
   limitations, 13–14
   purpose of, 10, 12
   responsibility for contents of, 14
Bereiter, C., 71
Bissex, Glenda, 50, 140, 186–87
Britton, James, 48, 49–50, 53, 55
Bush, George, 120–21

Cairney, T., 86
Calkins, Lucy, 46, 50, 56, 72–74, 92, 106, 133, 164, 192–95
Cambourne, B., 10, 12, 23, 34, 208
capitalization, 189, 191, 198, 199, 202
   children's self-assessment of, 64
capital letters, children's preference for, 186
Carter, M., 18
centering, in story writing, 77–78
chain narratives, 61–62
   focused, 79, 90–91
   unfocused, 79
character development, 99–104
characters
   friends, 103
   generic, 103

275